Approaches to Second Language Acquisition

Richard Towell and Roger Hawkins

MULTILINGUAL MATTERS LTD
Clevedon • Philadelphia • Adelaide

Library of Congress Cataloging in Publication Data

Towell, Richard
Approaches to Second Language Acquisition/Richard Towell and Roger Hawkins
p. cm.
Includes bibliographical references and index.
1. Second language acquisition–Methodology.
I. Hawkins, Roger (Roger D.) II. Title
P118.2.T68   1994
418–dc20   93-50615

British Library Cataloguing in Publication Data

A CIP catalogue record for this book is available from the British Library.

ISBN 1-85359-235-8 (hbk)
ISBN 1-85359-234-X (pbk)

Multilingual Matters Ltd

UK: Frankfurt Lodge, Clevedon Hall, Victoria Road, Clevedon, Avon BS21 7SJ.
USA: 1900 Frost Road, Suite 101, Bristol, PA 19007, USA.
Australia: P.O. Box 6025, 83 Gilles Street, Adelaide, SA 5000, Australia.

Typeset, printed and bound in Great Britain by the Longdunn Press, Bristol.

Contents

Acknowledgements..vii
Introduction 1

1. The Observable Phenomena of Second Language
    Acquisition 7
    There is transfer of properties of the L1 grammar into
        the L2 grammar 7
    There is staged development in second language
        acquisition..10
    There is systematicity in the growth of L2 knowledge
        across learners...11
    There is variability in learners' intuitions about, and
        production of, aspects of the L2 at certain stages of
        development 13
    Second language learners stop short of native-like
        success in a number of areas of the L2 grammar 14
    Summary..15

2. Early Linguistic Approaches to Explaining the Observable
    Phenomena of Second Language Acquisition.............................17
    The Contrastive Analysis Hypothesis......................................17
    Evaluation of the Contrastive Analysis Hypothesis 18
    The Natural Order Hypothesis 23
        The morpheme studies 23
        Krashen's five hypotheses 25
    Evaluation of the Natural Order Hypothesis..........................28
    Summary..31

3. Sociolinguistic Approaches to Explaining the Observable
    Phenomena of Second Language Acquisition.............................33
    Tarone's approach 34
    Ellis's approach..36
    The acculturation/pidginisation approach..............................37
    Evaluation of sociolinguistic approaches to second
        language acquisition..39
    Summary..43

4. Cognitive Approaches to Explaining the Observable
   Phenomena of Second Language Acquisition............................45
   Pienemann's account 46
   Wolfe Quintero's account 48
   Evaluation of cognitive approaches to second language
      acquisition...50
   General evaluation of the early linguistic, sociolinguistic
      and cognitive approaches to explaining the observable
      phenomena of second language acquisition 54

5. The Approach to Second Language Acquisition Based on
   Universal Grammar...57
   Goals and assumptions of work on Universal Grammar 58
   Principles and parameters..61
      An analogy...61
   The structure of phrases 61
   Phrase structure and first language acquisition.....................65
   Phrase structure and second language acquisition.................68
   Summary...71

6. Parametric Variation and Transfer in Second Language
   Acquisition 74
   The structure of clauses 75
   Parametric differences between German/Dutch and
      English/French..79
   The transfer of L1 parameter values in the second
      language acquisition of word order properties in
      French and German 84
   Transfer, parametric variation and differences between
      second and first language learners 87
   Two kinds of parameter and differences between second
      language learners speaking different first languages..........92
   Inclusive parameter values and the problem they pose
      for learnability in first language acquisition......................97
      Markedness..98
      The subset principle 101
   Transfer, inclusive parameter values, and the resetting
      of parameters in second language acquisition 103
   Adverb placement in English and French 104
   Parameter resetting versus parameter 'activation' in
      second language acquisition 106
   Summary... 107

7. Parametric Variation and Incompleteness in Second
    Language Acquisition 110
        The pro-drop parameter 114
        Verb movement in French and English 120
        Summary 127

8. Parametric Variation, Staged Development and Cross-
    learner Systematicity in Second Language Acquisition 129
        The logical and developmental problems in language
        acquisition 129
        The logical and developmental problems in second
        language acquisition 132
        Summary 140

9. Parametric Variation, Variability and the Limits of the
    Explanatory Power of Universal Grammar in Second
    Language Acquisition 142
        Summary 151

10. Explanations of Variability 153
        Variability is a pervasive phenomenon 154
            Variability caused by differences in cognitive
            abilities and learning environments 155
            Variability caused by the demands of different tasks ... 155
            Variability caused by variable focus of attention 157
            Variability caused by the use of formulaic language 158
            Variability caused by the use of strategies 159
            Three explanations for variability 159
        Psychological Mechanisms 162
            Short-term and long-term memory, controlled and
            automatic processing 162
            A model of language production 165
        Summary 171

11. Hypothesis Creation and Revision 174
        Explicit instruction and negative feedback 177
        Exposure to authentic data 183
            Mental representation 185
            Formulaic language seen in the light of changes in
            mental representation 192
        Hypothesis revision 197
        Summary 199

12. The Development of Language Processing................................201
    ACT*...202
    A production system 204
    Declarative knowledge, working memory and
        interpretive procedures 205
    Production memory and compilation 209
    Matching, execution and application......................211
    Tuning: generalisation and discrimination 211
    Processing different kinds of knowledge................213
        Processing competence 213
        Processing learned linguistic knowledge...........215
        Combining different kinds of knowledge in
            processing..216
    Evaluation 217
    Application 218
    Summary..224

13. Approaches to Learner Strategies................................226
    Reduction and achievement strategies...................229
    The Nijmegen project..232
    Analysis and control..235
    Strategies based on declarative and procedural
        knowledge..238
    Discussion 243
    Summary..243

14. Towards a Model of Second Language Acquisition...................245
    An overall model..246
        The role of exposure to authentic data 252
        The role of explicit instruction 255
    Research methods and directions for further research 259
        Investigating the role of Universal Grammar...............259
        Investigating the role of the first language 261
        Investigating the role of information processing..........263
        Investigating interaction between the parts of the
            model..265
    Summary..266

Bibliography 267
Index..277

Acknowledgements

The authors acknowledge the considerable input of other people, both direct and indirect, to the formulation of the ideas presented in this book. In particular, Richard Towell would like to thank Vivian Cook for his comments on part of the text and the students following the MA in Applied Language Studies at the University of Salford for their reactions to many of these ideas.

Roger Hawkins would single out several of his colleagues at the University of Essex who, through discussion and interaction over several years now, have helped him clarify his thinking about Universal Grammar, principles and parameters theory, and their explanatory role in language acquisition research: Martin Atkinson, Keith Brown, Vivian Cook, Andrew Radford and Andy Spencer. A first draft of the manuscript underwent considerable revision in the light of the comments of an anonymous referee for Multilingual Matters, and we would like to thank that person.

Introduction

Human beings have the capacity to acquire not only a mother tongue, but also one or more second languages. This potential for acquiring second languages seems to last throughout one's lifetime, and there are some spectacular examples of prolific second language (L2) learners.[1] For example, Farwell (1963) (cited in Taylor, 1976: 258) reports that a nineteenth-century British explorer — Sir Richard Burton — claimed to have spoken more than 40 languages and dialects, and describes his method of acquiring second languages in the following way:

> First he bought a simple grammar and vocabulary and underlined the words and rules he felt should be remembered. Putting these books in his pocket, he studied them at every spare moment during the day, never working more than fifteen minutes at a time. By this method he was able to learn 300 words a week. When he acquired a basic vocabulary, he chose a simple story book and read it, marking with a pencil any new words he wanted to remember and going over these at least once a day. Then he went on to a more difficult book, at the same time learning the finer points of the grammar . . . When native teachers were available, he claimed that he always learned the 'swear words' first and laughingly said that after that the rest of the language was easy.

Dulay, Burt & Krashen (1982: 21), reporting work by Sorenson (1967), describe the L2 learning situation that exists among the Indians living in the area of the Vaupes River in South America:

> The Vaupes River Indians may well be the world's leading experts in practical language learning. Almost two-dozen mutually unintelligible languages are spoken in a small area populated by a group of about 10,000 people. Furthermore, it is the custom in this Indian culture to marry outside one's language group — people must find mates who do not speak their language! As a consequence, children must learn at least three languages from the start: their mother's, their father's, and the lingua franca of the area (Tukano). More languages are typically acquired as the individual grows up, and this extraordinary language learning continues throughout adolescence, adulthood, and even into the later years.

Appel & Muysken (1987: 22) report on the multi-L2 situation that exists in Mauritius:

> On an island with less than a million inhabitants, over ten languages have sizable groups of speakers. Most of these are associated with particular ethnic groups . . . a businessman with a Bhojpuri ethnic background may use English on the telephone when dealing with a large company, French when negotiating a building permit with a government official, joke with his colleagues in Creole, and then go home to speak Hindi with his wife and both Hindi and Creole with his children: Creole when making jokes, Hindi when telling them to do their homework.

More recently a number of studies of particularly talented L2 learners have begun to appear in print. Obler (1989: 147) reports on CJ, a 29-year-old male whose 'first true experience with a second language came at the age of 15 with formal instruction of French in high school'. Thereafter CJ went on to learn German, Spanish, Latin, Moroccan Arabic and Italian, either in the classroom or in informal environments in the country in question, reportedly picking up Spanish and Italian 'in a matter of weeks'. Tsimpli & Smith (1991) are in the process of studying a particularly talented L2 learner, Christopher, whom they refer to as a 'polyglot savant'. Although he is unable physically to look after himself, and has therefore been institutionalised, Christopher has some competence in about 16 languages. He acquires new second languages remarkably quickly, and has an extraordinary facility for translating between them rapidly.

For most of us the acquisition of second languages is less spectacular. If we are past the age of around 7–10 years the acquisition of an L2, in marked contrast to the way we acquired our first language (L1), can turn out to be rather slow, laborious and, even in talented L2 learners, tends to stop short of native-like proficiency. This 'stopping short' has been referred to as fossilisation (Selinker, 1972) or incompleteness (Schachter, 1990). It is one of the noticeable characteristics of second language acquisition (SLA). Even after many years of exposure to an L2, in a situation where the speaker might use that L2 every day for normal communicative purposes, even to the extent of 'losing' the native language, it is not uncommon to find that the speaker still has a strong 'foreign' accent, uses non-native grammatical constructions, and has non-native intuitions about the interpretation of certain types of sentence.

For example, Krashen (1988: 13) describes the L2 English of a native

Chinese speaker referred to as 'P'. P was in her forties, and had begun learning English when she first arrived in the United States in her twenties. Even after 20 years of exposure to English, however, P's English was not entirely native-like in spontaneous production, as was revealed in a study of her English over a three-week period: 'Observers, native speakers of English (usually P's son), simply recorded her errors from utterances she produced in normal family living or in friendly conversational situations. The data were gathered over a three-week period and about 80 errors were tabulated.' The types of errors made by P were: omission of the third person singular ending on verbs (e.g. 'she walk' instead of 'she walk -s'); incorrect irregular past tense forms; failure to make the verb 'be' agree with the subject; use of 'much' with countable nouns (e.g. 'much books'), and so on — types of errors which native speakers rarely make, although they do make plenty of slips of the tongue, false starts and other 'performance' errors. Thus after 20 years of exposure to English as an L2, and having brought up a native English-speaking son, this L2 learner still makes a considerable number of non-native 'errors' in spontaneous speech.

Coppieters (1987) investigated in some detail the intuitions of a group of 21 L2 speakers of French from diverse L1 backgrounds about the grammaticality and interpretation of a range of French constructions, and compared their intuitions with those of a group of 20 native speakers of French. The L2 speakers were very near-native speakers, as judged by their native French-speaking friends, colleagues, students, and by Coppieters himself (who is a native French speaker). Although none of them had been exposed to real communicative situations involving French before the age of 18, six of them had no clearly detectable foreign accent, and all of them had been resident in France for at least 5.5 years, with an average length of residence of 17.4 years. Nevertheless, Coppieters found major differences between the intuitions about French of this near-native group and those of the native speakers. To cite just a couple of examples: adjectives usually follow nouns in French, but some can appear both before and after nouns, with a difference in meaning. For example, *sale* does not mean the same thing in (1a) as it does in (1b):

1a *une sale histoire*
   a sorry story, a mess

 b *une histoire sale*
   a dirty story

While the native speakers Coppieters tested had stable and consistent intuitions about meaning differences induced by the different placement of adjectives in the contrasting sentences they were presented with, the near-native speakers sometimes failed to detect any meaning differences at all, or had idiosyncratic interpretations. The third person subject pronouns *il/elle*, 'he, she or it', and *ce*, also 'it', can alternate freely in some environments but only one or the other is possible in other environments. The native speakers again had stable intuitions about these cases, but the near-native speakers showed a strong tendency to interpret *il/elle* as referring to people, and *ce* as referring to things, which is not the contrast relevant to the distribution of *il/elle* and *ce* in native French.

We have, then, a situation where people have the potential to learn second languages throughout their lives, but where that learning is not as successful as it is in the case of the acquisition of one's native language. One of the central goals for any theory of SLA must be to account for this. L2 learners typically acquire second languages slowly, with some effort and incompletely. There have been a number of approaches adopted by researchers in SLA towards explaining such phenomena. They fall into three broad categories: linguistic approaches, sociolinguistic approaches, and psychological or cognitive approaches.

Linguistic approaches to the nature of SLA are of a single broad type: they assume that infants are born with a 'language faculty' which equips them with biologically determined grammatical tools for the task of acquiring, natively, the language that is spoken around them. In SLA this language faculty has undergone some structural changes with the course of time, either as the result of the general biological development of the individual ('maturation'), or as the result of an L1 having been acquired. These structural changes which take place in the mental language faculty are what leads to differences between L2 and L1 acquisition.

Sociolinguistic approaches have been concerned with at least two issues: one is the attitudes which L2 learners have towards the L2, the people who speak it, or the culture with which the language is associated. Whether those attitudes are positive or negative may be involved in determining a learner's motivation to learn the L2, and indirectly influence the nature of SLA itself. The second issue is the effect that the context in which the learner encounters or uses the L2 has on the process of acquisition.

Psychological or cognitive approaches have also been concerned with at least two issues: one is the general cognitive maturity of L2 learners as compared with L1 learners. L1 learners acquire knowledge of language and knowledge of the world simultaneously, whereas L2 learners already know quite a lot about the world when they come to the task of SLA.

General cognitive differences may be involved in differences in language acquisition between the two groups. The second issue is the nature of the mental devices which comprehend, store and produce language, and how this might be related to the way that L1 and L2 learners acquire particular languages.

It is our intention in this book to assess these various approaches – the linguistic, the sociolinguistic and the psychological — to how people learn second languages, the levels of success they achieve, and the relationship between L2 and L1 learning. Our starting point will be that there are (at least) five core areas of observed L2 behaviour for which a theory of SLA must account:

- (subconscious) *transfer* of grammatical properties from the L1 mental grammar into the mental grammar that learners construct for the L2.
- *staged development* in SLA: L2 learners in the general case do not acquire properties of the L2 immediately, but go through a series of 'transitional stages' towards the target language
- *systematicity* across L2 learners in the way that knowledge about the L2 being learned grows (i.e. the stages of development are common to many L2 learners).
- *variability* in the intuitions about and production of the L2 at various stages of L2 development
- *incompleteness* for the majority of L2 learners in the grammatical knowledge about the L2 attained in relation to native speakers of that target language.

In line with certain recent trends in work on language acquisition (see for example Chomsky, 1986a; White, 1991b; Hyams, 1991) the central thesis of this book will be that linguistic knowledge is an autonomous component in SLA, distinct from the socially determined use of the L2, and distinct from psychological capacities for understanding, storing and producing utterances in the L2. The investigation of each of the three areas has different insights to offer, and the interaction of the three areas produces the five types of observed behaviour in SLA. But there are major advantages to be gained from keeping them apart, both on the descriptive and theoretical levels. Our own approach will therefore be to consider them separately.

In Chapter 1 examples of the observed behaviour in need of explanation outlined above will be considered — this will not be an exhaustive list, but will illustrate phenomena which any theory of SLA would have to account for. Then a number of attempts to account for these phenomena from the 1960s onwards will be surveyed in Chapters 2–4. In Chapters 5–9 we shall review research which has made use of the theory of Universal Grammar developed in works such as Chomsky (1981, 1986a, b) (see Haegeman, 1991, for an introductory overview), and give examples of how this approach to language, appropriately interpreted for the context of SLA, can provide insight into several of the observations. At the same time, a number of problems which Universal Grammar apparently cannot handle have to be dealt with in a framework based on language use and language processing. Chapters 10–13 examine how those problems might be handled, and begin to explore the points of contact between linguistic knowledge and other knowledge systems. In Chapter 14 we shall bring together the strands of the argument in a single model and propose further directions for research.

Notes

1. Some writers on second language acquisition make a distinction between second language *acquisition* and second language *learning*. They do so often for two reasons: (1) to distinguish people who learn second languages naturalistically (that is, from exposure to samples of the L2 in their daily lives) from people who learn second languages in the classroom — they would say that naturalistic learners 'acquire' second languages, but tutored learners 'learn' them; or (2) to distinguish different types of knowledge that L2 learners might have — knowledge which they have 'acquired' unconsciously through using the L2, and knowledge which they have consciously 'learned' from their teachers, from textbooks, from grammars and dictionaries, and so on. The evidence to support making such distinctions, however, is not strong, as will become clear as the book proceeds. For this reason we make no such distinction and use 'acquisition' and 'learning' interchangeably throughout.

1 The Observable Phenomena of Second Language Acquisition

Any serious approach to the construction of a theory of SLA, it seems to us, would (minimally) need to offer some plausible account for five observations that can be made about SLA.

There is Transfer of Properties of the L1 Grammar into the L2 Grammar

When we hear non-native speakers using English we are frequently able to make a good guess about the native language of those speakers. This may be the effect of a particular 'foreign accent', or of particular syntactic, morphological or lexical features characteristic of the native language in question. Transfer of linguistic properties from a speaker's L1 into the L2 is a pervasive feature of SLA. Odlin (1989) has devoted a whole book to the topic, and up to the 1960s it was the main focus of attention for anyone involved with thinking about the nature of second languages. Transfer seems to affect all linguistic levels: phonetics/phonology (pronunciation), syntax (the construction of sentences), morphology (the internal structure of words), lexicon (vocabulary), and discourse (the communicative use that sentences are put to). We are most aware of transfer in SLA where the L1 and L2 differ on a particular property, because this leads to patterns in the speech of the non-native speaker not found in the speech of the native speaker.

For example, at the phonological level, nasal vowels and /y/ exist in French words like those in (1.1a). Diphthongs and /ð/ exist in English words like those in (1.1b):

1.1a *bon*, good; *sang*, blood; *fin*, end; *pur*, pure; *sud*, south
   b fail, soil, bout; this; there

It is a noticeable feature of many L1 English speakers of L2 French that they pronounce words like *fin* as English 'fan', or words like *sud* as English 'sued', and of many L1 French speakers of L2 English that they pronounce words like 'fail' a bit like 'fell', and 'this' as 'zees'. This is clearly because they are transferring phonological properties of English into French, and French into English.

There are also more subtle forms of phonological transfer. Spanish, for example, has the sound [ð] intervocalically in words like *todo*, 'all', and therefore in principle Spanish learners of English should have little difficulty with this sound in words such as 'this' and 'there'. However, [ð] is not a phoneme in Spanish, but only a positional variant (an allophone) of the phoneme /d/ when it appears intervocalically, as in *todo*. In word-initial position, or after /l/ or /n/, Spanish /d/ is pronounced as English [d]. Many L1 Spanish speakers have trouble with word-initial or post-consonantal [ð] in L2 English, and this is the direct result of transfer.

At the level of syntax and morphology, consider the following cases: Selinker, Swain & Dumas (1975), studying seven-year-old English-speaking children learning French in a Canadian-French immersion programme (in which English-speaking children are taught the normal school curriculum through the medium of French) found that after two years of immersion their subjects were making errors such as those in (1.2) and (1.3).

1.2a **Le chien a mangé* les.[1]
The dog has eaten them.
(Native French: *Le chien les a mangés.*)

b **Il veut* les *encore.*
He wants them again.
(Native French: *Il les veut encore.*)

1.3 **Le chat* toujours *mordre.*
The cat always bites.
(Native French: *Le chat mord toujours.*)

These would appear to be cases of the transfer of syntactic properties from English to French: in (1.2) the postverbal position of unstressed object pronouns has been transferred, rather than learners using the required preverbal position for pronouns in French, and in (1.3) the adverb is located in a position possible in English but not in French. As a case of morphological transfer, consider the example (1.4) observed by Dulay & Burt (1983) in the L2 English of an L1 Spanish speaker.

1.4 **Now she's putting *hers* clothes on.*

Spanish possessive determiners inflect for both gender and number, whereas English possessive determiners only inflect for gender.

In the area of the lexicon most of us have come across examples such as those in (1.5) produced by L1 French speakers learning L2 English.

1.5a *I have very hungry.
  b *I have twelve years old.

In French the verb which appears in these constructions is the one which corresponds to English 'have': *avoir; J'ai très faim, J'ai douze ans.* French speakers, it seems, often transfer this lexical choice from French into English. A more amusing example of the same type is offered by Selinker (1983), who observed a Hebrew speaker produce sentence (1.6) in L2 English.

1.6 I shall order two girls for dinner.

It seems that in Hebrew the verb *lehazim* has two meanings — 'to invite' and 'to order' — and the speaker who uttered sentence (1.6) has assumed that the same lexical range applies to 'order' in English.

Transfer is even visible at the level of discourse. The French for 'if', for example, is *si*, but the discourse functions of *si* go beyond those of 'if'. This is notably the case in invitations: *si on allait au cinema?* literally means 'if one went to the cinema?', but it is used regularly to mean 'Shall we go to the cinema?'. L1 French speakers often transfer inappropriately this discourse function into their L2 English use of 'if' (Riley, 1981).

The examples of transfer offered up to this point have been cases where the L1 and L2 differ on a given property. But transfer of properties of the L1, where the L1 and the L2 are structurally identical, may also have observable effects in SLA. For example, it may facilitate and speed up the learning process for the L2 learner. Zobl (1984) has noted that the acquisition of the determiners 'a'/'the' in English is faster for L2 learners whose native language also makes a distinction between indefinite and definite determiners (such as French and Spanish) than for those L2 learners whose native language does not make such a distinction (such as Chinese or Russian).

White (1986a) compared L1 Spanish and L1 French speakers learning English as an L2, and found that the French speakers acquired English subject pronouns more rapidly than the Spanish speakers. This follows from the fact that Spanish is a language which allows phonetically unspecified (null) subjects, but English and French do not. While the Spanish speakers transfer null subjects initially into their L2 English grammars, inappropriately as it turns out, the French speakers transfer the notion of phonetically specified subjects, enabling them, it seems, to acquire English subject pronouns more rapidly.

There is Staged Development in Second Language Acquisition

The acquisition of second languages is typically 'staged'; that is, from the initial-state grammars that L2 learners construct (often heavily influenced by transfer) they go through stages of development towards the target language. In this respect L2 learners resemble L1 learners, who also typically go through stages of development towards the target language, although more often than not starting from a different initial-state grammar.

For example, word order patterns in German are relatively complex. In main clauses the tense-inflected and person-inflected verb must appear in second position in the clause, whether the first position is occupied by the subject or some other phrase such as an adverb. This is usually referred to as 'verb-second' or V2. But any non-finite verb form accompanying the inflected verb (a participle, an infinitive or a verb particle) must appear in clause final position. This is often referred to as 'verb-separation'. V2 and verb-separation are illustrated in (1.7a) and (1.7b). In subordinate clauses any tense-inflected and person-inflected verb must appear generally in clause-final position (as in (1.7c)). This is referred to as 'verb-final':

1.7a *Er hat heute ein Buch gekauft.*
     He has today a book bought.

  b *Heute hat er ein Buch gekauft.*
     Today has he a book bought.

  c *Ich glaube dass er heute ein Buch gekauft hat.*
     I think that he today a book bought has.

Clahsen & Muysken (1986) have observed that adult L2 learners of German (speakers of Italian, Spanish, Portuguese and Turkish as first languages) go through a number of stages in acquiring these word order patterns. Initially they assume the word order patterns illustrated in (1.8), none of which are grammatical in native-speaker German.

1.8a *Er hat gekauft ein Buch heute.*

b *Heute er hat gekauft ein Buch.
c *Ich glaube dass heute er hat gekauft ein Buch.

These word orders in the early grammars of the L2 speakers in question are probably the result of transfer from their first languages (although Clahsen & Muysken do not think that this is the reason; see discussion in Chapter 6). Subsequently, however, learners acquire the appropriate target patterns in the following stages. First they acquire verb-separation; then they acquire V2; and in a third stage they acquire verb-final.

Interestingly, Clahsen & Muysken compare this development in L2 learners with development in child L1 learners of German, as reported in Clahsen (1984). Although L1 learners of German do not produce word order patterns like those in (1.8), suggesting that their initial-state grammars are different from those of the L2 learners in question, the development of the L1 learners involves an identical staged development: they acquire verb-separation first, then V2, and finally verb-final. Both L2 and L1 learners, then, display a staged development on this particular phenomenon. Many other examples of L2 staged development have been observed by L2 researchers, and we shall consider several of them in the course of the book.

There is Systematicity in the Growth of L2 Knowledge Across Learners

We have just seen in the case of German word order patterns that speakers of several different first languages — Italian, Spanish, Portuguese and Turkish — seem to go through a series of stages in moving towards the target language. They acquire verb-separation first, V2 next, and verb-final last of all. This is not only an example of staged development, but also an example of cross-learner systematicity. Learners from different L1 backgrounds develop L2 linguistic knowledge in a way that is not directly attributable either to their L1, or to the L2 input (there is nothing given in German word order patterns to tell learners that verb-separation should be acquired before V2, rather than vice versa, for example). The L2 speakers in question were, as it happens, all immigrant workers to Germany, acquiring German naturalistically (Meisel, Clahsen & Pienemann, 1981). But an identical order of development has been found by Ellis (1989) in a group of 29 adult L1 English speakers learning German in the classroom (in fact learners starting German as part of an undergraduate degree programme). Ellis found that these learners also acquired German word order in the sequence verb-separation, then V2, finally verb-final, even though this was not the sequence in which they encountered German word order patterns in the classroom.

As a second example, a number of studies in the 1970s and early 1980s found consistent patterns in the development of accuracy on grammatical morphology in English across a range of L2 learners from different language backgrounds, of different ages, and learning English under different conditions. Examples of the types of morphological phenomena in question are illustrated in (1.9).

1.9   Progressive: The boy is eating.
       Plural: The boys are hungry.
       Past regular: The boy shouted.
       Past irregular: The boy sang.
       Possessive: The boy's horse.
       Third person singular: The boy runs.
                               and so on.

Dulay & Burt (1973) first noticed that L2 learners systematically produced some grammatical morphemes more accurately than others across three groups of L1-Spanish speaking 5–8 year-olds in the United States. They subsequently replicated their findings with a group of 6–8-year-old Cantonese-speaking learners of L2 English, finding a significantly similar accuracy order (Dulay & Burt, 1974). Bailey, Madden & Krashen (1974) found a significantly similar accuracy order in a group of adult L2 learners of English from diverse L1 backgrounds. Makino (1980) studied 777 adolescent Japanese classroom learners of English in Japan, and not only found a high correlation between his subjects and those of Dulay & Burt, but also found that there was no relationship between this order and the order in which the Japanese learners were taught the grammatical morphemes in the classroom (on the basis of the textbooks they were using).

What it is important to retain from examples like this is that learners from different L1 backgrounds, acquiring an L2 under different conditions of exposure — naturalistic versus classroom — can go through the same stages of development. That is, there is systematic development which is independent either of the first language a learner speaks, or the type of input a learner has received. This is an important feature of SLA which any serious approach will have to account for.

There is Variability in Learners' Intuitions About, and Production of, Aspects of the L2 at Certain Stages of Development

The mental grammars of L2 learners at certain stages of development appear to allow more than one structural variant for a given construction where the target language has only one form. For example, Ellis (1992) reports an example of an 11-year-old Portuguese learner of L2 English who, while playing a card game, produced two separate utterances with apparently the same meaning:

1.10a No look my card.
   b Don't look my card.

Here the learner is variably using 'no' and 'don't' to perform the task of sentence negation, where the native speaker has only one construction: 'don't'. Another example is also offered by Ellis in the same book (p. 126):

> I have observed Zambian learners of English use the third person singular of the present simple tense correctly in simple sentences or in the initial clause of complex sentences but use the uninflected form in the second clause of complex sentences. For example:
>
> Moses lives in Lusaka.
> Moses lives in Lusaka, but he work in Kafue.

Such cases of variability may be of temporary duration in L2 development, or they may continue over long periods. For example, a study by Towell, Bazergui & Hawkins (1993) found that L1 English-speaking learners of L2 French (undergraduate students) had trouble with a contrast between the forms *de* and *à* in sentences like the following:

1.11a *C'est ennuyeux de lire des livres techniques.*
   It's boring to read technical books.

   b *Les livres techniques sont ennuyeux à lire.*
   Technical books are boring to read.

The crucial difference between the two is that when the subject of the clause in which adjectives like *ennuyeux* appear is also interpreted as the direct object of *lire*, as it is in (1.11b), the infinitive-introducing complemen-tiser *à* must be used. Elsewhere *de* must be used. However, several of the subjects in Towell, Bazergui & Hawkins' study failed to acquire this fact, although they recognised that *à* and *de* are required in this environment. Rather they randomly alternated the two forms, and they did so over several years.

Second Language Learners Stop Short of Native-like Success in a Number of Areas of the L2 Grammar

Very few L2 learners appear to be fully successful in the way that native speakers are. We noted this in the introduction, and gave two examples there. Consider another example from a study by Johnson & Newport (1989). Johnson & Newport administered a grammaticality judgement task to a population of 46 L1 Chinese and L1 Korean speakers who had acquired English as an L2. All subjects in the test had been in the United States for a minimum of five years (some considerably longer) with at least three years of continuous residence. The test itself covered a range of the grammatical properties of English: determiners ('a'/'the'), plural, verb subcategorisation (the selection of verb complements, for example: 'allow someone to/*Ø watch something', 'let someone Ø/*to watch something'), past tense, pronoun selection, particles (such as 'up' in 'pick the book up'), choice of auxiliary verbs, third person singular

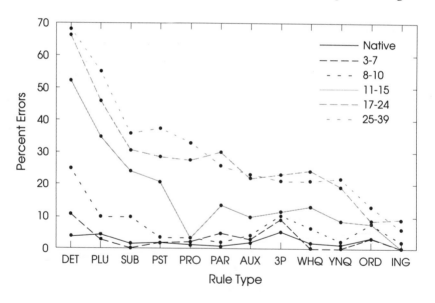

Key: Det = determiner, Plu = plural, Sub = subcategorisation, Pst = past, Pro = pronoun, Par = particle, Aux = auxiliary, 3P = 3rd person singular present, WHQ = wh-question, YNQ = yes/no question, Ord = word order, ING = present progressive inflection -ing.

Figure 1.1 Mean percentage of errors on 12 types of English rules

Source: Johnson & Newport, 1989

('run -s') wh- questions, yes-no questions, word order, and progressive ('-ing').

Johnson & Newport broke down the scores that their subjects achieved on the test by 'age of arrival' in the United States (which, in the case of their subjects, ranged from 3 to 39 years), and compared those scores with the scores of a group of 23 American-born native speakers of English who also took the test. The results are given in Figure 1.1 (taken from Johnson & Newport, 1989: 87).

The striking thing about these results is that they show that holding length of exposure to an L2 constant (a minimum of five years), the major factor which is influential in determining degree of success in attaining native speaker-like judgements is the age at which the learner is first exposed consistently to the L2. L1 Chinese and Korean speakers who were consistently exposed to English before the age of seven years (i.e. arrived in the US before that age) make as few errors on the test as native speakers. The older an L2 learner is when first consistent exposure starts, the more errors he or she makes, indicating a progressive failure to acquire native-like grammatical knowledge. But it is interesting to note that this failure does not affect all areas of grammatical knowledge equally. All of the L2 subjects make fewer errors on progressive -ing and word order patterns than on some of the other grammatical properties tested.

Summary

Approaches to the study of SLA must be able to account for a number of its observable properties:

- People can learn second languages throughout their lives, and can use those second languages for effective communication, although it seems that beyond the age of around seven years learners are not going to be as successful as pre-seven-year-olds at acquiring all its grammatical properties.
- Early L2 grammars are characterised by a considerable influence from the grammatical properties of the L1.
- In acquiring the L2, learners often go through transitional stages of development.
- The same stages can be found in different groups of L2 learners, of different ages, and learning the L2 under different conditions.
- L2 learners often go through phases of variability.

There have been three general approaches to an explanation of these factors in SLA — the linguistic, the sociolinguistic, and the psychological or cognitive — and it is the intention in the early chapters of this book to consider how these approaches might go about handling them. In the next chapter we review some early linguistic approaches to explaining the observable phenomena of SLA.

Note

1. Throughout we shall use the standard conversion of placing an asterisk before sentences which are considered ungrammatical by native speakers of the language in question.

2 Early Linguistic Approaches to Explaining the Observable Phenomena of Second Language Acquisition

The Contrastive Analysis Hypothesis

One of the first attempts to account for some of the observable phenomena of SLA has come to be known as the Contrastive Analysis Hypothesis. This was an enterprise built in the 1950s on the twin bases of structural linguistics and behaviourist psychology. Structural linguistics set about providing detailed linguistic descriptions of particular languages from a collection of utterances produced by native speakers: a 'corpus'. The rationale for this corpus-based approach derived from the notion of science which dominated at that period: everything had to be demonstrable in terms of the visible behaviour of whatever was being analysed, be it the behaviour of molecules, animals or humans. Behaviourist psychology held that the ability to perform in a first language represented a set of habits which had been acquired by linking language forms with meanings via reinforcement and reward.

The meeting of the two approaches — structural linguistics and behaviourist psychology — in researchers' thinking about SLA gave rise to the Contrastive Analysis Hypothesis. The logic was relatively simple: if acquisition of the L1 involved the formation of a set of habits, then the same process must also be involved in SLA, with the difference that some of the habits appropriate to the L2 will already have been acquired in the L1; others will have been acquired in the L1 but will need to be modified or eradicated in the context of the L2; and yet others will need to be acquired from scratch for the L2.

It followed from this that the basic information required to organise the learning of an L2 would be to know which habits were the same and which were different. This would allow a concentration on those which were different. It would simply remain to find ways and means of changing those habits which were different so that new, appropriate, L2 habits would be acquired. The purpose of contrastive analysis was to compare the structure of languages and to state where the differences lay so that teachers of foreign languages and course designers of foreign language syllabuses could focus the content of their classes on those structures where the language differed and use methods of reinforcement and reward to change those habits in the L2. The teaching method related to the approach was, of course, audio-lingualism as it was applied in language laboratories all over the world, particularly in America.

The term used to describe the way in which the learner related the first set of language habits to the second set of language habits was *transfer*: in cases where the languages were similar the transfer would be positive and would not need a lot of drilling/teaching for it to be acquired: in cases where the languages were different, the transfer would be negative and would need a great deal of drilling before the new set of habits could be automatised. Contrastive analysis would provide the essential information about the relationship between pairs of languages so that the real areas of difficulty — those where negative transfer or interference occurred — could be predicted.

Evaluation of the Contrastive Analysis Hypothesis

For a time the Contrastive Analysis Hypothesis appeared to make good predictions, not surprisingly, about one of the core observations noted in Chapter 1: transfer. But it had little to say about the other observations, and researchers became aware that even in the domain where it should make appropriate predictions, it also made inappropriate predictions. For example, not all areas of contrast between an L1 and an L2 lead to automatic learning difficulty. Consider again example (1.2) of native English-speaking learners of French negatively transferring English postverbal pronoun placement to produce ungrammatical examples, such as: *Le chien a mangé les*, 'The dog has eaten them' (native French: *Le chien les a mangés*), *Il veut les encore*, 'He wants them again' (native French: *Il les veut encore*). According to the Contrastive Analysis Hypothesis one would expect the same kind of difficulty for learners going in the other direction, i.e. for native speakers of French learning L2 English, who should produce errors like: *'The dog them has eaten', *'He them wants again'. Zobl (1980: 52) suggests, however, that one does not typically find such errors in French-speaking (or Spanish-speaking as it happens) learners of English, even though both languages have preverbal object pronouns. This is a case of a one-way learning difficulty. Although the Contrastive Analysis Hypopthesis can explain the behaviour of English learners of French, it cannot explain the behaviour of French or Spanish learners of English on this property.

Sorace (1993) reports that L1 Italian learners of L2 French have more trouble acquiring the distribution of the auxiliary verbs *avoir/être*, 'have'/'be', than L1 French learners of L2 Italian do in acquiring the Italian equivalents *avere/essere*. Although *avoir/avere* and *être/essere* are cognates, *être* has a more restricted distribution than *essere*. Since the two languages contrast on this property, the Contrastive Analysis Hypothesis predicts that both groups of learners should have difficulty in acquiring the appropriate distribution in the other language, and not that there will be a one-way learning difficulty.

A second problem for the Contrastive Analysis Hypothesis is that not all areas of similarity between an L1 and an L2 lead to immediate positive transfer. Odlin (1989), for example, reports that although Spanish has a copula verb similar to English 'be' in sentences such as 'That's very simple', 'The picture's very dark', L1 Spanish learners of L2 English characteristically omit the copula in early stages of acquisition, saying: 'That very simple', 'The picture very dark'.

A third problem for the Contrastive Analysis Hypothesis is that when researchers began systematically to classify errors in L2 learners' oral and written productions, they found that the number of errors which could unambiguously be attributed to contrasting properties between the first and second languages was only a relatively small proportion of all errors. Lococo (1975) for example suggests that in the corpus she studied errors which result from L1/L2 contrast are no more than 25% of the total number of non-native forms produced by the learners she studied.

A study by Jackson (1981) of the acquisition of L2 English by L1 Punjabi speakers living in central England, which assumes the Contrastive Analysis Hypothesis as an instrument of explanation, brings out well the problems that arise, and so we shall consider this study in some detail. Jackson first describes key points of contrast between the grammars of English and Punjabi, and then effects a comparison between these points of contrast and a corpus of errors in the L2 English of Punjabi speakers supplied by their English teachers.

English and Punjabi differ in (at least) the following areas:

(a) English has prepositions, such as 'in', 'on', 'to', 'at', and so on, whereas the equivalent forms in Punjabi are postpositions. This means that whereas English has phrases such as 'in the garden', 'at the post office', Punjabi's equivalent phrases are 'garden in' and 'post office at' (no definite article exists in Punjabi).

(b) English has two ways of expressing the possessive. One where the possessor precedes the possessed and there is a 'possessive inflection', -'s, as in 'the horse's mouth', and another where the possessor follows the possessed, and the two are linked by the preposition 'of': 'the mouth of the horse'. In Punjabi there is only one possessive construction, which consists of placing the possessor before the possessed and linking the two by a particle, in the manner: 'the horse [particle] the mouth'.

(c) In yes/no questions in English (that is, questions which require a 'yes' or 'no' answer) there is usually inversion between the subject and an auxiliary verb such as 'may', 'must', 'can', 'do', and so on, as for example in (2.1).

2.1a I may come. → May I come?
   b She comes here often. → Does she come here often?

In Punjabi, not only is there no subject–verb inversion of this kind in yes/no questions, but the verb normally also comes at the end of the clause, giving equivalent yes/no question forms in Punjabi such as: 'I come may?', 'She here often comes?'

(d) In wh- questions in English (that is, questions which involve a wh-word such as 'who', 'what', 'when', 'why'), the wh- word usually comes first in the sentence, followed by an auxiliary verb, as shown in (2.2).

2.2a Who is coming to the party?
   b What did you have for breakfast?
   c Why has he gone home?

In Punjabi, there is again no inversion of subject and verb, and the wh- word comes immediately before the verb, which is usually the last item in the clause, as shown in (2.3).

2.3a Party to who-coming is?
   b You breakfast for what-have?
   c He home why-gone has?

(e) The English simple present tense verb has the inflection -s in the context of third person singular subjects, for example: 'I walk', 'you walk', 'he/she/it walks', and so on. In Punjabi, the only verb forms which inflect for person and number are the future and subjunctive forms.

Following this outline of key points of contrast between the two languages, Jackson then notes the following error patterns in the L2 English of Punjabi speakers:

(a') Despite the fact that English has prepositions and Punjabi postpositions, there were no instances of learners saying things such as 'garden in' or 'post office at' in the corpus of errors.

(b') With respect to the possessive construction, errors found in the corpus were of the type shown in (2.4).

> 2.4a There's a shoe of a pair, *for* There's a pair of shoes.
> b Some crisps of packets, *for* Some packets of crisps.
> c His hand of the fingers, *for* The fingers of his hand.

(c') In yes/no questions errors such as those in (2.5) were produced.

> 2.5a You can run? *for* Can you run?
> b You know where they finding? *for* Do you know where to find them?

(d') In wh- questions errors such as those in (2.6) were produced.

> 2.6a What this is? *for* What is this?
> b How I do this? *for* How do I do this?
> c How big he was? *for* How big was he?

(e') In the case of the English singular third person present tense -s inflection, errors such as those in (2.7) were found in the corpus.

> 2.7a He clean his face, *for* He cleans his face.
> b We cleans his face, *for* We clean his face.
> c Does a cat drinks water? *for* Does a cat drink water?

Jackson's account of the pattern of errors runs as follows. First, although non-native-like forms arise in the L2 English of the subjects in cases (b)-(e), none appears to arise in case (a). Since there is a noticeable difference between prepositions and postpositions, the first problem for the Contrastive Analysis Hypothesis is to explain why a grammatical difference between the two languages does not give rise to learning difficulty and error on the part of the learners. Jackson attributes this to the fact that the distinction preposition/postposition is a 'gross' difference between languages. Where there are 'gross' differences learners will notice them straight away, and will not be led to negatively transfer the L1 property.

Secondly, in cases (b)–(e), Jackson suggests that the errors that arise are all directly attributable to negative transfer: the odd possessive construction — 'some crisps of packets'; non-inversion of subject and auxiliary verb in questions — 'you can run?', 'what this is?'; and uncertainty about what to attach the third person singular present tense inflection to — 'we cleans his face', 'does a cat drinks water?'.

However, this account leaves a number of questions unanswered. What makes particular contrasts between languages 'gross', and others not? In what way is the contrast between prepositions and postpositions 'more gross' than the contrast between subject–verb inversion and non subject–verb inversion? Furthermore, in the case of questions, it seems that many, if not all, L2 learners of English, speaking whatever first language, go through a phase in acquiring questions when they do not invert the subject and an auxiliary verb, *even if* their L1 has subject–verb inversion. Also, why do Punjabi speakers not negatively transfer the position of the wh- word, producing sentences such as 'This what is?', which they appear not to. Here Jackson (1981: 201) has recourse again to the notion of 'grossness': 'the contrast in position of the wh- word appears to be a gross enough difference not to cause interference errors: but the lack of inversion causes errors here.' Similarly, problems with the third person singular present tense inflection -s are common to all L2 learners of English, even for native speakers of languages with rich present tense verbal inflection systems. How is the Contrastive Analysis Hypothesis to explain this kind of systematic behaviour across a range of learners of L1s with properties both different from and similar to English?

The one case from the list where there are reasonable grounds for suggesting that negative transfer is involved is the case of the possessive construction. Errors such as 'there's a shoe of a pair' are not, to our knowledge, frequently found in the L2 English of native speakers of languages other than Punjabi.

Assessing the Contrastive Analysis Hypothesis as an approach to explaining the five core observations about SLA, it could be said that it provides some account of transfer, but it both overpredicts (some contrasts between languages do not lead to negative transfer), and underpredicts (some similarities between languages pose learning problems for L2 learners). One might try to modify the account, as Jackson (1981) does, to distinguish cases of 'gross' contrast between languages which (presumably) are so noticeable for L2 learners that they do not constitute an area of potential difficulty. But 'grossness' is hardly a usable concept: any area of contrast between two languages which does not induce learning difficulty would have to be an area of 'gross' contrast, but this is merely to apply a label to a problem and not to explain it. The notion of 'transfer', as it is used within the Contrastive Analysis Hypothesis, at best classifies but does not explain why learners construct certain grammatical representations, but not others.

The Natural Order Hypothesis

The growing awareness of the failure of the Contrastive Analysis Hypothesis to predict a number of observations in SLA led to a shift in perspective on the part of researchers in the late 1960s and early 1970s from a primary interest in transfer (the first of our observations about SLA) to a primary interest in staged development and cross-learner systematicity (the second and third observations). This shift in perspective was signalled in two landmark papers of the period, one by Corder (1967) on 'The significance of learners' errors', and the other by Selinker (1972) on 'Interlanguage'. Both papers stress the autonomy of the L2 learner's mental grammar, which has come to be known (pace Selinker) as his or her *interlanguage grammar*, a grammatical system with its own internal organising principles which may or may not be related to the L1 and the L2, that being a matter for empirical and theoretical investigation.

The morpheme studies

This shift in perspective led to an interest on the part of researchers in conducting empirical research on staged development and systematicity in L2 learning. The L2 'morpheme studies' were among the first of this kind of study (Dulay & Burt, 1973, 1974; Bailey, Madden & Krashen, 1974), inspired by the work on L1 acquisition of Brown (1973). At around about this time Brown and his colleagues were investigating the acquisition of grammatical morphology by child L1 learners of English. Brown made two important discoveries. First, that in three unrelated children acquiring L1 English in different households (and therefore probably exposed to different samples of English) the order in which the grammatical morphemes of English appeared in the speech of the children was the same. To illustrate, the first 9 of the 14 morphemes Brown studied emerged in the order shown below:

1. Progressive -*ing*   The boy (is) eat*ing*.
2. Plural   The boy*s* are hungry.
3. Irregular past   The boy *sang*.
4. Possessive   The boy*'s* book.
5. Article   He saw *the/a* boy.
6. Regular past   The boy shout*ed*.
7. Third person singular   The boy run*s*.
8. Copula *'s*   The boy*'s* hungry.
9. Auxiliary *'s*   The boy*'s* going.

Second, that there was no correlation between this order of emergence of grammatical morphology and the frequency with which each morpheme occurred in the speech addressed to the child learners. These findings lent considerable empirical support to an emerging view in linguistic theory at that time that a large part of human linguistic ability is innate, such that L1 acquisition and the eventual grammatical knowledge attained by native speakers is determined by abstract internal mental structures, and is considerably under-determined by the input. Brown's findings lent support to this view because even in development, it seems, child L1 learners of English proceed in ways which are independent of input, but similar across learners, at least in the area of grammatical morphology.

The work of Brown strongly attracted L2 researchers who were disillusioned with the explanatory power of the Contrastive Analysis Hypothesis, and who were now themselves focusing on staged development and systematicity across learners. Dulay & Burt (1973) were the first researchers to investigate the acquisition of grammatical morphemes in L2 English. Using a technique called the Bilingual Syntax Measure, in which subjects are presented with a series of cartoon drawings and are asked questions about them, Dulay & Burt first elicited spontaneous speech from three groups of 5–8-year-old L1 Spanish speakers in three locations in the United States. They then checked the productions of their subjects for the frequency with which grammatical morphemes were being produced in contexts where native speakers would obligatorily produce morphemes. On the basis of this checking Dulay & Burt were able to establish an 'order of accuracy' for their subject groups going from the morpheme on which they were most like native speakers descending to the morpheme on which they were least like native speakers. They found a similar 'order of accuracy' in the use of English grammatical morphemes across the three groups of L1 Spanish-speaking children, although this order was different from the acquisition order found by Brown for L1 learners of English.[1]

In case this initial finding was an artifact of the L1 Spanish language background of the subjects, Dulay & Burt (1974) repeated the task with a group of 115 L1 Cantonese-speaking 6 8 year-olds. The order of accuracy found for these subjects was remarkably similar to the order found with the Spanish speakers. Bailey, Madden & Krashen (1974) repeated the same task with a group of 73 adult learners of L2 English (aged 17-55) from diverse L1 backgrounds, again finding a remarkably similar order of accuracy. What these findings seemed to indicate was that both child and adult learners of the same L2, from differing L1 backgrounds, and learning under different conditions of exposure (naturalistic, classroom and mixed environments), developed accuracy on grammatical morphology in a 'natural' order.

Other studies began to appear suggesting that systematic staged development in SLA was a common phenomenon, for example: Ravem's (1974) case study of a Norwegian-speaking child learning English; Cazden, Cancino, Rosanksy & Schumann's (1975) study of L1 Spanish-speakers learning L2 English; Hakuta's (1976) study of a Japanese-speaking child learning English; Wode's (1976) study of L1 German child learners of L2 English.

Krashen's five hypotheses

The discovery of clear examples of staged development led a number of researchers to conclude that the Contrastive Analysis Hypothesis about SLA had been mistaken, and that the course of SLA, like the course of L1 acquisition, is determined by innate principles of linguistic knowledge, what Corder (1967: 166) called in relation to SLA a 'built-in syllabus'. Krashen (1985: 1) formulated the observation as a hypothesis:

Natural Order Hypothesis
To my knowledge, this hypothesis was first proposed for second language acquisition by Corder (1967). It states that we acquire the rules of language in a predictable way, some rules tending to come early and others late. The order does not appear to be determined solely by formal simplicity, and there is evidence that it is independent of the order in which rules are taught in language classes.

But it soon became clear that the Natural Order Hypothesis needed to be supplemented by ancillary hypotheses. For a start, it was found that while 'natural' orders were often displayed in the spontaneous, unplanned productions of L2 learners, when learners were allowed to plan their productions, or when the task was not spontaneous production, but a grammar exercise, a drill or a translation, those orders could change. Typically learners display different degrees of approximation to target language norms under different task conditions. As an example, consider a study by Ellis (1987b). Ellis asked 17 adult learners of L2 English from diverse L1 backgrounds to perform three tasks: (a) to write a story based on a picture composition, where subjects were allowed one hour to complete the task; (b) to retell orally in the language laboratory the story they had written; (c) to tell orally in the language laboratory a story about another picture composition without prior planning. One of the grammatical pheonmena that Ellis considered in the samples collected from subjects was the use of the regular past tense -ed. He found that subjects were most target-like in their use of this morpheme in the planned written composition, less target-like on the oral retelling, and least target-like on the unplanned telling of a different picture composition. Task-based differences in accuracy of this sort are common in SLA (see Tarone (1988) for discussion).

Similarly, if L2 speakers are asked to produce the L2 spontaneously, but are subsequently asked to review what they have said/written making corrections where necessary, it is found that they are aware of discrepancies between what they have said/written and what they know about target-language norms. Dulay, Burt & Krashen (1982: 64), for example, found that, depending on the study, L2 subjects could increase their accuracy by between 6% and 47% with this kind of *post hoc* reviewing procedure.

Variability in L2 performance of this sort across tasks led Krashen (1982, 1985, 1988) to supplement the Natural Order Hypothesis with the hypothesis that L2 learners are capable of developing two types of distinct grammatical knowledge about the L2: *acquired* L2 knowledge, which develops subconsciously in learners as the result of exposure to the L2, and *learned* L2 knowledge, which L2 learners acquire consciously, either through learning about the language from textbooks or teachers, or through forming their own 'rules of thumb'. Krashen's view is that 'real' L2 knowledge of the kind found in learners' spontaneous, meaningful productions can be initiated only by the acquired system, which develops as the result of the learner being involved with the L2 in spontaneous, meaningful interactions. The acquired system of knowledge is the one which displays natural orders of development. Under certain circumstances, however, knowledge about the L2 which has been consciously learned can be used by L2 learners to *monitor* the output initiated by the acquired system, to check for discrepancies, and to correct the output where such discrepancies are found. The circumstances in which such monitoring can occur, according to Krashen's early work, are where the learner has enough time to access the learned knowledge which he or she possesses, and where the learner is focused on the form of what he or she is producing. Putting natural orders, acquired versus learned knowledge, and monitoring together, we have the first three hypotheses of Krashen's (1985) model for SLA:

The Acquisition-Learning Hypothesis
The Natural Order Hypothesis
The Monitor Hypothesis.

To these Krashen adds a further hypothesis:

The Affective Filter Hypothesis.

This is 'that part of the internal processing system that subconsciously screens incoming language based on what psychologists call "affect": the learner's motives, needs, attitudes, and emotional states', which sets in around puberty (Dulay, Burt & Krashen, 1982: 46). It determines whether a person is more or less inhibited in situations of L2 use. Where people are very inhibited, the filter is 'high' and prevents a lot of L2 input from being converted into acquired knowledge. Where people are less inhibited, the filter is 'lower', allowing a greater proportion of L2 input to be converted into acquired knowledge.

The Affective Filter Hypothesis allows some account to be given of individual differences between L2 learners who, although ostensibly receiving the same L2 input, can show wide differences in their development of both acquired and learned knowledge (for example in a classroom situation where the input is effectively the same for all class members, but where the outcomes in individual learners can be quite different). Given the Affective Filter Hypothesis it could be suggested that the less successful learners have a 'higher' filter than the more successful ones. The Affective Filter Hypothesis could also permit some account to be given of incompleteness in SLA: learners who fail to achieve native-like intuitions of grammaticality have been hampered by their affective filters, which have not allowed them to take in the range of input necessary for the acquired system to develop fully. On this account the acquired system is in principle as powerful in SLA as it is in L1 acquisition. The difference in 'completeness' between L2 and L1 learners arises because infants, by hypothesis, do not have an affective filter and are therefore untroubled by inhibitions. (For fuller details see Krashen (1985), who also discusses a fifth hypothesis — the Input Hypothesis — which relates specifically to the kind of L2 exposure which will optimally allow learners' acquired knowledge to develop.)

Evaluation of the Natural Order Hypothesis

Krashen's system of hypotheses attracted enormous interest, at least in the 1980s. It was one of the first attempts to provide an integrated account of some of the core observations about SLA which we have suggested any serious approach to providing a theory of SLA would need to account for. Although, as we shall see shortly, on closer inspection the hypotheses that make up Krashen's system (excluding for the purposes of exposition the 'Input Hypothesis') fail in crucial ways to make the right predictions, the account was pioneering, and helped to focus thinking about what the key issues requiring explanation in SLA are.

Consider now how his system deals with the five core observations in which we are interested: transfer, staged development, systematicity, variability and incompleteness. First, transfer has disappeared from the account. This was probably an historical consequence of the evolution in thinking that had taken place in SLA research; once researchers had become disillusioned with the Contrastive Analysis Hypothesis which treated all L2 phenomena as transfer effects, the pendulum swung to the other extreme: no L2 phenomena are the result of transfer effects. They are either 'acquired' or 'learned' effects. This is clearly implausible, given the range of evidence we have already considered. No doubt the Acquired/Learning Hypothesis could be modified to incorporate some notion of transfer, but since we shall argue that the whole system is ill-founded we shall not do this here.

Secondly, although staged development and systematicity have been given a label — 'acquired knowledge' — this is an entirely mysterious phenomenon in Krashen's system. Why learners go through the stages they do receives no explanation. To say that L2 knowledge is acquired through meaningful interactions involving the L2 is to do no more than observe that there is staged development, and learners are systematic in going through those stages. A serious approach to SLA needs to tell us much more about development and systematicity than this.

Thirdly, variability in performance across tasks is crucially dependent in Krashen's system on the learned component of knowledge which, given the right conditions (consciously knowing the rule in question, being focused on form, and having enough time), monitors the output initiated by the acquired system, checks for discrepancies between it and learned knowledge, and corrects where there are such discrepancies. However, there are good reasons to believe that L2 learners are variable across tasks even where they do not appear to consciously know the rules, and even when they are under pressure of time.

A study by Hulstijn & Hulstijn (1984) investigated the influence of time pressure, attention to form, and conscious knowledge of L2 rules on the performance of a group of 32 adult L2 learners of Dutch in Holland in a story retelling task. Subjects heard a series of short stories, each consisting of four pieces of information, and afterwards each was asked to retell the story. For some stories they were told to recall the information in the story as accurately as possible, while for others they were told to recall the form in which the story was presented as accurately as possible. Simultaneously, for some stories they were told to perform the retelling as quickly as possible, while for others they were told they could take as long as they liked. This provided the researchers with information about story retelling under four conditions: where learners are form-focused and where they are not, and where learners are under pressure of time and where they are not. After the retelling task, Hulstijn & Hulstijn interviewed the subjects to determine whether they were able to talk about the particular rules of Dutch grammar involved in what they had produced; i.e. they established whether subjects had conscious knowledge or not about certain rules of Dutch.

Hulstijn & Hulstijn examined the results of this task for the accuracy of their subjects on a number of word order properties of Dutch, but we shall report here only their findings about performance on the verb-final placement of inflected verbs in subordinate clauses. Like German, Dutch requires that a finite verb be clause final when that clause is subordinate, for example:

2.8 *Deze dame zegt dat er een inbraak was.*
   This lady says that there a burglary was.

They found that while it was the case that those subjects who 'knew the rules', as demonstrated by their ability to verbalise them after the task, were globally more accurate (i.e. more target-like) than those who were unable to verbalise them, the accuracy of *both* groups on verb-final increased when they were asked to focus on recalling the form of the story as accurately as possible, and decreased when they were asked to focus on recalling the information in the story as accurately as possible. They also found that time pressure made no difference to this perform- ance: accuracy increased when subjects were focused on form whether they were under time pressure or not. It would appear, then, that the learned component of knowledge, in Krashen's sense, is not involved in task-based variability in the way predicted by the Monitor Hypothesis.

Finally, incompleteness in Krashen's system is accounted for by the Affective Filter Hypothesis, which postulates that learners' 'motives, needs, attitudes, and emotional states' (Dulay, Burt & Krashen, 1982: 46) act as a screen or barrier which limits the extent to which internal mental organising mechanisms receive L2 data. But this is extremely implausible in the light of a study such as that of Johnson & Newport (1989). Johnson & Newport found a steady and progressive decline in ability to achieve native-like grammatical intuitions in the L2 with increasing age. Consider, for example, their graph of the relationship between 'age of arrival' in the United States (that is, first consistent exposure to the L2 in everyday communicative situations) and mean score on the grammar test they administered to their L1 Chinese-speaking and L1 Korean-speaking subjects shown in Figure 2.1:

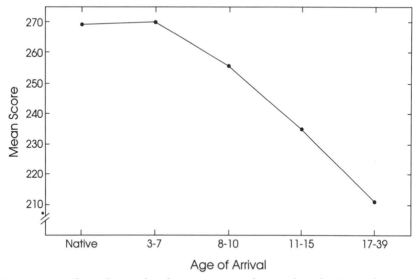

Figure 2.1 The relationship between age of arrival in the United States and total score correct on the test of English grammar

Source: Johnson & Newport, 1989

If 'inhibitions' determined the degree of grammatical success of L2 learners, we would expect to see both successful and unsuccessful learners in the 11–15-year-old group and in the 17–39-year-old group, so that scores on the test would be at the same level for both age groups (unless one wished to maintain that 17–39 year olds are more inhibited than 11–15 year olds, which seems hardly likely). Gregg (1984: 93) also picks up on this point in relation to the Chinese subject 'P' reported in Krashen (1988) who, recall, despite 20 years' residence in the United States, and having brought up a native English-speaking son, still makes grammatical errors in spontaneous oral production on properties such as the third person singular marker on verbs: 'she walk-s'. Gregg says:

> Evidently we are to believe that P's 'non-acquisition' of certain rules, such as third person singular -s, is owing to the Affective Filter. What could this mean? What is P's problem? Low motivation? Anxiety? Lack of self-confidence? These seem odd characteristics to predicate of a person who took a BA in Linguistics at an American university even though she started learning English only at the age of twenty. Perhaps she has an unconscious dislike of certain morphemes?

Although Krashen's integrated hypotheses were, then, a good first attempt to account for the core observations of SLA in which we are interested here, there are serious empirical and conceptual problems with them.

Summary

The Contrastive Analysis Hypothesis about SLA arose from the meeting of behaviourist psychology and structural linguistics. It assumed that language acquisition involved the formation of a set of habits. In the case of SLA, habits formed in the L1 would initially be transferred into the L2. Some of those habits would be appropriate (positive transfer), some would be inappropriate (negative transfer) and in need of modification, and others would need to be established from scratch.

It turns out, however, that not all areas of difference between the L1 and L2 lead to negative transfer, and not all areas of similarity lead to positive transfer. Furthermore, many of the errors produced by L2 learners cannot be attributed unambiguously to transfer. These constitute serious empirical problems for the Contrastive Analysis Hypothesis as an approach to SLA.

Problems with the Contrastive Analysis Hypothesis led researchers in the 1970s to consider the L2 learner's mental L2 grammar as an autonomous entity, and to investigate how it grows over time. Some of the early studies from this perspective were influenced by the work of Brown (1973) on the L1 acquisition of English grammatical morphology, and focused on L2 morphology. It was found that different groups of L1 speakers of different ages displayed 'accuracy orders' which were highly similar, suggesting to researchers that L2 morphology is acquired in a 'natural order'. Studies of other areas of grammar also strongly suggested natural orders.

It soon became clear that other hypotheses besides the 'natural order' hypothesis were also needed. Accuracy orders cl...nge where learners perform under different task conditions, for example where they are able to plan their productions. Krashen, in a series of studies (summarised in Krashen, 1985), has proposed the Acquisition/Learning Hypothesis, and its corollary, the Monitor Hypothesis. To these Krashen further adds the Affective Filter Hypothesis, in order to explain both individual differences between learners where input is constant, and incompleteness. Learners who fail to acquire native-speaker-like intuitions about the target language are hampered by their 'affective filters'.

However, these hypotheses fail to account for transfer. 'Acquired knowledge', which is supposed to account for 'natural orders', is mysterious. Variability is crucially dependent on the 'monitoring' function of 'learned knowledge', but it has been shown by Hulstijn & Hulstijn (1984) that such variability exists in the absence of 'learned knowledge'. It is implausible to argue that incompleteness results from the application of an 'affective filter' in view of the findings of Johnson & Newport (1989) that incompleteness increases progressively with age of first exposure to the L2.

Note

1. One of the reasons why Dulay & Burt opted to study 'order of accuracy', rather than 'order of emergence' as Brown had done, may have been because de Villiers and de Villers (1973) had conducted a cross-sectional study with L1 learners of English and had found that the accuracy order in the cross-sectional study was the same as Brown's order of emergence. At this period a number of L2 researchers seemed to assume that cross-sectional L2 results also reflected order of emergence, but without testing this hypothesis empirically. This led subsequently to a number of criticisms of the L2 morpheme studies related to this issue, but since technical details of this sort have become rather superfluous in more richly articulated current theories of SLA, we shall consider them no further here.

3 Sociolinguistic Approaches to Explaining the Observable Phenomena of Second Language Acquisition

Krashen's (1985) approach to SLA assumes that it crucially involves a discrete, or encapsulated (to borrow a term from Fodor, 1983) module of linguistic knowledge — the language faculty — which is to a considerable extent a biological endowment, and which constrains the form that grammars take in both L1 and L2 acquisition, thus accounting for staged development and cross-learner systematicity in both kinds of acquisition. The differences between L2 and L1 learners arise in Krashen's system as the result of interference from other cognitive domains which do not interfere with L1 acquisition: learned knowledge, which can make L2 learners' productions look more target-like than the grammatical knowledge which they have in their 'acquired' component would warrant, and the affective filter, which comes between an L2 learner's language faculty and data from the L2, preventing the free interaction of the two and distorting acquisition. Another way of describing Krashen's position is to say that he assumes a single underlying grammatical competence, or homogeneous competence, which can be distorted in performance by the 'monitor' and by the affective filter.

Another type of approach to accounting for the phenomena of SLA in which we are interested, and which we shall call broadly 'sociolinguistic approaches', because they take their inspiration from work in socio-linguistics of the 1960s and 1970s, views variability itself to be at the core of what L2 speakers know about the L2, rather than an epiphenomenon induced by interference at the level of performance. That is, they view competence as variable and not homogeneous.

Tarone's Approach

One version of this approach is Tarone's (1983, 1985, 1988) idea that L2 learners acquire a continuum of grammars for the L2 (which she calls 'styles') ranging from the most informal or 'vernacular' style, to the most 'careful' style, used when an L2 speaker is focusing on form, and trying to be as correct as possible. Tarone refers to this as the capability continuum; it is illustrated in Figure 3.1.

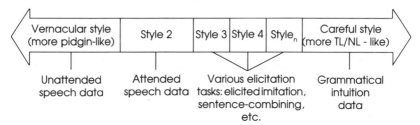

Figure 3.1 Interlanguage capability continuum

Source: Tarone, 1988: 41

The vernacular style is usually the least target-like, but the most internally consistent, while at the other pole the careful style is more target-like, perhaps incorporating grammatical knowledge which has been consciously learned by the L2 speaker. It will also be less internally consistent, involving acquired knowledge, consciously learned knowledge, and perhaps also careful style norms transferred from the L1.

To illustrate these notions consider two hypothetical examples. Suppose that L1 English learners of L2 French, in their use of unstressed object pronouns, produce them postverbally in their vernacular style, just like Selinker, Swain & Dumas's (1975) subjects described in Chapter 1: *Le chien a mangé les*, 'The dog has eaten them' (native French: *Le chien les a mangés*). In their careful style, however, they are consciously aware (through lessons in French, perhaps) that French does not allow postverbal unstressed object pronouns. At the same time their grammars may not yet be sufficiently developed to allow preverbal pronouns, with the result that they simply omit them on occasions in the careful style, sometimes producing sentences such as *Le chien a mangé* for the intended 'The dog has eaten them', alongside *Le chien a mangé les*. Omission of unstressed object pronouns in French is in fact an attested stage in L2 development (Adiv, 1984; Schlyter, 1986; Véronique, 1986). On this scenario the vernacular style of a speaker will be different from the careful style of the same speaker, and it will also be more consistent internally, always displaying postverbal object pronouns, rather than an alternation between a pronoun and Ø; both styles will in addition be non-target-like, although the careful style has moved one stage down the path towards the target language.

The second example again concerns L1 English learners of L2 French. Suppose that in the vernacular style these learners reproduce two properties characteristic of English: the optional deletion of the complementiser 'that' in cases such as: 'I thought (that) he had left', and the 'stranding of prepositions' in examples such as: 'Who did she go out with?' Neither of these are possible in native speaker (European) French, but they may nevertheless appear in the vernacular style of these learners as, respectively, *Je croyais il était parti (native French Je croyais qu'il était parti) and *Qui est-elle sortie avec? (native French Avec qui est-elle sortie?).[1] At the same time many (British) English speakers are taught to think of deletion of 'that' and preposition stranding in English as less careful forms of English. If they transfer this knowledge into their careful style for French, then they will produce target forms. Thus there will be a constrast between their target-like careful style, and their non-target-like vernacular style.

The kind of example that Tarone cites herself in support of the capability continuum is illustrated in a study by Schmidt (1980) of second verb deletion or ellipsis in examples such as (3.1).

3.1 Mary is eating an apple and Sue . . . a banana.

Native speakers of English allow both (3.1), in which the second verb has been deleted, and sentences where it has not: 'Mary is eating an apple and Sue is eating a banana'. Schmidt found that the non-native speakers of L2 English varied in their use of second-verb ellipsis depending upon the linguistic task they were engaged in. Schmidt's nine subjects were required to perform four tasks: free oral production, elicited imitation, written sentence combining and grammaticality judgement. The proportions in which they produced second-verb ellipsis in these tasks were: free oral production: 0%; elicited imitation: 11%; written sentence combining: 25%; grammaticality judgement: 50%.

Observed variability of this sort in the productions of L2 learners, according to Tarone (1988: 41), 'is caused by style-shifting along this [capability continuum], which in turn is caused by variable shifts in the degree of attention which the learner pays to language form'. L2 learners' knowledge of the L2 is, then, multiple. They have internalised different types of grammar for different types of situation.

Tarone also suggests that this conceptualisation of the nature of linguistic knowledge in SLA allows an account of staged development. According to Tarone (1988: 41), new forms can enter the continuum in two ways:

> (1) forms may be spontaneously produced first in the vernacular style; it is possible that such forms could gradually spread over time into more and more formal styles. Or (2) new forms may appear first in the most formal style where the learner can pay attention to speech production, and gradually spread over time into less and less formal styles.

Before considering Tarone's account for its ability to handle the five observations about SLA, two other versions of the sociolinguistic approach will be briefly considered. One is the approach of Ellis (1985a, b, 1992), who proposes a variable competence model.

Ellis's Approach

Like Tarone, Ellis does not seem to believe in an underlying homogeneous competence in SLA, as Krashen does, but nor does he believe in a continuum of styles. Rather, he opts for a view of L2 linguistic competence which allows variable rules where the target grammar does not. For example, we have already described a case cited by Ellis where in the L2 English of Zambian learners the third person singular marker of the simple present tense of verbs is used in main clauses by these speakers, or in the first clause of a complex sentence, but not necessarily in the second or subsequent clauses of a complex sentence. This gives rise to sentences such as (3.2).

3.2 Moses lives in Lusaka, but he work_ in Kafue.

In Ellis's view this results because the 'rule' that a speaker who utters such a sentence has internalised is variable, something along the lines of (our guess) (3.3.).

3.3 Verb + 3p sing → V + -s
                        V + Ø

Such variable rules, according to Ellis, not only explain the observed variability of learners, but are also the agents of staged development in SLA. In early stages of learning, an L2 learner has rules which have only one realisation, in the case in point, say:

3.4 Verb + 3p sing → V -∅

But then the learner begins to notice that native speakers use -s in (at least some) cases of third person singular verbs. Rather than -s replacing ∅ at this point in the learner's developing grammar, it comes to 'co-exist with previously acquired forms, at least initially' (Ellis, 1992: 121). This can result in either *free variation* (i.e. forms alternating in all environments in an apparently random fashion) or *systematic variation* (one of the alternants appearing in one environment, the other in others, and where 'environment' means either 'linguistic context', as in the case of the Zambian learners of L2 English, or 'context of utterance', as in the case of Schmidt's study of variability across four tasks).

Ellis views free and systematic variation as important keys to understanding staged development. The learner starts off with some early non-variable representation for a grammatical property in the L2, perhaps the result of transfer from the L1, perhaps the result of general strategies (we are not aware that Ellis is specific on the source of early non-variable rules). Some form is noticed in the input which is in conflict with that representation, and so the form is freely added to the representation. But then 'learners seek to maximise the communicative effectiveness of their interlanguage systems by eliminating free variation' (Ellis, 1992: 122). Here Ellis is basing his account on 'the economy principle of linguistic organisation. This states that in ideal form a linguistic system will contain enough and no more distinctive features than are required to perform whatever functions the user wishes to communicate' (p. 134). Learners eliminate free variation by associating each variant with a specific set of environments, either linguistic or social. 'Thus free variation serves as a precursor of systematic variation' (p. 122).

The Acculturation/Pidginisation Approach

The third version of the sociolinguistic approach that we wish to consider briefly here is what has been referred to as the 'Acculturation/ Pidginisation Hypothesis'. It appears that this version grew out of work describing 'the general process of acculturation as involving modification in attitudes, knowledge, and behaviour . . . Part of this process involves learning the appropriate linguistic habits to function within the target-language group' (McLaughlin, 1987: 110). The primary focus in this approach appears to be incompleteness in ultimate attainment of knowledge of the L2, and individual differences between learners in their levels of ultimate attainment. It suggests that these phenomena can be accounted for in terms of the social distance between the learner and the native speakers of the target language. If there is a large social distance, then the learner's interlanguage will be of a very rudimentary kind, of the sort characteristic of 'pidgin' (or 'contact') languages — for example, lacking morphological inflections, lacking function words such as determiners and auxiliaries, lacking subordinate clauses, and so on. Development towards target language norms is dependent on the social distance between the learner and native speakers of the target language decreasing. If it fails to decrease, the L2 learner's grammar will fossilise. Individual learners will vary, too, depending on the extent to which they are willing or able to reduce social distance. The reason why social distance is so important in this account is that it determines the extent to which learners are able to avail themselves of L2 input from native speakers. The greater the social distance, the less interaction there will be between the learner and native speakers. It is an approach to incompleteness and learner differences in SLA, then, which regards quantity of input as the primary determinant of success.

One of the best-known studies of the effect of acculturation (or rather lack of it) on SLA is Schumann's (1978) study of Alberto, a 33 year-old Costa Rican immigrant to the United States. Alberto seemed to see himself as socially quite distant from Americans, interacting largely with Spanish speakers, not wishing to own a television, and working both day and night. During the course of Schumann's nine-month study of him, Alberto showed very little development in his L2 English, which seemed to have fossilised at a rudimentary level (for example, sentence negation being effected by placing 'no' in front of the verb, there being no subject–verb inversion, and there being only erratic use of grammatical morphology).

Another study which stresses the role of social distance between the L2 learner and native speakers of the target language, although from a slightly different perspective, is that of Meisel, Clahsen & Pienemann (1981). Studying the development of L2 German among immigrant workers speaking L1 Spanish and L1 Italian, Meisel, Clahsen & Pienemann suggest that differences between individual learners arise as the result of learners being either *integratively oriented*, displaying positive attitudes towards the speakers of the L2, and seeking out contact with them, or *segregatively oriented*, displaying a less outgoing attitude, and not actively seeking contact with native speakers of German.

Crucial to both accounts — Schumann's, and Meisel, Clahsen &

Pienemann's — is the idea that the greater the social distance between the L2 learner and the speakers of the target language, the more likely the former is to produce language which is minimally communicatively effective, and no more, and this means that learner language will display 'omission of various grammatically obligatory but communicatively redundant items ("Julia happy", "She eat sandwich")' (Larsen-Freeman & Long, 1991: 282). In this they are similar to Ellis. All three assume that in the earliest stages of L2 learning, learner language is the way it is because of the elimination of all grammatical items not relevant to communication. The more the social distance is overcome, the more likely a learner is to produce the 'communicatively redundant' grammatical items because of a desire to speak like the native speakers of the target language.

Actually, Meisel, Clahsen & Pienemann's account is more complex than this brief description would suggest, because it links the idea that social distance is involved in predicting incompleteness in SLA with a view that staged development in SLA is the product of general psychological processing strategies. We shall consider the processing strategies in the next chapter when we look at 'cognitive approaches' to SLA.

Evaluation of Sociolinguistic Approaches to Second Language Acquisition

Consider now how these sociolinguistic approaches deal with the five observations about SLA in which we are interested: transfer, staged development, systematicity, variability and incompleteness. First, transfer seems to be rarely considered in these approaches. For example, neither 'transfer' nor 'interference' even figure in the indexes of two representative texts like Tarone (1988) or Ellis (1992). Doubtless transfer could be given some kind of account within these approaches, just as it could be in the case of Krashen's system, but because we shall argue that the idea of a continuum of styles or of variable rules is itself an implausible interpretation of variability, we shall not do this here.

Both Tarone and Ellis seem to assume that new items enter the developing L2 grammar freely, when the learner notices a discrepancy between the predictions of his or her grammar and actual samples of the L2. For example, a learner allowing sentences such as 'Moses live in Lusaka' suddenly notices that English uses a verbal inflection -s in some cases, and this enters the grammar. Once in, this form then 'spreads', either along the continuum, in Tarone's case, or to linguistically or task-determined contexts, in Ellis's case. Both authors, then, seem to assume that the order in which items enter the L2 grammar, and the subsequent stages of development which result from those forms entering the grammar are essentially random.

But we have already seen that this appears generally not to be the case. Recall the L1 French learners of L2 English and L1 English learners of L2 French acquiring unstressed object pronouns. The French learners of L2 English appear to have little trouble acquiring the postverbal pronouns of examples such as 'The dog has eaten them', whereas the English learners of L2 French have considerably more difficulty acquiring the preverbal pronouns of examples such as: *Le chien les a mangés*, going through a phase of postverbal pronouns, such as **Le chien a mangé les*. The notion that new forms 'randomly' enter the L2 grammar of learners at a random point of development, and then spread through the grammar, again randomly, cannot account for observed differences like this without recourse to some further theoretical construct(s).

Secondly, it is clearly the case that some areas of variability in SLA are more quickly resolved by L2 learners than others. Recall Ellis's example of the Portuguese-speaking 11 year-old learning L2 English who, within the same discourse, alternated 'No look my card', and 'Don't look my card'. The development of negation in the speech of this learner actually started with the generalised used of 'no', then 'don't' appeared in free variation with 'no'. This is a typical pattern found with many learners of L2 English. Following this stage, learners begin to add other forms to their repertoire, such as 'can't', 'won't', 'isn't', 'hasn't', and eventually analyse English negation into auxiliary verb + n't, which is correct for English. What is usually found is that this process is quite rapid; the stage of free variation rapidly gives way to systematic variation, which rapidly gives way to target-like invariance. Moreover, the majority of L2 learners of English, given sufficient exposure to English, do not fail to acquire it (setting aside atypical cases such as Alberto).

This is in marked contrast to some other variable aspects of L2 grammars. Recall the alternation studied by Towell, Hawkins & Bazergui (1993) between *de* and *à* in French examples such as: *C'est ennuyeux de lire les livres techniques*, 'It's boring to read technical books', and *Les livres techniques sont ennuyeux à lire*, 'Technical books are boring to read'. Towell, Hawkins & Bazergui found that (un-target-like) variability in the use of *de/à* was a persistent feature of the L1 English learners of L2 French they studied. Indeed Towell (1987b), in a previous study of the same phenomenon, had a subject who failed to acquire the distinction even after 11 years of classroom exposure to French, of which four years were an undergraduate degree programme in French, with one of the years spent in France. These are not isolated examples. Some properties of L2 grammars appear to be persistently variable (where the target language is not), whereas others are variable only for short periods. Neither Tarone's capability continuum nor Ellis's variable competence model have mechanisms for predicting these differences. They would need to have recourse to some further theoretical construct(s) in order to explicate them.

Thus, although both Tarone and Ellis 'appear' to have models for handling the variable productions of L2 learners, and 'appear' to be able to link variability to staged development, in essence why particular L2 forms enter L2 grammars when they do, and how they spread through L2 grammars, are as mysterious as the notion of 'acquisition' in Krashen's system. As a measure of the failure of both accounts to offer any real explanation for even rather straightforward generalisations about variability consider this: why is it that, in the case of Ellis's third person singular verb inflection example, learners are always observed to alternate precisely between -s and Ø, and never between, say, Ø and -en, or Ø and -ly, or Ø and -ish, as in 'Moses work'/*'Moses work-en', 'Moses work'/*'Moses work-ly', or 'Moses work'/*'Moses work-ish'? These are all inflections that learners will encounter from English, and which attach to the ends of lexical stems. How do learners know to restrict -s to tensed verbs, -en to participles (such as 'broken'), -ly and -ish to adjectives (such as 'quickly' and 'reddish')? The answer is, of course, that these forms do not randomly enter L2 grammars and then spread just under the influence of environment. Learners need to be equipped with a rich system of grammatical knowledge involving notions like 'noun', 'verb' and 'adjective'. They have to know the difference between free and bound morphemes. And they have to know that bound morphemes have a grammatically determined distribution — that is, that verbal inflections do not normally attach to nouns or adjectives, and vice versa. At the core of accounts of variability and staged development there needs to be, then, a theory of grammatical structure and how grammatical structure is acquired in SLA.

But once one admits that a theory of grammatical structure is necessary, it becomes possible to offer a rather different perspective on variability and staged development. We shall pursue such an account in the later chapters of this book. Further criticisms of the models of Tarone and Ellis along the same lines, but of a rather more conceptual kind, can be found in Gregg (1990).

The Acculturation/Pidginisation Hypothesis takes both variation and incompleteness as its central focus. But like the models of Tarone and Ellis, the approach suffers from the absence of a theory of the nature of grammatical structure. In both the Schumann, and Meisel, Clahsen & Pienemann approaches there is an assumption that if there is a great social distance between the L2 learner and native speakers of the target language, this will result in a 'simplified' L2 grammar, sufficient only for communicative success and lacking 'redundant' grammatically relevant properties. Quite apart from the difficulty of defining the notion of 'social distance' in any way which is not circular (a learner who is socially distant has a simplified grammar, therefore a learner who has a simplified grammar must be socially distant), a paradoxical implication of the approach is that L2 learners with simplified grammars must in some sense know what grammatically relevant properties in the L2 are, so that they can avoid them, otherwise we should find all sorts of randomised linguistic elements in 'simplified' grammars. Crucially we do not find such random elements. This is a general problem for any approach which links the nature of early L2 grammatical productions with a notion of 'communicative economy', as Ellis also does. Such a view necessarily imputes to the learner the ability to segment data from the L2 into lexical items and grammatical morphemes, and then reject grammatical morphemes on the grounds that they are not relevant to communication. But this seems bizarre. More plausible, it seems to us, is that all L2 learners from the beginning of L2 acquisition (subconsciously) construct grammatical representations for the L2 on the basis of the input they receive, and probably under heavy influence from the L1 (see Chapter 6). Initially the grammars will be rudimentary because the input will have been rudimentary. The fact that they appear 'simplified' is merely an effect of what Bley-Vroman (1983) calls the 'comparative fallacy', that is the analyst making a comparison between the L2 learner's grammar and the target language grammar, when a more appropriate comparison would be between the L2 learner's grammar and the input that had been available in the construction of that grammar. We shall be directly concerned with the nature of grammatical growth in SLA in Chapters 5–9.

The acculturation/pidginisation approach to incompleteness seems to offer only a partial explanation of the phenomenon. Certainly, if L2 learners are 'segregative' and encounter the L2 only in very limited contexts (for example, in shops), it is self-evident that their knowledge of the L2 will only ever be rudimentary. It cannot approach native-speaker-like knowledge because the range of linguistic experience has been so limited. But the acculturation/pidginisation approach would seem to have nothing to say about incompleteness in learners who appear to be 'integrative', and who have had considerable exposure to the L2. Krashen's (1982) subject 'P', for example, or Johnson & Newport's (1989) L1 Chinese and L1 Korean speakers of L2 English. Recall that Johnson & Newport found a progressive decline in completeness as a function of the age of arrival of these subjects in the United States. Assuming a normal distribution of integrative/segregative learners across ages, however (and there seems to be no reason why one should not assume such a normal distribution), the progressive decline in completeness would not be expected.

Summary

Work by Tarone (for example, 1988) argues that L2 learners acquire a 'capability continuum' of styles ranging from the 'vernacular' to the more attention-demanding 'careful' style. In production, different conditions of use will induce in the learner different degrees of attention to linguistic form, resulting in the accessing of different styles. This will create the impression of variability in an L2 learner's use of the L2. Styles towards the careful end of the continuum are more target-like than those towards the vernacular end, but they are internally less consistent. Development over time occurs because new forms may enter any one of the 'styles', and spread from there into the other 'styles'.

Ellis (for example, 1992) suggests that learners have just one 'style' or grammar, but rules within this grammar may be variable. Initially, rules are constructed which have a unique output. But as the learner gets more exposure to the L2, competing forms may be associated with the same rule. This gives rise to free variation. With yet longer exposure to the L2, the learner may come to restrict each variant to a specific context of use or a specific grammatical function. In this way development in the learner's grammar occurs.

The problems that were found with these accounts are these. Transfer from the L1 receives no explanation. New forms enter the grammar freely (randomly), but this is in conflict with the considerable evidence for systematic staged development, which would be inexplicable if new forms freely entered the grammar. No account is offered for why some kinds of variation are resolved more quickly than others.

The acculturation/pidginisation approach suggests that the social distance between a learner and the community speaking the target language is what gives rise to lack of development, and individual differences between learners. When the distance is great learners will tend to use 'simplified' or 'pidginised' language lacking grammatical function words. This is because they omit items which are 'communicatively redundant'. Paradoxically, however, if learners omit grammatical items which are communicatively redundant, they must in some sense already 'know' what those items are. But this seems bizarre. The approach also implies that where there is no social distance between the L2 learner and the community speaking the target language, the learner ultimately will be as successful as native speakers. This is implausible in the light of research which suggests that older learners ultimately will not be as successful as native speakers, whatever the conditions under which learning takes place.

Note

1. (Colloquial) European French allows constructions like *Tu viens avec?* 'Are you coming with?' ('us' implied). These are different from preposition stranding constructions. In cases of preposition stranding an item has been moved from a position following the preposition leaving it stranded, for example: *Elle a parlé à quelqu'un*, 'She spoke to someone', **Qui a-t-elle parlé à?*, 'Who did she speak to?' (where *quelqu'un* has become *qui*, and has moved to the front of the sentence). In cases such as *Tu viens avec?* an item following the preposition is implied, and has not been moved.

4 Cognitive Approaches to Explaining the Observable Phenomena of Second Language Acquisition

Cognitive approaches to SLA have focused primarily on staged development and systematicity across L2 learners. Typically they argue that these phenomena can be accounted for by postulating psychological 'strategies' that human beings use generally for analysing, understanding and learning perceptual information of various kinds, including linguistic information. The view taken by these approaches is that it is not necessary to recognise in SLA an encapsulated module of linguistic ability different in nature from other cognitive abilities, as Krashen does for example. Rather, the processes involved in SLA are common to a number of cognitive domains. They are of the type referred to by Fodor (1983) as central processes.[1]

Two exemplars of cognitive approaches to SLA will be considered here (although the role of non-language-specific psychological processing in SLA will be reconsidered in chapters 11–13). The first exemplar is a series of studies emanating from the initial work of Meisel, Clahsen & Pienemann (1981) and Clahsen, Meisel & Pienemann (1983) on the acquisition of L2 German in largely naturalistic circumstances by speakers of Italian and Spanish (the learners in question being immigrant workers and their families). Pienemann has also extended the approach to Italian-speaking classroom learners of L2 German (for example in Pienemann, 1989). The second exemplar is work by Parker (1989, cited in Larsen-Freeman & Long, 1991), and Wolfe Quintero (1992, who is the same researcher under a different name) on learning strategies in SLA, and the exploration of the predictions made by those strategies in the learning of L2 English by L1 Japanese speakers.

Common to both versions of the cognitive approach is the idea that L2 learners initially decode, analyse, store and produce — i.e. process —

material from the new language in ways which are determined by general cognitive factors like the 'perceptual saliency' of the material, the 'continuity' of elements in that material, the basic 'conservatism' of learners in not extending hypotheses to domains not warranted by the input. This approach considers that people perceive events in terms of 'actors', 'actions' and 'persons or things acted upon', and that these are more 'salient' than the place where the event took place, or the time it took place, or the manner in which it took place. By extension it is considered that L2 learners will attend to and acquire ways of expressing 'actors', 'actions' and 'people or things acted upon' before they will attend to and acquire adverbials dealing with the place, time and manner of the event. Meisel, Clahsen & Pienemann further propose that the beginnings and ends of sentences are more perceptually salient than the middles of sentences, so that L2 learners will attend to and acquire phenomena at the beginnings and ends of sentences before they attend to and acquire phenomena in the middles of sentences. Wolfe Quintero contends that 'continuous' phenomena are more salient than 'discontinuous', so that learners are more likely to attend to and acquire phrasal verbs such as 'pick up' when they are continuous constituents in sentences such as 'She picked up the book', than when they are discontinuous constituents in sentences such as 'She picked the book up'.

In order to be specific in our assessment of the ability of cognitive approaches to account for the five observations about SLA, illustrated in Chapter 1, we shall consider two particular studies: that of the stages of development in German word order to be found in Pienemann (1987, 1989), and the account of wh- questions (who, what, which, etc.) in Wolfe Quintero (1992).

Pienemann's Account

Recall that the stages which learners of L2 German reportedly go through in acquiring word order are those outlined below (with examples from Pienemann — although in standard written German the first letter of nouns is capitalised, Pienemann cites examples of learner language without capitalisation, presumably to reflect their non-standard status; *mim* is the contracted form of *mit dem*, 'with the'):

Stage 1 S(ubject) V(erb) O(bject) word order
Die kinder spielen mim ball.
The children play with the ball.

Stage 2 (Adverb) SVO order
Da kinder spielen.
There children play.

Stage 3 V-SEP(aration)
Aller kinder muss die pause machen.
All children must the break have.

Stage 4 V2
Dann hat sie wieder die knoch gebringt.
Then has she again the bone brought.

Stage 5 V-Final
Er sagte dass er nach hause kommt.
He said that he home comes.

What causes this particular staged development and not some other? Pienemann suggests that Stage 1 is the result of the L2 learners organising sentences on the basis of the 'natural' order in which events are perceived, and this is assumed to be: 'actor – action – acted upon'. The construction of sentences in Stage 1 is determined by a strategy which maps this perceptual order on to L2 words or phrases; this is therefore essentially a pre-linguistic phase of acquisition. It is a strategy referred to by Clahsen (1984) as the *Canonical Order Strategy*:

Actor — Action — Acted Upon
Die kinder spielen   mim ball

With continued exposure to the L2, however, learners soon notice discrepancies between what they can produce with the Canonical Order Strategy and the input. But the areas of the input in which they notice such discrepancies are themselves constrained by perceptual saliency: learners first notice differences at the beginnings or the ends of sentences, because it is held that these are more salient portions of the input than the middles of sentences. What learners notice in the case of German word order is that adverbs as well as subjects appear in first position in sentences, and non-finite verb forms (participles, infinitives and particles) appear in sentence-final position. This leads to the postulation of a second strategy, the *Initialisation–Finalisation Strategy* (Clahsen, 1984): movements of constituents to the beginnings and ends of sentences are allowed. But notice that both Stage 2 and Stage 3 involve movement to the ends of sentences. Why does adverb fronting appear earlier than V-SEP? The answer is that V-SEP does not just involve movement to the end of the sentence, it also involves disruption of a continuous constituent, the [V + participle, infinitive, or particle].

Therefore a strategy of continuity of elements within the same constituent must be involved, delaying the acquisition of V-SEP, which violates this strategy.

Movement into sentence-internal positions is held to be less salient perceptually than movement to the end of the sentence, and so V2 will be acquired only after considerably more exposure to German. One last strategy, the *Subordinate Clause Strategy* is required to predict why V-Final is acquired as the last stage. This strategy suggests that permutations of elements in subordinate clauses which make the word order in main and subordinate clauses different will be avoided. Thus L2 learners tend to assume that German subordinate clauses have the same word order properties as main clauses, even into advanced stages of acquisition.

To summarise, informally, we have the following proposed account of why the stages of development of German word order are as they are:

- Word order reflects a (presumed universal) manner of perceiving events.
- Movement is allowed to the ends of sentences if it does not lead to discontinuity.
- Movement is allowed to the ends of sentences even if this does lead to discontinuity.
- Internal movements are allowed.
- Movement specific to subordinate clauses is allowed.

Wolfe Quintero's account

A similar kind of approach is adopted in Wolfe Quintero (1992) to account for the stages of development that L2 learners of English go through in acquiring wh- questions. The stages in question are illustrated in (4.1), using Wolfe Quintero's own classification by type: type 0 sentences are the first acquired, and type 3 are the last acquired. (She found that in a study focusing on types 1–3 with a group of 21 adult native speakers of Japanese learning L2 English, accuracy in performance on a sentence manipulation task was greatest at the type 1 level, and declined progressively towards the type 3 level.)

4.1 Type 0 John [VP saw whom]?
    Type 1 Whom did John [VP see ___]?
    Type 2 Whom did John [VP think [PP about ___]]?
    Type 3 Whom did John [VP read [NP a book [PP about ___]]]?

(VP = verb phrase, PP = prepositional phrase, NP = noun phrase. These grammatical notions are discussed more fully in Chapter 5.)

Wolfe Quintero proposes that a set of 'learning principles', similar to the strategies of Meisel, Clahsen & Pienemann, are involved in determining why learning takes place in this order rather than some other. The principles are:

- *conservatism*: 'the initial hypothesis will be the most conservative possible . . . even if a learner notices complexity in the input data' (Wolfe Quintero, 1992: 44)
- *continuity*: 'a preference for items that combine to be adjacent' (p. 44)
- *uniqueness*: an 'initial preference for one-to-one correspondences between forms and their meaning' (p. 45)
- *cumulative development*: 'development must proceed in stages and . . . each stage will contain the previous stage plus something more' (p. 45)
- *generalisation*: 'avoid exceptions' (p. 45)
- *pre-emption*: 'when a structure is generalised to related lexical items without direct evidence from the input, the hypothesis will be noted as tentative . . . If there is never confirming evidence, the hypothesis will be lost' (p. 46).

The interaction of these learning principles, according to Wolfe Quintero (1992: 46), leads to a characterisation of staged L2 development and cross-learner systematicity:

> Provided with input, learners will initially form conservative hypotheses based on an assumption of the continuity and uniqueness of language structures. They will develop a full representation of target language structures only though a process of cumulative development through stages of complexity. The structures at any given stage will also gradually extend through the lexicon via the process of generalisation, which will result in many correct generalisations as well as. certain overgeneralisations. Eventually, through the process of either pre-emption by further input or loss of a tentative hypothesis, the overgeneralisation will be lost.

Consider now how this system of learning strategies might account for the stages of development in the acquisition of wh- questions illustrated in (4.1). Wolfe Quintero suggests that learners start with the most 'conservative' hypothesis, which is 'continuity': the wh- phrase 'whom' appears in the position in which an object noun phrase would appear — next to the verb. This gives type 0 sentences as the first stage. When learners start to notice that in the input wh- phrases appear in sentence-initial position they acquire this structure, but are 'conservative' about 'generalising' it. They restrict fronting of wh- phrases initially to the least embedded structure (type 1 sentences), and only with further input and evidence of the extraction of wh- phrases from PPs and NPs will they extend the rule to these contexts as well.

> Learners must first learn to produce structures with extraction from VPs, then from PPs in VPs, and finally from PPs in certain NPs, with each stage building upon the last. It is not probable that a learner could produce extraction within three levels of embeddedness, without already being able to produce extraction within fewer levels (Wolfe Quintero, 1992: 51).

Since development is held to be 'cumulative' each extension of the hypothesis will not replace but will include the previous hypotheses, so that eventually the learner will have acquired all four types of wh-question.

Evaluation of Cognitive Approaches to Second Language Acquisition

How able are cognitive approaches to SLA to offer an account of the five observations with which we are now familiar: transfer of properties of the L1 grammar into the L2 grammar; staged development; systematicity across learners in development; variability; and incompleteness?

First there is a conceptual problem. Cognitive approaches require us to assume that the underlying general perceptual model on which they are based is correct — for example, that people do perceive events as 'actor–action–acted upon' arrays, that people do have a preference for continuous as opposed to discontinuous entities, that the beginnings and ends of sentences are indeed more salient than the middles of sentences, and so on. But none of this is self-evident, although it may be correct; one of the problems with the cognitive approaches with which we are familiar is that they rarely offer justification for making these assumptions. They require us to take on faith assumptions about the nature of perception. The perceptual constructs are essentially 'mysterious' in precisely the same way that Krashen's acquired system is mysterious, and the mechanisms by which new forms enter the variable competences proposed by Tarone and Ellis are mysterious. And what is more, any number of new ones may be invented in an unconstrained way.

Cognitive approaches would seem to predict that transfer is not an important property in SLA. Learners are assumed to construct initial hypotheses about the L2 which are 'driven' by perceptual factors presumed to be universal. The early stages in the acquisition of a given L2 should therefore be identical across learners from any L1 background. There are indeed some cases where the prediction that L2 learners behave in the same way in early stages of acquisition offers an interesting account of the difficulty or the ease for learners of acquiring cross-linguistic differences. For example, it offers a potential explanation for the developmental difference we have noted between L1 French learners of L2 English and L1 English learners of L2 French in acquiring unstressed object pronouns. Recall that French speakers have little trouble acquiring postverbal pronouns in sentences such as 'The dog has eaten them', but English speakers have considerably more trouble acquiring the French pattern: *Le chien les a mangés*. It could be suggested that in both cases learners are adopting the Canonical Order Strategy of Meisel, Clahsen & Pienemann, and are mapping phrases in the L2 on to the perceptual array 'actor–action–acted upon'. This would lead both groups to postulate a generalised SVO order, even for pronouns, which turns out to be appropriate for English, but inappropriate for French. (For an alternative account for this developmental difference between French and English learners see Chapter 5.)

On the other hand, there are also cases where differences between different L1 speaking populations learning L2s are not so easily explained by cognitive approaches. We have briefly considered the studies of L1 Spanish-speaking and L1 Italian-speaking learners of L2 German, in the context of which Meisel, Clahsen & Pienemann first elaborated their learning strategies. A study by Hulk (1991), which will be considered in more detail in Chapter 6, considers acquisition going in the other direction. Hulk examined the acquisition of L2 French (a Romance language like Spanish and Italian, with similar word order properties in relevant respects (none of these languages allow verb separation, V2, or verb final in subordinate clauses)) by speakers of L1 Dutch (a language similar to German in relevant word order properties (it requires verb separation, V2 and verb final in subordinate clauses)). She found that in the earliest stages of development her subjects adopted Germanic word order, and did not display a preference for so-called Canonical Word Order. Or consider the case of the placement of manner and frequency adverbs in L2 English and L2 French discussed earlier. French-speaking learners of L2 English have persistent problems in eliminating the postverbal placement of such adverbs in sentences such as: *'Mary eats often oysters', whereas English-speaking learners of L2 French find it easier, relatively, to acquire the fact that French allows sentences such as: *Marie mange souvent des huîtres*. If learners were adopting a Canonical Order Strategy, one might expect the perceptual array 'actor–action–acted upon' to resist intrusion from non-canonically relevant elements such as adverbs. Indeed, the placement of an adverb between the verb and its object complement, as in the French case, also violates 'continuity'. So that the persistence of the French speakers in placing adverbs between the verb and its object in their L2 English is doubly surprising on the learning strategy account. Examples like this, and they are common (see Chapter 6 for several examples), are straightforward counterexamples to the assumption that early stages of L2 acquisition are driven by presumed universal perceptual properties.

With respect to staged development and cross-learner systematicity, observations about SLA with which cognitive approaches are primarily concerned, there are also problems. One of the problems is that the status of grammatical knowledge within the learning strategies is ambivalent. One of the strengths of cognitive approaches should be that they can account for developmental and systematic phenomena in SLA which appear not to be easily reducible to grammatical factors. The cognitive approaches considered so far, however, are not at all clear about the role that grammatical knowledge plays in relation to the learning strategies/principles. Sometimes grammatical knowledge appears to be appealed to solely for the purpose of getting the account out of a hole when the strategies/principles make the wrong predictions. Recall that in the acquisition of German word order it is proposed that the very last stage — the acquisition of verb-final location of the tensed verb in subordinate clauses is identical to that of main clauses, until evidence to Strategy which leads learners to assume that the word order in subordinate clauses is idential to that of main clauses, until evidence to the contrary is noticed in the input. But what is the status of the Subordinate Clause Strategy? It is in fact required to prevent the Initialisation–Finalisation Strategy making the wrong predictions in the case of subordinate clauses. V-final is an instance of movement to the end of a sentence: a salient position. V-final should therefore be predicted to be acquired before V2, which is movement to a sentence-internal, less salient position. But it is not acquired before V2, so appeal has to be made to some other strategy. But the Subordinate Clause Strategy is a strategy which involves purely grammatical information: the notion 'subordinate clause'. In what sense is this explanatory? The answer is, it isn't, because the interface between grammatical knowledge and perceptual dispositions is unclear in this theory.

Wolfe Quintero's system is also problematic because of the ambivalence of the interaction between learning principles and grammatical knowledge. Recall that in her account of the stages of development of wh- questions illustrated in (4.1), the order is predicted to be the result of learners being 'conservative' about fronting wh- phrases. They start with fronting from within VPs, then from within PPs inside VPs, finally from within PPs inside certain NPs, this being determined (presumably) by the supposition that 'continuity' is less strong between a verb and its complement than between a preposition and its complement, or between a noun and its complement. Given this account, compare the examples in (4.2):

4.2a Whom did John [vp see ___]?
   b About whom did John [vp think ___]?

In both cases we have fronting of a wh- phrase from within a VP. According to Wolfe Quintero's learning principles both sentences should be equal in developmental terms for L2 learners, because both are possible in English. However, Wolfe Quintero shows clearly that her own subjects do not ·acquire structures such as (4.2b) (in which the preposition is carried along when the wh- phrase is fronted) early. In fact such structures are acquired well after 'preposition stranded' structures like the type 2 sentence of (4.1), repeated here as (4.2c):

4.2c Whom did John [vp think about ___]?

Now, it is the case that preposition stranded structures like (4.2c) are far more frequent in the spoken English of native speakers than structures like (4.2b) (and hence more frequent in the input to L2 learners), and this leads Wolfe Quintero (1992: 51) to suggest that '. . . preposition stranded structures will develop earlier than nonstranded structures because preposition stranded structures provide a far more frequent target of acquisition in oral and informal input.'

But the problem is that the strategy of 'generalisation' should lead learners to produce forms like (4.2b) as soon as they produce forms like (4.2a), because both involve fronting from VP. Just as in the German word order case, the interaction of the proposed principles produces an unwanted result. In order to rescue the account some appeal would need to be made to the idea that learners have rather subtle grammatical knowledge which underlies the operation of the learning principles. In this case they would need to be able to distinguish between NP complements and PP complements to verbs, and limit wh- phrase fronting to NP complements initially. The problem reveals that there is a lack of a clear view about the interface between grammatical knowledge and the proposed learning principles in L2 development.

With respect to variability and incompleteness in SLA, cognitive approaches would appear to offer the means of providing some account, but in the studies we have considered this is not explored in any clear way. Variability might be accounted for by the idea that hypotheses determined by the strategies/principles are 'cumulative'. Every time a learning strategy/principle is relaxed, a new hypothesis will enter the grammar and be in competition with a previous hypothesis. This would give rise to variability. But the accumulation of hypotheses is not so much an explanation as a claim. Incompleteness might be predicted if it were assumed that L1 acquisition were qualitatively different from L2 acquisition. For example, if L1 acquisition were to involve an innately determined 'language faculty' (see Chapter 5), whereas L2 acquisition (in the case of post-seven-year-old learners) were not. On this scenario it could be claimed that general learning strategies/principles are not sufficient to allow L2 learners to acquire the full range of grammatical competence that L1 learners do.

Overall, then, cognitive approaches make a strong attempt to provide an account of a number of the core observations in which we are interested, but appear unsatisfactory because they do not offer a clear account of transfer, because their predictions about staged development and systematicity are vague, lacking an explicit theory of the role that grammatical knowledge plays, and because predictions about variability and incompleteness have not been explored.

General Evaluation of the Early Linguistic, Sociolinguistic and Cognitive Approaches to Explaining the Observable Phenomena of Second Language Acquisition

In Chapters 2–4 we have considered a number of approaches to the five observations about SLA with which we started: transfer, staged development, systematicity across L2 learners, variability and incompleteness.

The Contrastive Analysis Hypothesis focuses primarily on transfer, but it fails not only to offer an account of the other observations, but also in making correct predictions about transfer. Krashen's Monitor Model focuses on staged development, systematicity, variability and incompleteness. While the strength of the system is that it addresses a range of observations, its weakness is that a theory of 'acquired L2 knowledge', which is at the core of the system, is nonexistent, that wrong predictions are made about the source of variability, and that an implausible prediction is made about the source of incompleteness. Transfer is not addressed in the account.

The sociolinguistic approaches focus primarily on variability, staged development and incompleteness. But the account of how new linguistic phenomena enter the L2 grammar and how they spread through the grammar is marred by the nonexistence of a theory of grammatical structure. The account given of incompleteness in these approaches is as implausible as it is in Krashen's model, relying on the idea that incompleteness is the result of the attitudes of L2 learners. Sociolinguistic approaches appear to have little to say either about transfer or about cross-learner systematicity.

The cognitive approaches primarily address the observations of staged development and systematicity, but by extension offer the means for accounting for variability (on the assumption that development is 'cumulative'), and incompleteness (on the assumption that L1 acquisition is qualitatively different from L2 acquisition). However, it appears difficult to reconcile transfer with the view that early L2 grammars are constructed on the basis of presumed universal learning strategies/principles. Furthermore, the interaction of these strategies/principles can sometimes make wrong empirical predictions which are then either resolved within the models we have considered via *ad hoc* appeal to grammatical knowledge (as in the case of the Subordinate Clause Strategy) or are left unresolved.

What recurs as problematic in all of these approaches is the lack of a sophisticated theory of the nature of grammatical structure, and a clear view about how knowledge of the L2 grammar interacts with other factors in SLA. There is one approach to SLA which we have not yet considered: the current linguistic approach, based on work in *Universal Grammar*. The reason is that we shall devote the next five chapters to considering the ways in which a detailed theory of grammatical structure might provide a key to understanding and explaining the five observations about SLA. It will be our contention that by looking at concrete proposals for what the elements of a grammar are, and how those elements are acquired by L2 learners, the picture of what can and what cannot be properly attributed to the grammar in SLA becomes sharper. It will also be our contention that a theory of grammatical structure and how grammatical structure is acquired in SLA needs to be supplemented by a theory of how that knowledge is put to use. We shall return to this question in Chapters 10–13.

Note

1. Some SLA researchers within this paradigm make a distinction, though, between first and second language acquisition in this respect. Clahsen & Muysken (1986), Felix (1987) and Meisel (1991) for example suggest that L1 acquisition involves an encapsulated language faculty, which then disappears as the child grows, perhaps as the result of biological maturation, leaving L2 learners with only general psychological strategies to help them acquire second languages, and it is this which determines the differences which exist between L1 and L2 learners.

5 The Approach to Second Language Acquisition Based on Universal Grammar

In Chapter 1 it was suggested that there are five observations about SLA for which any theory of SLA should offer some account:

- *transfer* of grammatical properties from the L1 grammar into the L2 grammar
- *staged development* between the initial L2 grammars that L2 learners construct and the eventual knowledge that they attain of the target language
- *systematicity* in the growth of L2 linguistic knowledge across L2 learners
- *incompleteness* in acquiring native-speaker-like competence for the majority of (post-seven-year-old) L2 learners
- *variability* in L2 learners' performance in the L2.

In this central part of the book we shall examine how a detailed theory of grammatical structure might be employed to explore some of these observations. The particular theory of grammatical structure that will be explored is the theory of Universal Grammar (UG) stemming from the work of Chomsky (1981). If plausible explanations for L2 phenomena can be offered within this framework, they will be *principled* — i.e. the theoretical constructs used in the explanations have independent motivation. UG is a theory which has not been specially constructed for the purpose of explaining SLA. It is required anyway to account for the structural properties of the world's languages: their similarities and their differences. It also seems that it is required for explanation in L1 acquisition. If it turns out that the theory is relevant in the domain of SLA, then this would be a considerably more interesting account than one in which an *ad hoc* theory is devised for the sole purpose of explaining SLA. If the theory of UG is involved in SLA, then observed L2 behaviour could be said to follow from properties inherent to the human language faculty itself.

At the same time an attempt will be made to sketch the potential limits of the explanatory power of UG in SLA, so that the points of contact in L2 learning between the language faculty and other cognitive domains become sharper. Anticipating, it will be suggested that while UG has something interesting to say about aspects of transfer, staged development, systematicity across learners, and some aspects of incompleteness, it has little to say about variability.

The approach will be as follows: the goals and assumptions of work on UG will be briefly outlined, some examples will be given to illustrate the kind of approach adopted in such work, and these examples will then be related to specific studies drawn from the SLA literature.

Goals and Assumptions of work on Universal Grammar

To understand how UG might provide some insight into at least some of the five observations, it is necessary first to consider the goals of work on UG. They are to characterise those grammatical properties which all human languages share, and to determine the limits within which all human languages vary. Although superficially it might seem that human languages are extremely diverse (and the inability of most of us to speak more than one or two of them with any ease would seem to support this impression), the assumption of many researchers who work on UG is that human languages are, in fact, considerably alike in their grammatical properties, and where they vary they do so in quite restricted ways.

One reason why this view is attractive has to do with L1 acquisition. All infants acquire their first languages *rapidly* (barring physiological impairment, and given normal exposure to language). Within three years they have mastered the major structures, and by age five their understanding of complex and subtle structural distinctions is effectively adult-like, although at this age their topics of conversation are limited by experience. They also acquire them *effortlessly*: mere exposure is sufficient for them to do this. Further, they acquire them *uniformly*: it is now known that children go through the same kinds of stages of development in learning specific grammatical properties. Finally, they acquire them with *remarkable success*: they attain a state of subconscious knowledge about the language they are exposed to which closely resembles other native speakers' subconscious knowledge about the language.

Children appear to do all of this not only without receiving any formal instruction about what can and what cannot be said in the language, but without any apparent need for, or sensitivity to, correction of their productions by adult speakers. This particular feature of L1 acquisition is often referred to as the 'no negative evidence' condition. Children acquire their first languages on the basis of positive evidence only.

Here are two classic cases from the L1 acquisition literature which suggest that the role played by negative evidence is of restricted importance for the child's developing linguistic knowledge. The first is reported by McNeill (1966), who recorded a mother trying to get her small son not to use a double negative:

Child: Nobody don't like me.
Mother: No, say 'nobody likes me'.
C: Nobody don't like me.
[This exchange is repeated eight times]
M: No, now listen carefully: say 'nobody likes me'.
C: Oh! Nobody don't LIKES me.

Even where there is explicit, and repeated, instruction the child appears not to be sensitive to it. And most of the time children are not exposed to anything like this level of repetition. The second case is a study by Brown & Hanlon (1970) of parental speech to children. Brown & Hanlon found that the amount of corrective feedback that parents give to grammatical errors in the speech of their children is negligible. They will mostly let pass utterances such as 'Daddy rided bike' without correcting them. On the other hand, parents apparently do correct the factual accuracy of their children's speech, so that if in fact Daddy had gone on the bus, rather than on his bike, they would correct that. Children, it seems, acquire their native languages perfectly without the benefit of either consistent instruction or correction.

Children also appear to do all of this under a wide variety of conditions of exposure. In the middle-class strata of industrialised societies parents and care-givers normally direct a lot of talk to infants. But in some societies it is not the norm to talk to infants in the same way. Yet children in such societies still learn the language of their community rapidly, effortlessly, uniformly, and successfully. For example, Pye (1983, cited in Ingram, 1989: 128) suggests that among the Quiché people of Guatemala 'the parental attitude is to ignore the infant until it is producing recognisable adult-like language', and reports other cases from around the world where it is not the norm for adults to mix conversationally with children. Slobin (1979: 161) reports that Norwegian children living on isolated farms in rural areas spend most of their time in solitary play, having little verbal contact with anyone other than the mother, who typically does not prompt or encourage children to talk, does not ask questions or suggest activities, or even read stories. This is in contrast to Norwegian town and village children who have considerably more exposure to Norwegian from a variety of sources. Nevertheless, 'the language development is similar in the three settings — farm, village and town'. Even more striking are cases reported by Schiff (1979, cited in Hyams, 1991: 77-8) 'of hearing children of deaf parents who received less than 20 hours a week of oral language input. By several standard measures of linguistic development these children showed no delay in oral language development when compared to children from homes with hearing parents'.

Finally, children acquire language in this remarkable way whatever their ethnic origin, and no matter which language they are exposed to. Take any child at birth, born in any part of the world, transport that child into any speech community, and he or she will learn the language of the community rapidly, effortlessly, uniformly, and successfully (barring physiological impairment, and given normal exposure to the language).

These observations about L1 acquisition would follow if the structural properties of human languages — which from now on we shall refer to technically as their *grammars* — are essentially alike, with limited variation between them, and if the properties that the grammars of human languages share are in some way determined by the structure of the minds of those who speak them; that is, if what is common to the grammars of human languages follows from the innately determined structure of the human language faculty. Children would then come to the task of L1 acquisition already equipped with subconscious expectations about the form that the grammars of human languages take. They would not have to learn those features of the particular language to which they are exposed which are universal, because they know them already. They would have to learn only those features which vary between languages, and about which they will need positive evidence from the language spoken around them.

If this were the appropriate view of language acquisition, it would follow that although language learning takes time, because children will need to accumulate evidence about how the variable properties are to be fixed, it should be relatively rapid, uniform in development, and effortless, and it should require neither instruction nor corrective feedback because an important part of the requisite knowledge is part of the child's innate biological endowment.

Principles and Parameters

This leading idea, that much in the grammars of human languages is fixed and innate, and that variation itself falls within narrow limits, has given rise to the principles and parameters approach to UG first elaborated in Chomsky (1981). *Principles* are the universal design features of human language, and the research task of linguistics is to uncover and describe those principles. Principles are invariant. *Parameters*, by contrast, are the limited possibilities for variation allowed within the principles of UG. A parameter will have two or more values, and particular languages will make different choices among the values allowed by the parameter. We shall illustrate the notions of 'principle' and 'parameter' first by an analogy, and then by a series of examples. Because it would be impossible, given that this book is about second language acquisition and not about linguistic theory, to provide a comprehensive account of the principles and parameters approach, the choice of the examples has been guided by whether they allow insight to be gained about SLA, and each example of a proposed principle or parameter will be directly related to a particular empirical problem in SLA.[1]

An analogy

Automobile wheels are driven by a motor linked to the axle to which the wheels are attached. This is a universal feature — a 'principle' — of automobile design. But different types of automobile allow different possibilities for organising the manner in which the motor drives the axle to which the wheels are attached. Some vehicles have front wheel drive, some have rear wheel drive, and some have four wheel drive. Thus, although there is a design principle that the motor is linked to an axle which drives the wheels, there is a 'parameter' of variation in the realisation of that principle; a parameter with three 'values': front wheel drive, rear wheel drive, or four wheel drive.

The Structure of Phrases

The component — or subtheory — of UG which deals with the structure of phrases is known as *X-bar theory*. The reason for this arcane title will become clear in a moment. Recent work on this theory suggests that the structure of phrases that go to make up sentences in the world's languages is of a single basic type consisting of a main or head category, which is the core of the phrase, and two different kinds of modifiers, one called a specifier and the other called a complement, as illustrated in (5.1):

5.1 [PHRASE Specifier — Head — Complement]

Complements are modifiers closely associated with the head, and form with it a constituent. Specifiers modify this [head + complement] constituent to form another constituent: [specifier + [head + complement]]. This constituent structure can also be represented hierarchically in the form of a tree, as in (5.2), where the constituents are labelled, arbitrarily for the moment, X and Y. Our discussion below will clarify the status of these constituents.

5.2

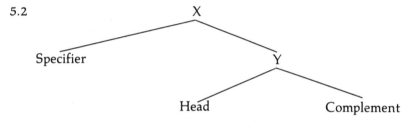

The justification for proposing this organisation of phrases into subconstituents will become clear as we proceed. It should also be noted at this point that specifiers and complements, because they are modifiers, are not obligatory in phrases. They may or may not be present.

Head categories include some of the major syntactic categories recognised in traditional grammatical theory, such as noun (N), verb (V), adjective (A), preposition (P) (and also some non-traditional categories to which we return later). Because the head is the core of the phrase, it plays a crucial role in selecting appropriate specifiers and complements, and it also plays a crucial role in determining the possible distribution of the phrase in sentences. For this reason it is standard practice to reflect the importance of the head in the structural labels given to the phrase. Ns head noun phrases (NPs), Vs head verb phrases (VPs), As head adjective phrases (APs), and Ps head prepositional phrases (PPs). In between the heads (which are sometimes called zero-level categories: N°, V°, A°, P°) and the maximal projections (NP, VP, AP, PP) occurs the constituent composed of the head and its complement. It is conventional to label this constituent as the head plus a diacritic bar: head' (or head-bar): N' (N-bar), V' (V-bar), A' (A-bar), P' (P-bar). So, for example, the structure of an NP in English would be that illustrated in (5.3).

5.3

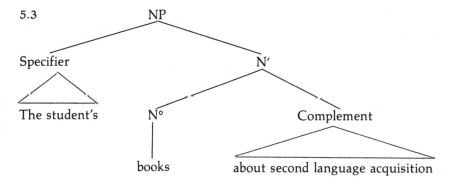

It is hypothesised that the structural configurations illustrated in
(5.2) and (5.3) are common to all phrases, whatever the head. We can
describe this schematically by saying that in the world's languages any
head X° projects into another constituent of type X' (i.e. X-bar — hence
'X-bar theory'), consisting of the head and its complement, and this
constituent projects into the maximal projection XP, consisting of the X'
and its specifier. VPs, APs and PPs in English will then have the same
structure as NPs, as illustrated in (5.4), (5.5) and (5.6).[2]

5.4

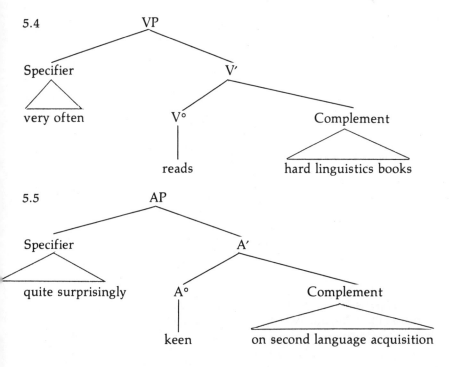

5.5

5.6

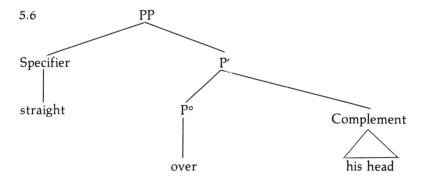

The structure of phrases, then, is determined by an invariant universal principle which requires that X° project into X′, and that X′ project into XP. At the same time, individual languages vary as to whether the head appears to the left or right of its complement, and whether the specifier appears to the left or to the right of X′. For example, in languages such as English, French and Italian, typically specifiers precede the head and complements follow it, as in (5.7a).

5.7a

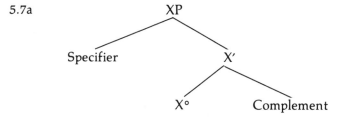

This gives rise to word orders like 'several books about second language acquisition', 'surprisingly keen on linguistics' and 'away up there'. In languages such as Japanese, Turkish and Burmese, typically both specifiers and complements precede the head, as in (5.7b).

5.7b

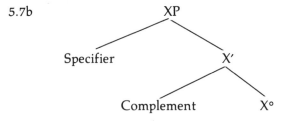

This gives rise to word orders like 'several second language acquisition about books', 'surprisingly linguistics on keen' and 'away there up'. In languages such as Malagasy, Gilbertese and Fijian, typically heads precede their specifiers and complements, as in (5.7c) (J.A. Hawkins, 1980: 201).

5.7c

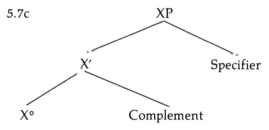

This gives rise to word orders like 'books about second language acquisition several', 'keen on linguistics surprisingly' and 'up there away'.[3]

The linear ordering of specifier with respect to X' constituents, and X° with respect to complements is a parameter of variation allowed within the invariant principle of UG determining phrase structure. Particular languages have selected different values of the parameter.

Phrase Structure and First Language Acquisition

How is an account of phrase structure along these lines of interest in the investigation of language acquisition? Recall that in the case of L1 acquisition it is hypothesised that invariant principles will not have to be learned by children because they will already know them innately. This predicts that infants will come to the task of language acquisition already endowed with the knowledge that word-level categories (X°) project into X' level categories, and that X' level categories project into XP (Maximal) categories. Once children have learned a sufficient number of words of the language to which they are being exposed, and have correctly categorised them as N, V, and so on, it should be an automatic process for them to build phrase structure, because they already know the principle determining what form phrases take. This prediction appears to be borne out. Studies which have addressed the question find that children are able to build phrase structure from a very early age. For example, in a study of the acquisition of English as a first language Radford (1990: 62–82) cites many examples of two, three and four-word utterances produced by children between the ages of 18 and 23 months which suggest that they know how to project productively X° categories into X' categories, and X' categories into XP categories. Just a few examples of the many that Radford cites are given in (5.8).

5.8	X^0	Complement		
	cup	tea	(N')	'a cup ot tea'
	ball	wool	(N')	'a ball of wool'
	open	box	(V')	'open the box'
	get	toys	(V')	'get my toys'
(put)	in	there	(P')	'put it in there'
(get)	out	cot	(P')	'I want to get out of the cot'

	Spec	X'		
	Mummy	car	(NP)	'Mummy's car'
	Hayley	dress	(NP)	'Hayley's dress'
	Dolly	hat	(NP)	'Dolly's hat'
	Daddy	gone	(VP)	'Daddy has gone'
	Hayley	draw (boat)	(VP)	'Hayley is drawing (a boat)'
	Paula	play (with ball)	(VP)	'Paula is playing (with a ball)'

He goes on to suggest (Radford, 1990: 81) that:

> . . . the initial grammars formulated by young children show clear evidence of the acquisition of a well-developed set of symmetrical lexical category systems, in that young children at the relevant stage (typically between the ages of 20 and 23 months ±20%) seem to 'know' how to project head nouns, verbs, prepositions and adjectives into the corresponding single-bar and [XP] categories.

On the other hand, children do not know in advance what the relative positions of specifier to X' constituent, and X^0 to complement will be; this can be determined only on the basis of exposure to positive evidence from the particular language being learned. It might, then, take children a little longer to work out the appropriate linear orderings than it does for them to project phrase-structure, because linear orderings have to be learned, while the projection of phrase structure does not. Tsimpli (1991) has argued that this is the case. Surveying young children in the early stages of learning a range of first languages (English, Greek, German, French) she suggests that while they can project phrase structure, they are not always consistent in where they put specifiers or complements, even though the language they are exposed to has a consistent order. For example, (5.9) shows some utterances taken from children learning French (Pierce, 1988) and German (Clahsen, 1988) as first languages.

5.9 *French*   *German*

papa travaille (Spec X°)   mama sitzen (Spec X°)
Daddy work   Mummy sit

lit maman (X° Spec)   sitzen puppa (X° Spec)
read Mummy (= Mummy is   sit doll (= the doll is sitting)
reading)

bébé veut papa (Spec X° Comp)   ich ziehn (Spec X°)
baby want Daddy   I pull

promener bébé (X° Spec)   so ziehn pferd ((Adv) X° Spec)
walk baby (= Baby is walking)   like this pull horse (= The horse
                                       pulls like this)

In practice, languages appear generally to have a preferred or canonical position for head and specifier for all phrases, in the sense that if, say, a V° appears to the left of its complement, N°s, A°s, and P°s will also appear to the left of their complements; conversely, if, say, a V° appears to the right of its complement, so will N°s, A°s and P°s. This property was first brought to the general attention of linguists by Greenberg (1966), and has been given the name of 'cross-category harmony' (J.A. Hawkins, 1980). Although it is not clear what the status of cross-category harmony in language acquisition is (i.e. whether it is part of the child's biological endowment, in the sense that the child will expect all categories to display the same specifier–head–complement ordering, or not) if it were available to the child L1 learner as some kind of aid to learning, and if the child were to assume that the language he or she was exposed to was uniformly directional, learning should proceed rapidly and swiftly.

But some languages are not uniformly directional; some types of head or specifier are in the opposite direction to the language's canonical order. That is, some languages have superficially mixed orders. French is a case in point. French has a canonical ('preferred') order of specifier–X°–complement, as shown in (5.10).

5.10 *Specifier*   X°   *Complement*

plusieurs   livres (N°)   sur la Révolution
several   books   on the Revolution

Claude   paraît (V°)   triste
Claude   appears   sad

très	*fort* (A°)	*en langues*
very	good	at languages
droit	*vers* (P°)	*la mairie*
straight	towards	the Town Hall

But in the case of unstressed direct and indirect object pronouns (the equivalent of the English forms 'him', 'her', 'to them', 'to us', and so on) these appear not to the right of the V° head, but to its left — see (5.11).

5.11 *Specifier* *Complement* V°

Claude	*le*	*connaît*
Claude	him	knows
Kim	*le lui*	*donne*
Kim	it to him	gives

In this case, the child L1 learner of French will have to learn to discriminate those areas of the grammar of French where the V° head is to the left of its complement (as in (5.10)), from those where it is to the right (as in (5.11)). And this task does indeed seem to pose a learning problem for child L1 learners of French. Clark (1985: 714–15) reports that 'clitic object pronouns are a fairly late acquisition', and that 'what children appear to rely on in the early stages is the predominant order [i.e. SVO], so their errors consist of relying on the orders used with full noun phrases'.

The adoption of the principles and parameters approach to the study of L1 acquisition therefore allows a principled account of why children might rapidly, effortlessly, uniformly and without instruction acquire the organisation of words into structured phrases: they know the principle guiding the projection of phrase-structure innately. It also predicts why they may have trouble acquiring certain linear orderings of specifier–head–complement: these are not given in advance, but must be learned on the basis of evidence from the language being learned.

Phrase Structure and Second Language Acquisition

How is an account of phrase structure along these lines of interest in the investigation of SLA? Earlier in this chapter we described a finding that child L1 learners of French take time to acquire preverbal unstressed direct and indirect object pronouns, and we suggested that this was because the location of such pronouns goes against the canonical ordering of heads and complements in French. Consider now an initially puzzling case of L2 development concerning precisely the placement of unstressed object pronouns which was described in Chapter 2. Zobl (1980) has noticed a difference in development between L1 French and L1 Spanish speakers acquiring L2 English, and L1 English speakers acquiring L2 French. The French and Spanish speakers find it easier to acquire the fact that in English unstressed direct and indirect object pronouns follow the verb, as in 'Bill knows him', 'Kim gives it to him', than English speakers do to acquire the fact that in French unstressed direct and indirect object pronouns precede the verb, as in *Claude le connaît* and *Kim le lui donne.*

Suppose we assume that L2 learners initially transfer the properties of their L1 grammars into their L2 grammars. (We shall present clear evidence for the transfer of L1 parameter settings into L2 grammars below.) What might explain this differential difficulty, because the task for both sets of learners is to establish that direct and indirect object pronouns occupy a different position in the L2? The account of phrase structure offered above allows a principled account of this difference. Head position with respect to the complement has to be learned on the basis of evidence from the language, so that a learning task is involved for both sets of learners. But in English the position of unstressed direct and indirect object pronouns falls in line with the canonical 'head first–complement last' pattern, whereas in French the position of unstressed direct and indirect objects runs counter to the canonical pattern. French and Spanish learners of L2 English have only to realise that English is uniformly directional in this case to get the pattern right, whereas English learners of L2 French will have to learn to delimit the class of items which run counter to the canonical ordering in French, and this will take evidence and time. In fact, the stages of development that L1 English speakers go through in acquiring this pattern in L2 French are very similar to the stages that child L1 learners of French go through in acquiring it. Following an initial stage where learners leave object pronouns postverbally in the position occupied by full noun phrases, e.g. *Le chien a mangé les,* 'The dog has eaten them' (Zobl, 1980; Clark, 1985), they go to a stage of omission of the pronoun: *Le chien a mangé Ø* (Adiv, 1984; Schlyter, 1986; Véronique, 1986) before eventually acquiring preverbal object pronouns: *Le chien les a mangés.* Developmental similarity across L1 and L2 learners might be expected in this case because the learning task is essentially the same for both sets of learners.[4]

So, by assuming that the grammars constructed by L2 learners are constrained by X-bar theory, which dictates the nature of phrase structure, but allows some parametric variation between languages (variation which has to be learned by the language learner), and by assuming that L2 learners initially transfer the grammatical properties of their L1 into their L2 grammars, it is possible to offer a principled account of observed differential development between French and Spanish speakers acquiring L2 English, and English speakers acquiring L2 French where one might not superficially have expected a difference. Note that this renders an account in terms of learning strategies — such as the Canonical Order Strategy described in Chapter 4 — redundant in this case. The nature of the grammatical knowledge involved is sufficient to predict the observed development.

A similar kind of account has been offered by White (1991b) for another 'odd' observation about SLA. Clahsen & Muysken (1986), studying L1 Romance-language-speaking and L1 Turkish-speaking learners of L2 German noticed that the Turkish speakers passed through an early phase of development where they treated German as a language in which V° is to the left of its complement, i.e. a head–complement language. This is surprising because Turkish is a complement–head language, and most current accounts of the syntax of the German verb phrase also suggest that it displays complement–head order. This is on the basis of the word order that German displays in subordinate clauses, where the verb clearly follows its complement, as in: *Ich glaube dass er ein Buch gekauft hat*, literally 'I believe that he a book bought has'. (German differs from Turkish, however, in that Turkish is uniformly complement–head across all categories, whereas German has both complement–head and head–complement orderings; the latter, for example, is the order for the verb and its complement in main clauses: *Er kaufte ein Buch*, 'He bought a book'. We shall discuss German word order at length in Chapter 6). With both the L1 and L2 displaying complement–V° order, one might have expected the Turkish speakers to initially transfer the word order pattern of their L1, recognise that German V°s and their complements conform to the same pattern, and continue with that pattern. White (1991b: 184–5) suggests, however that:

> . . . there is a potential explanation of the L2 learner's initial assumption of SVO order [for German] . . . It relates to the fact that the head position parameter usually operates consistently across syntactic categories, German being an exception in this respect. Suppose that L2 learners have to set the headedness parameter for the L2, and that in their L1s this parameter is set consistently across categories . . . Suppose, in addition, that the L2 learner assumes that the L2, like the L1, will show consistent head position across

categories, and that the L2 learner is responsive to a number of properties of the L2 input, but is misled by this assumption of consistency. The position of specifiers and complements in NPs and PPs in German is such as to suggest that German is head initial. This configuration plus the consistency assumption will be enough to yield VO order, even for Turkish learners of German.

Turkish speakers, then, according to White, have the task of learning, on the basis of evidence from the language itself, which value of the ordering parameter for heads and complements German has selected, and they are misled early on in this task by conflicting evidence from the L2, together with the assumption, transferred from Turkish, that German will be uniformly directional.

Summary

We have begun to explore how the principles and parameters approach might offer an explanation for five core observations about SLA: that learners transfer grammatical properties from the L1 grammar into their L2 grammar, that they go through stages of development, that they do so systematically, that learners' eventual L2 grammars are nevertheless incomplete relative to the grammars constructed by L1 learners, and that L2 learners go through phases when their grammatical knowledge appears to be variable.

Principles and parameters theory assumes that human languages are cut basically to the same pattern, in that the grammars of particular languages fall within a class defined by invariant universal principles. One such principle was briefly described, that of the projection of phrase structure of a specific type from head categories: head categories, X°, project into X' constituents of the form $[x'\ X^\circ$ complement], and X' constituents project into XP constituents of the form $[xp$ specifier $X']$.

Although the phrase structure of all languages is of this type, particular languages vary as to whether the head precedes or follows its complement, and as to whether the X' constituent precedes or follows its specifier.

In much current work on L1 acquisition it is assumed that children know the invariant principles of UG at birth, i.e. such principles are innate. If this were the case it would be one explanation for the remarkable speed, effortlessness, uniformity and success that characterises L1 acquisition. In a general sense, children know what a human language is likely to be like in advance of any contact with one (where 'know' means 'subconsciously know', of course). The learning task for children comes with establishing the settings for the parameters of variation allowed within the domain determined by the invariant principles.

This general approach was illustrated by considering the way that children from a very early age can productively project phrase structure, but take longer to establish the ordering of specifiers, heads and complements, particularly where a language is not uniformly directional, as for example in the placement of unstressed object pronouns in French, in examples such as: *Claude le connaît.*

It was then argued that this approach can very neatly be extended to the observation of a rather bizarre difference in SLA between French and Spanish learners of L2 English who have no problems, it seems, with the location of unstressed object pronouns in English, and English learners of L2 French (and presumably Spanish) who have considerable difficulty acquiring unstressed preverbal object pronouns in the L2. The assumption that L2 learners' grammars are constrained by the invariant principles of UG, but that parametric variation has to be learned on the basis of positive evidence from the L2, just as for L1 learners, offers an immediate account of this difference.

We have, then, a potential initial hypothesis about the nature of SLA: that it is essentially like L1 acquisition in that learners' construction of L2 grammars will be determined by the principles of UG, but that they will have to learn the appropriate settings for the parameters of the L2. At the same time, L1 and L2 learners are strikingly different in a number of areas. One of them is transfer, which is dealt with in the next chapter.

Notes

1. For a general introduction to principles and parameters see Haegeman (1991); for an introduction to their application to first language acquisition see Atkinson (1992); and for an application of UG to SLA see White (1989b). For a critical debate of whether UG has a role to play at all in SLA, see the contributions in Eubank (1991).
2. It should be noted that specifiers and complements are themselves maximal projections; thus, 'the student's' in (5.3) is a specifier which is an NP, and 'about second language acquisition' is a complement which is a PP; in (5.4) 'very often' is a specifier which is an AdvP (adverbial phrase) and 'hard linguistics books' is a complement which is an NP; and so on.
3. It appears that the ordering complement–head–specifier is either very rare or non-existent in the world's languages.

4. There is an alternative to the account of the syntax of unstressed direct and indirect object pronoun placement given in the text, and this is that pronouns are generated at an abstract level of structure in the canonical postverbal position, and are moved to their surface structure position, for example: *Claude connaît le* → *Claude le connaît t* (where t is the 'trace' left behind by the movement of *le*). On this account French would be uniformly directional at this abstract level. This alternative account does not affect the learning problem which remains the same for the language learner on either analysis: to delimit the class of complements which, on the surface, appear to the left of V^{o} from those which appear to its right.

6 Parametric Variation and Transfer in Second Language Acquisition

Do L2 learners transfer the parameter settings of their first languages into their initial L2 grammars? It appears that they do. Despite a number of studies in the early 1980s which attempted to show that L2 learners initially assume 'open' parameter values (i.e. that the settings of the L1 are not influential in SLA) — for example, see a series of studies by Mazurkewich (1984a, b, 1985) — studies have been accumulating since the early 1980s which suggest that L2 learners do indeed initially transfer their L1 parameter settings.

Transfer of L1 parameter settings into the L2 can have two effects. If the setting in the L2 happens to be the same as the setting in the L1, then the learner should get grammatical properties of the L2 which are dependent on that parameter setting right from the very beginning of acquisition. Where the settings differ between the L1 and the L2 the learner would initially be expected to get wrong grammatical properties of the L2 dependent on that parameter setting. Where there is a parametric conflict of this sort between a learner's initial L2 grammar and the target language, what happens as the learner receives more input from the L2 is currently far from clear. All L2 learners show development away from the L1 grammatical properties in this situation, but the extent to which this involves them in resetting parameter values is an open and controversial question (to which we return in Chapter 7).

Later in this chapter we present two sample studies of L2 word order acquisition to illustrate the transfer of L1 parameter settings into L2 grammars. The studies in question are one by Hulk (1991) of L1 Dutch speakers acquiring L2 French, and a cluster of studies concerning the acquisition of L2 German by L1 Romance-language speakers (Clahsen & Muysken, 1986; duPlessis, Solin, Travis & White, 1987; Schwartz & Tomaselli, 1988). Before we consider these cases we need to expand a little upon the account of phrase structure outlined in Chapter 5.

The Structure of Clauses

In current linguistic theory, clauses (that is, the smallest sentences) are held to have the same structural properties as NPs, VPs, APs and PPs: they consist of a specifier–head–complement structure. There are, in fact, two categories which are crucial to the construction of clauses; neither of them are categories which appear in traditional grammars. The first is a category referred to from the 1980s onwards (cf. Chomsky, 1981) as Infl or I°, which is short for 'inflection', and refers to the person and number (and sometimes gender) of the subject of the clause, which are realised as an agreement inflection on verbs. English is not particularly rich in the subject agreement properties it realises on verbs. For example in the present tense most verbs inflect for -Ø or -s: 'I run', 'she runs'. Other languages have much richer conjugations, for example Spanish: *hablo* 'I speak', *hablas* 'you [sing.] speak', *habla* 'he speaks', *hablamos* 'we speak', *habláis* 'you [plur.] speak', *hablan* 'they speak'. In addition to the features of person and number, agreeing with the subject, I° also carries tense features [± past]. I° is a head which, when it projects into an IP,

6.1

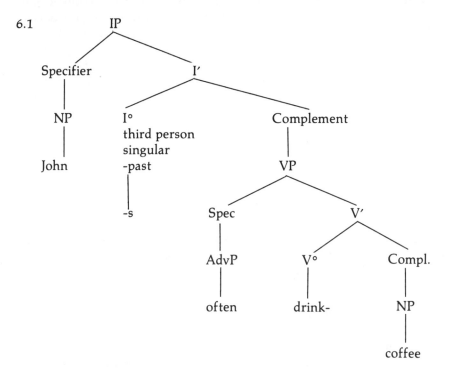

takes the subject of the clause as its specifier, and the VP as its complement, as illustrated in (6.1).

The structure (6.1) underlies the sentence 'John often drinks coffee'. The features of person, number and tense of I° are realised as -s in this case. Obviously a syntactic operation is required to ensure that -s is appropriately attached to the verb 'drink', but we shall deal with this later.

Although IP is central to clauses, I° is not the head of the clause. The head of the clause determines the type of clause that it is going to be. For example, we need to distinguish at least four major types of clauses in the world's languages. First, main or root clauses need to be distinguished from subordinate or embedded clauses, as illustrated in (6.2).

6.2a *John often drinks coffee.*   (root clause)
   b I believe *that John often drinks coffee.*   (embedded clause)

Embedded clauses can have syntactic properties quite different from root clauses. For example, in English they may be introduced by a complementiser, like 'that' in (6.2b), while root clauses in English are never introduced by a complementiser. Inversion of the subject and verb in questions, which is possible in root clauses in English, is usually impossible in embedded clauses, for example: 'Why did he do it?' (root clause), *'I wonder why did he do it?' versus 'I wonder why he did it' (embedded clause). In some languages certain forms of the verb are possible only in embedded clauses, for example the subjunctive mood in French is available only in embedded clauses. And so on.

Secondly, declarative clauses (statements) need to be distinguished from interrogative clauses (questions), as in (6.3).

6.3a John often drinks coffee.   (declarative clause)
   b Does John often drink coffee?   (interrogative clause)

The declarative–interrogative distinction cuts across the root–embedded distinction so that we can have root declaratives and root interrogatives, and embedded declaratives and embedded interrogatives, as illustrated in (6.4).

6.4a John often drinks coffee.   (root declarative)
   b Does John often drink coffee?   (root interrogative)
   c I believe that John often drinks coffee.   (embedded declarative)
   d I wonder if John often drinks coffee.   (embedded interrogative)

To capture these major distinctions between clause types in languages, current linguistic theory proposes that the head of clauses is another non-traditional category called 'complementiser' or C°, which projects into a CP. Clauses are in fact CPs, as (6.5) shows.

6.5

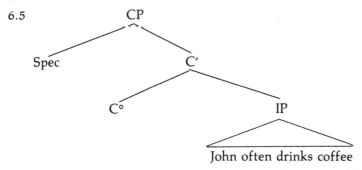

John often drinks coffee

C° determines the kind of clause it is: whether it is a root clause or an embedded clause; whether the clause is a declarative or an interrogative. These options can be represented as features of the category C° (just as person, number and tense are features of the category I°). Thus C° has the features [± root] and [± wh] (where [+ root] = root clause, [– root] = embedded clause, [+ wh] = question, and [– wh] = declarative). The different selections of these features will produce the range of clause types that we have described, as shown in (6.6).

6.6a A declarative root clause

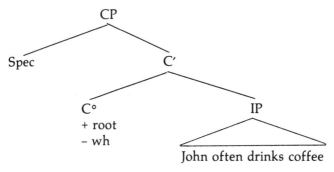

John often drinks coffee

Notice that although in (6.6b–d) C° is realised as a phonetically specified lexical item ('that', a form of 'do', and 'if' respectively), in declarative root clauses like (6.6a) in English there is no lexical item realising C°. What is the justification for proposing that declarative root clauses in English are headed by C° when there is no evidence of this C° on the surface? One justification is theoretical uniformity: we can say

6.6b A declarative embedded clause

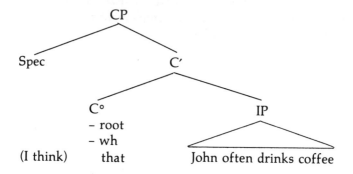

6.6c An interrogative root clause

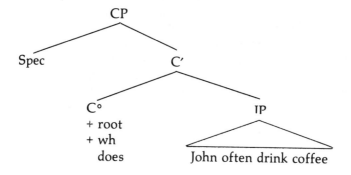

6.6d An interrogative subordinate clause (indirect question)

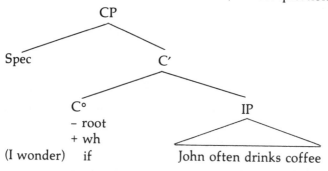

that the complementiser 'that' selects subordinate declarative IPs, the complementiser 'do' selects root interrogative IPs, the complementiser 'if' selects subordinate interrogative IPs, and the complementiser Ø selects root declarative IPs. Another justification is that in some languages of the world the complementiser that selects root declarative IPs is phonetically specified, for example Ross (1970), gives examples from Classical Arabic and Spanish, as shown in (6.7) and (6.8).

6.7 Classical Arabic:
   ?inna lwalada qad taraka lbayta.
   that the-boy did leave the-house.
   'The boy left the house.'

6.8 Spanish:
   Que mi gato se enratonó.
   that my cat got-sick-on mice.
   'My cat got sick from eating too many mice.'

It can then be suggested that English simply has a null version of this complementiser.

The invariant principles of UG involved here are that clauses are CPs whose structure is determined by X-bar theory, with $C°$ taking IP as its complement (the structure of IP also being determined by X-bar theory), and that $C°$ carries (at least) the features [± root] and [± wh]. The parameters of variation involved (i.e. those realisations of CP and IP which may differ between languages) are, as in the case of other phrases, the position of the head and the specifier in CP and IP, and furthermore the classes of items which may appear under $C°$ given particular selections of its features.

Parametric Differences Between German/Dutch and English/French

Differences in the selection of parameter values for CP and IP can be illustrated by comparing the characteristic word order properties of German and Dutch on the one hand, and English and French on the other. This particular case has been chosen because it allows us to consider directly the L2 studies of the acquisition of German/Dutch and English/French word order properties.

Whereas in English and French all declarative clauses, whether root or embedded, are typically of the structure subject–verb–object (SVO) or adverbial–subject–verb–object (ASVO), as illustrated in (6.9) from English.

6.9a John bought a book.
  b Today John bought a book.

in root clauses in German and Dutch the verb always comes in second position, whatever comes in first position in the clause, whether it is the subject, an adverbial or even a direct object (illustrated from German in (6.10)).

6.10a *Johann kaufte heute ein Buch.*
   b *Heute kaufte Johann ein Buch.*
   c *Ein Buch kaufte Johann heute.*

Not surprisingly, this has led to German and Dutch becoming known as verb-second (V2) languages. But the characteristic differences between German/Dutch and English/French do not stop there. If the verb in a root clause in German/Dutch is in a compound tense (for example, *hat gekauft*, 'has bought'), or involves a modal verb and an infinitive (for example, *will kaufen*, 'wants to buy'), or is a verb with a particle attached to it (for example, *aufnehmen*, 'to pick up') then although the verb which is inflected for person, number and tense appears in V2 element position, the other — past participle, infinitive or particle — goes to the very end of the clause, i.e. there is what might be called verb separation, as shown in (6.11).

6.11a *Johann* hat *ein Buch* gekauft.
   b *Johann* will *ein Buch* kaufen.
   c *Johann* nahm *ein Buch* auf.

In English/French, by contrast, past participles and infinitives do not usually go to the end of the clause, and particles (found only in English) do so only optionally, as shown in (6.12).

6.12a John *has bought* a book.
   b John *wants to buy* a book.
   c John *picked up* a book/John *picked* a book *up*.

Finally, in embedded clauses introduced by a subordinating conjunction such as *dass*, 'that' (German), or 'that' (English), in German/Dutch the verb inflected for person, number and tense obligatorily appears at the end of the clause, and not in V2 position; embedded clauses are verb final — see (6.13).

6.13a *Er glaubt, dass Johann ein Buch* kaufte.
     He thinks that Johann a book bought.
   b *Er glaubt, dass Johann ein Buch gekauft hat.*
     "   *Johann ein Buch kaufen will.*
     "   *Johann ein Buch aufnahm.*

whereas in English/French, the inflected verb and other verbal elements occupy the same positions in embedded clauses that they do in main clauses, as in (6.14).

6.14 I think that John *bought* a book.
     "   John *has bought* a book.
     "   John *wants to buy* a book.
     "   John *picked up* a book/*picked* a book *up*.

The principles and parameters approach can offer an interesting account of these word order differences within the framework of phrase-structure that we have been outlining. (The account below draws elements from a number of different studies discussed variously in

6.15a German/Dutch

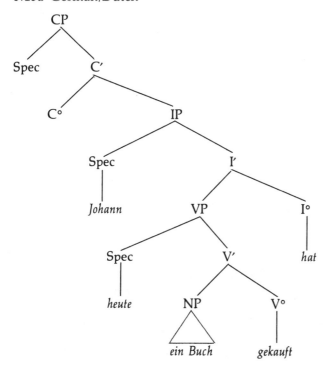

Clahsen & Muysken, 1986; duPlessis *et al.*, 1987; Schwartz & Tomaselli, 1988; Rizzi, 1990; Haegeman, 1991: 513–52.)

Suppose that at an underlying abstract level of structure — underlying structure was originally called the 'deep structure' of clauses (Chomsky, 1957) and is now called the D-structure — the heads V° and I° in German and Dutch are not to the left of their complements, as they are in English and French, but to the right of their complements. This would be a parametric difference between the two languages. The structure of clauses in German/Dutch at D-structure would then differ from the structure of clauses in English/French at D-structure in the way illustrated in (6.15).

6.15b English/French

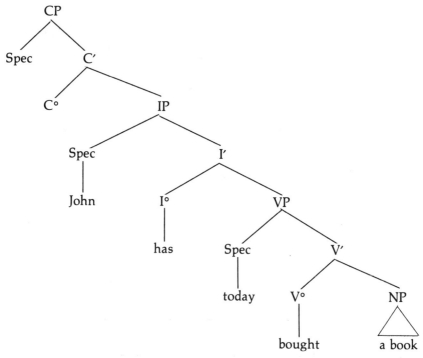

Assume further that German/Dutch and English/French differ parametrically in that in root clauses in German/Dutch the inflected verb moves from its D-structure position into a position under C°. This will give S-structures in German/Dutch (originally called 'surface structures') in which the inflected verb appears at the front of the clause. This movement can be characterised by saying that a C° with the feature [+

root] in German/Dutch attracts the inflected verb (i.e. the inflected verb moves from its D-structure position into the position under C°) whereas in English/French it does so only when C° is both [+ root] and [+ wh], i.e. in questions: 'Did John buy a book?', 'What did John buy?'. If it is also assumed that when C° is filled by an inflected verb some NP or adverbial must move into the specifier of CP, this will produce the V2 effect in German/Dutch, illustrated in (6.16).

6.16a [CP *Johann kaufte* [IP ___ *heute ein Buch* ___]]
   b [CP *Heute kaufte* [IP *Johann* ___ *ein Buch* ___]]
   c [CP *Ein Buch kaufte* [IP *Johann heute* ___ ___]]
   d [CP *Johann hat* [IP ___ *heute ein Buch gekauft* ___]]
   e [CP *Heute hat* [IP *Johann* ___ *ein Buch gekauft* ___]]
   f [CP *Ein Buch hat* [IP *Johann heute* ___ *gekauft* ___]]
   and so on.

By contrast, when C° in German/Dutch is [– root] (i.e. when the clause is an embedded clause) it is normally filled by some phonetically specified complementiser like *dass*, and the presence of this element under C° blocks the movement of the inflected verb into C°. Since the inflected verb is forced to stay in its D-structure position, this will give the verb-final effect in embedded clauses:

6.17 *Er glaubt* [CP dass [IP *Johann heute ein Buch kaufte*]]
         ″   [IP *Johann heute ein Buch gekauft hat*]
         ″   [IP *Johann heute ein Buch kaufen will*]
   and so on.

In English/French, on the other hand, a C° with the features [+ root], [– wh] (i.e. in root declarative clauses) does not license movement of the inflected verb into C°, so that at S-structure the verb remains in the same position it occupies in D-structure in both root and embedded clauses, for example:

6.18a [CP ___ [IP Today John bought a book]]
   b [CP ___ [IP Today John has bought a book]]
   c (I believe) [CP that [IP Today John has bought a book]]
   and so on.

There are, then, considerable differences in the word orders of German/Dutch on the one hand, and English/French on the other. But by assuming one invariant principle of UG, and two parameters of variation, all the differences can be predicted. The invariant principle is that head categories, X°, project into constituents consisting of a head and its complement, X-bar, and that X-bar categories project into constituents consisting of an X-bar category and its specifier, XP. The parameters are: (a) that the heads V° and I° are to the right of their complements in German/Dutch at D-structure, but to the left of their complements at D-structure in English/French; (b) that C° [+ root], [– wh] in German/Dutch attracts the inflected verb, with an NP or adverbial simultaneously moving into the specifier of CP, whereas in English/French it does not. Since it is assumed that this principle and the parameters are required more generally to account for the word order properties of the world's languages, not only do we arrive at a relatively simple account for the word order differences between the two language types, but we do so on the basis of a theory which has wider application.

The Transfer of L1 Parameter Values in the Second Language Acquisition of Word Order Properties in French and German

A group of studies investigating the acquisition of word order properties in French and German allow us to consider directly the role of L1 parameter settings in early SLA. Hulk (1991) studied the development of L2 grammatical intuitions about French word order in a group of L1 Dutch-speaking subjects via a grammaticality judgement task. There were four groups in her study: 26 pupils in the first year of secondary school (first graders) who had just started French; 21 second grade pupils in their second year of French; 25 third grade pupils in their third year of French; and 16 university students who had continued with French throughout the secondary school curriculum and were studying French at the Free University in Amsterdam at the time of testing. The grammaticality judgement task required subjects to judge a randomised set of grammatical and ungrammatical sentences of French, where the ungrammatical sentences were possible word orders in Dutch, for example (the asterisk means that these sentences are ungrammatical in native-speaker French):

6.19a *Anne a *la télévision* regardé.   (V . . . V order)
      Anne has the television watched.   (i.e. verb
                                            separation)

   b *Ce soir* préparait *papa le dîner.*   (V2 order)
      This evening prepared father the dinner.   (as opposed to
                                            SVO)

   c *Je crois que Jean les fraises* mange.   (V–final order)
      I believe that Jean the strawberries is eating. (with a single V)

d *Je crois que papa le dîner préparé a.   (VV–final order)
  I believe that father the dinner prepared has. (with a
                                                 compound VV)

Hulk found that the first graders strongly preferred Dutch word order patterns in the L2. At the same time, this preference disappeared fairly rapidly (over the next two grades), so that by the time learners had reached the stage of L2 development represented by the university students, they appeared highly native-like in their judgements about clausal word order in French — see Tables 6.1, 6.2 and 6.3.

Table 6.1 Responses of correct to 'V . . . V' order (*Jean a les fraises mangé) and '. . . VV . . .' order (Jean a mangé les fraises)

	1st grade %	2nd grade %	3rd grade %	University %
V . . . V	73	40	2	0
VV	42'	86	100	100

Table 6.2 Responses of correct to 'V-final' order (*Je crois que Jean les fraises mange), 'VV-final' order (*Je crois que Jean les fraises mangé a), and 'VV-nonfinal' order (Je crois que Jean a mangé les fraises)

	1st grade %	2nd grade %	3rd grade %	University %
. . . V	89	31	8	0
. . . VV	65	26	0	0
VV . . .	27	87	100	100

Table 6.3 Responses of correct to 'V2' order after an adverb (*Hier mangeait Jean des fraises) and 'ASVO' (Hier Jean mangeait des fraises)

	1st grade %	2nd grade %	3rd grade %	University %
V2	92	50	32	10
ASVO	38	80	100	100

(Tables 6.1–6.3 adapted from Hulk, 1991: 22–4).

These findings suggest that in the early stages of acquisition of L2 French, Dutch-speakers (adolescents in this case) transfer the parameter values of head position and movement of the inflected $V°$ into [+ root] $C°$ into their L2 grammars for French, but recognise quite rapidly that these values are not appropriate to French, and move away from Dutch word order (over the first three years of classroom exposure in all cases in this study except for V2 after an adverbial, which is not fully eliminated even by learners at the university level of proficiency).

Looking at L2 acquisition going in the other direction, Clahsen & Muysken (1986) describe a series of stages that L1 Romance-speaking (Italian, Spanish and Portuguese) adult learners of L2 German, learning German naturalistically, go through in acquiring word order properties. It also turns out that exactly the same order of acquisition is found in classroom L1 Italian-speaking learners of German (Pienemann, 1989) and in classroom L1 English-speaking learners of German (Ellis, 1989). Representative examples are taken from a study by Ellis (1989); an asterisk in these examples means 'ungrammatical in native-speaker German'. It should be noted that the stages are somewhat idealised:

Stage 1 In root clauses learners assume SVO word order:
Ich bin gegangen ins Kino.
I   have gone to the cinema.
I went to the cinema.

Stage 2 Learners begin to front adverbials, while retaining SVO order:
Ich bin gegangen ins Kino.
Gestern ich bin gegangen ins Kino.
Yesterday I have gone to the cinema.
Yesterday I went to the cinema.

Stage 3 Learners begin to place nonfinite verbal elements (participles, infinitives, particles) in clause-final position in root clauses. This pattern is generalised to embedded clauses (V-separation):
Ich bin ins Kino gegangen.
Gestern ich bin ins Kino gegangen.
Er glaubt, dass ich bin ins Kino gegangen.
He thinks that I have to the cinema gone.
'He thinks that I went to the cinema'.

Stage 4 Learners acquire V2 in root clauses:
Ich bin ins Kino gegangen.
Gestern bin ich ins Kino gegangen.
Er glaubt dass ich bin ins Kino gegangen.

Stage 5 Learners acquire verb-final placement of the tensed verb in embedded clauses (i.e. all the relevant properties of target German are acquired):
Ich bin ins Kino gegangen.
Gestern bin ich ins Kino gegangen.
Er glaubt dass gestern ich ins Kino gegangen bin.

Given that the subjects were L1 Romance-language and L1 English speakers, and hence speakers of languages with specifier–head–complement order (SVO), it appears plausible to propose that transfer of L1 word order parameter settings into the L2 grammar is what determines the first two stages of acquisition. Subsequently, however, with continued exposure to German, learners move towards the target language, and according to duPlessis *et al.* (1987) and Schwartz & Tomaselli (1988) reset the parameter values.[1]

Odlin (1989) cites a number of other parallel cases of word order patterns in SLA where early transfer of L1 parameter settings would seem to be involved. For example, Bickerton & Givón (1976) found that L1 Japanese speakers (Japanese is a head-final SOV language) and L1 speakers of Philippine languages (which are head-initial VSO languages) who were immigrants to Hawaii, and acquiring Hawaiian Pidgin English as an L2, differed in their word order patterns in the L2. The Japanese speakers produced a large number of sentences in Pidgin English on the pattern SXV (i.e. head-final), while the Philippine language speakers produced a large number of sentences on the pattern VSX (i.e. head-initial) (where X = any category, including objects). Similarly, Nagara (1972) found that L1 Japanese-speaking immigrants to Hawaii produced SOV patterns in their use of Pidgin English. Another case is that of the L2 Spanish of Indians living in Peru and Ecuador who speak Quechua (an SOV language) natively (Luján, Minaya & Sankoff, 1984). The Spanish of these speakers is characterised by many SOV patterns.

These differences between different L1 speaking populations would seem to indicate very strongly that L2 learners transfer the head ordering parameter of their native language into their early L2 grammars.

Transfer, Parametric Variation and Differences Between Second and First Language Learners

The assumption that it is the norm for L2 learners to transfer parameter values already fixed in their first languages into their initial L2 grammars is a key factor in explaining differences between L1 and L2 learners.

L1 learners, by hypothesis, come to the task of acquisition with 'open' parameter values, which are then set on the basis of evidence from primary linguistic data (the language they are exposed to). If L2 learners come to the task of acquisition with already fixed parameter values, then they will differ from L1 learners in two ways. If the parameter setting of the L1 is the same as in the L2 then its appropriateness for the target language simply needs to be confirmed by compatible data from the L2; if it differs from the parameter setting of the L2 it will have to be reset, and from what we know this seems to be a more difficult task than the fixing of open parameter values for L1 learners.[2]

We should therefore expect to find observable differences in development between L1 and L2 learners which can be directly attributed to the influence of L1 parameter settings in the case of the latter. At the same time it is perfectly logical to maintain that both groups of learners, L1 and L2, are constrained in their task of grammar construction by Universal Grammar.

Consider again the acquisition of word order properties in German that we considered in the last section. As part of their study Clahsen & Muysken (1986) compared the early word order patterns produced by child L1 learners of German and those produced by L1 Romance-language-speaking L2 learners of German. They cite three main differences between the two groups:

(a) L1 learners assume verb separation in root clauses as soon as they are able to produce compound verbs, whereas L2 learners initially assume non-separation of compound verbs in root clauses. For example, as soon as L1 learners have acquired compound verbs such as *bin gegangen*, they place the second element at the end of the clause: *ich bin ins Kino gegangen*, 'I went to the cinema', whereas L2 learners start out with sentences like *ich bin gegangen ins Kino*.

(b) L1 learners assume verb-second in root clauses as soon as they are able to front non-subjects. For example, as soon as L1 learners are able to place an adverb like *gestern*, 'yesterday', at the front of the clause, they put the tense-marked verb in second position: *Gestern bin ich ins Kino gegangen*, 'Yesterday I went to the cinema'. L2 learners, however, allow fronting of adverbs without verb second: *Gestern ich bin ins Kino gegangen*.

(c) L1 learners assume verb-final position for tensed verbs in embedded clauses as soon as they are able to produce embedded clauses: *Er glaubt, dass ich ins Kino gegangen bin*, 'He believes that I went to the cinema'. L2 learners, by contrast, initially assume SVO ordering in embedded clauses: *Er glaubt, dass ich bin ins Kino gegangen.*

Clahsen & Muysken interpret the findings of this comparison to signify a fundamental difference in the constraints under which L1 and L2 acquisition takes place. They argue that while UG constrains grammar construction in L1 acquisition, L2 acquisition takes place as the result of the general problem-solving abilities of human beings, rather than as the result of the involvement of the language faculty. However, it should be clear that given the line of argument we have been developing, this is not a necessary conclusion. L1 and L2 learners can certainly differ initially because L2 learners start out with certain already fixed parameter settings, which L1 learners do not. This is bound to lead to developmental differences. However, the general constraints which subsequently guide the construction of a grammar — Universal Grammar — can, at the same time, still be operative. Indeed it is significant to note that the order of the stages that both L1 and L2 learners go through in this case are the same: the first property acquired is verb separation, followed by verb second, and the last property acquired is verb final in embedded clauses.

A similar L2/L1 difference is found going in the other direction. Hulk's (1991) L1 Dutch-speaking learners of L2 French begin by assuming that French allows verb separation (of finite and non-finite verbal elements in root clauses), that French allows V2 in root clauses, and that French allows verb final in embedded clauses. Children acquiring French as an L1 make none of these assumptions. Although early child L1 grammars of French appear to allow variable root clause word order, that variability is predominantly between SV(O) and V(O)S, and not SOV (Clark, 1985: 709–13). There is also no evidence of French children producing verb-second in root clauses or verb final in embedded clauses. Again this early developmental L2/L1 difference follows from the assumption that where L1 learners approach the learning task with open parameter values which require setting, L2 learners approach the task with already-set parameter values which require resetting. And again it is not necessary to conclude that L2 learners are not guided by UG.

In both of the examples just cited L2 learners come to the task of L2 learning with parameter settings transferred from the L1 which are in conflict with the parameter settings of the L2, and this leads to observable early L2/L1 developmental differences, even though ultimately it seems that the L2 learners arrive at a final-state grammar which is equivalent to the final-state grammar of the L1 learners (on these particular parameters); i.e. given sufficient exposure, the Romance-language speakers appear to reset the parameters so that they get the word order properties of German invariably right, and the Dutch speakers appear to reset the parameters so that they too get the word order properties of French invariably right. (For a critical consideration of the nature of ultimate success in SLA see Chapter 7.)

But what happens in the case where an L1-set parameter value is the same in both L1 and L2? It seems that this can lead to two kinds of situation. The first is where early L2/L1 grammars appear to be identical, even though child L1 learners start from open parameter values. If child L1 learners are able to fix the appropriate setting rapidly, then from very early on L2/L1 learners will behave identically on the properties determined by the parameter.

A case in point is head–complement ordering. Recall that although initially L1 learners can show some variability on head–complement ordering (see Chapter 5), it seems that they fix appropriate ordering quite rapidly. Child L1 learners of English and French recognise early on the VO ordering of English and French, child L1 learners of German recognise early on the OV ordering with non-finite verbal elements of German. L1 speakers of VO languages learning English and French almost never have problems with VO word order. For example, in the study by Selinker, Swain & Dumas (1975) referred to in Chapter 1, of L1 English-speaking children learning L2 French in a Canadian immersion programme, although the learners made many errors, and typical errors are illustrated in (6.20), none of these affected VO order.

6.20a *Il est trois ans*
   He is three years
   (Target: *Il a trois ans*)
   b *Il veut moi de dire français à il*
   He wants me to speak French to him
   (Target: *Il veut que je lui parle français*)
   c *La fille mettre du confiture sur le pain*
   The girl put jam on the bread
   (Target: *La fille met de la confiture sur le pain*)

Thus where L2 learners transfer a parameter setting appropriate to the L2, and L1 learners rapidly fix a parameter setting in the L1, L1 and L2 grammars can be identical from very early on in the developmental process.

A second kind of situation that the transfer of an L1-set parameter value appropriate to the L2 can lead to is that L2 learners may appear to acquire a grammatical property more easily than L1 learners, because the task of fixing open parameter values for the L1 learner requires time, while the effect of the transfer of an L1-set parameter value is immediate.

For example, there is a major difference in the world's languages between those which require obligatorily specified subjects, such as English, French, German and Dutch, and those which do not, such as Italian, Spanish and Greek, as illustrated in (6.21) and (6.22) through a comparison between Italian and English.

6.21a *Gianni ha telefonato.*
   b Gianni has telephoned.

6.22a *Ha telefonato.*
   b *Has telephoned.
   c He has telephoned.

English requires a phonetically specified referential pronoun 'he' (or 'she', 'I', 'you', 'we', etc.) in subject position in the absence of a lexical noun phrase, Italian does not.

An interesting observation that has been made about L1 child learners of English is that although English is an obligatory subject language, there appears to be a phase of early development during which child grammars allow null subjects. For example, children will produce utterances which allow both lexical noun phrase subjects and null subjects, like Italian — see (6.23).

6.23 Mummy throw it away. (Kathryn 21 months)
     Throw it away.
     Gia ride truck.   (Gia 22 months)
     Ride truck.
     Man sit down.   (Kathryn 22 months)
     Sit on piano.

(Examples from Bloom, 1970, cited in Radford, 1990: 206). Some studies have suggested that this occurs because children assume initially that all languages allow null subjects, and require time and exposure to encounter the triggering evidence that would allow them to determine English as an obligatory subject language (see, for example, Hyams, 1986;

although for a different interpretation of this early null subject phase see Radford, 1990).

There have been a number of studies of the second language acquisition of null and obligatory subject languages by L1 speakers of null or obligatory subject languages. While studies of L1 speakers of null subject languages (such as Italian, Spanish and Greek) learning an obligatory subject language as an L2 typically find a longish phase of development during which learners use null subjects, studies of L1 speakers of obligatory subject languages (such as English French, German and Dutch) learning an obligatory subject language find little evidence of null subjects, even in the earliest stages of L2 learning. In this case L2 learners develop more rapidly than L1 learners in an area of the grammar where a parameter setting is identical between the L1 and the L2.

So, if it is the norm for L2 learners' initial L2 grammars to be characterised by parameter settings transferred from the L1 which they speak, and for L1 learners initial L1 grammars to be characterised by open parameter values, then L2/L1 differences will follow on two levels: where the L1 parameter setting conflicts with the setting appropriate for the L2, L2 learners may appear to have more difficulty than L1 learners. Where the L2 and L1 parameter settings are congruent, L2 learners' early grammars may develop identically with L1 learners' early grammars, or L1 learners may appear to have more difficulty than L2 learners.

We have, then, the beginnings of a characterisation of the developmental differences that can be found between L2 and L1 learners as the direct result of the assumption that L1 parameter settings are transferred into the L2, while at the same time being able to maintain that grammar construction in both cases is constrained by UG. It turns out, however, that further refinement must be introduced into this tale of L2 development, because there are two types of parameter associated with UG, and distinguishing between them will enable us to account for some important developmental differences within the L2 population of learners itself: between learners from different L1-speaking backgrounds.

Two Kinds of Parameter and Differences Between Second Language Learners Speaking Different First Languages

Up to this point we have considered the following proposed parameters of variation allowed by UG:

- Head position in relation to its specifier and complement (i.e. whether the head is to the left or to the right).
- The status of C°: whether it attracts or does not attract the agreement-inflected and tense-inflected verb in root clauses.

Both are examples of what might be called parameters with exclusive values: a language selects one or the other option allowed by the parameter, but not both. It appears that, in addition to parameters with exclusive values, there are also parameters with inclusive values allowed by UG. In this case a language may select one value, or more than one value (both values, all three values, and so on, depending on how many values a parameter makes available); for example, standard accounts of questions such as that in (6.24) in English and French (which are direct translations of each other):

6.24a Who does he love?
   b *Qui aime-t-il?*

assume that they are derived by moving an inflected verb ('does' in the case of English, *aime*, 'loves', in the case of French) from the IP to the

6.25a

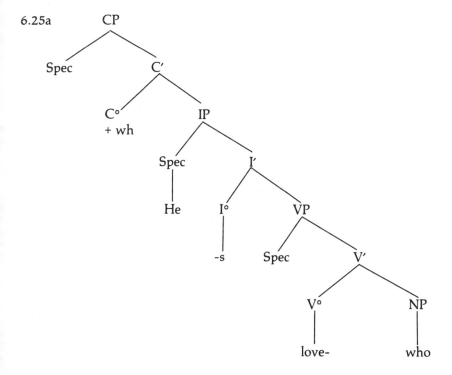

6.25b

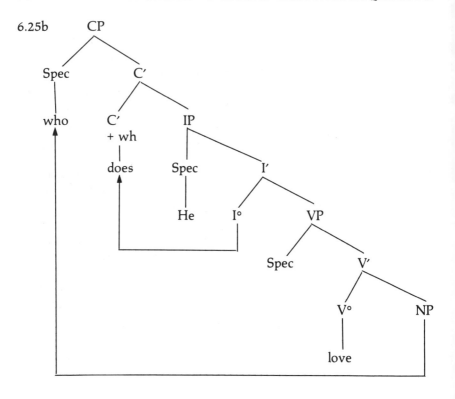

position under C°, and by moving a wh- phrase ('who' and *qui*) which has replaced a direct object NP in the VP, into the specifier position of CP. This is illustrated in (6.25), where (6.25a) and (6.25c) are the D-structure representations, and (6.25b) and (6.25d) are the S-structure representations after the items in question have moved.

Although the movement operations illustrated in (6.25) are basically the same in English and French, you will notice that there is an important distinction between them. Whereas in French the lexical verb *aime*, 'loves', ends up in the position under C°, in English the auxiliary verb 'does' ends up there. It is in fact impossible for the lexical verb 'loves' to move into this position in Modern English: *'Who loves he?' Notice also that in getting to C° the French verb undergoes two movements: first from V° to I°, and then from I° to C°. In Chapter 7 we shall discuss this difference between English and French, which, it has been proposed (Pollock, 1989), results from a parametric difference between the two languages. It is not relevant to the discussion here.

Making the assumption that wh- question formation applies in the

6.25c

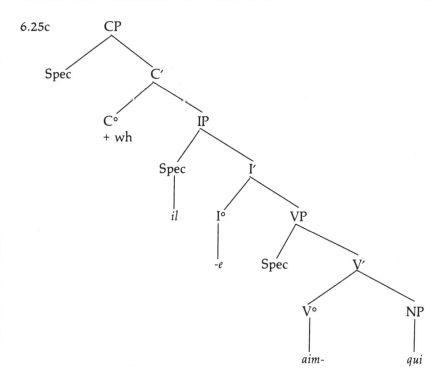

way just illustrated, consider the contrast between English and standard European French in (6.26) and (6.27).

6.26a To whom does he write?
   b A qui écrit-il?

6.27a Who does he write to?
   b *Qui écrit-il à?

Both (6.26) and (6.27) involve the movement of a wh- phrase from a prepositional phrase (PP) position in the complement of the verb 'write'/*écrire* to the specifier position of CP. In (6.26) the whole PP has been moved; in (6.27) a wh- NP from within the PP has been moved. These movements have been given the colourful names of 'pied-piping' (movement of the whole PP) and 'preposition stranding' (movement of the wh- NP from within the PP) (Ross, 1967). Why, though, is preposition stranding ungrammatical in French (6.27b), while it is grammatical in English (6.27a), when in both cases there is an appropriate movement of an inflected verb to C° and of a wh- phrase to the specifier of CP? It seems that the difference is that English allows both extraction

6.25d

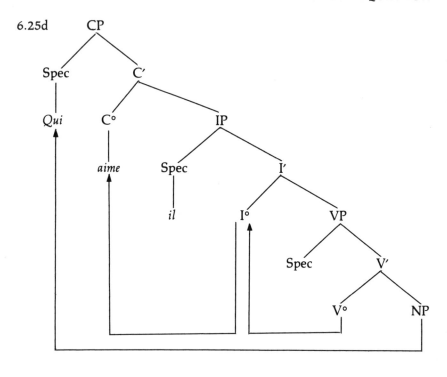

of a prepositional wh- phrase, and extraction of a wh- phrase from within a prepositional phrase, whereas French allows only extraction of the whole PP; it does not allow extraction from within a PP.[3]

    This syntactic difference between the two languages can be captured by assuming a parametric difference allowed by UG relating to the licensing of the positions from which items have been moved: the empty categories they leave behind. UG allows empty categories to exist (i.e. 'licenses' them) only under certain well-defined conditions. One of those conditions is that an empty category which results from the movement of some item, as in the cases under discussion, must be properly governed by another category. (The technical details of 'proper government' are beyond the scope of this discussion, but in essence proper government requires that an empty category which results from movement must be the complement to an immediately preceding head of a specific type.) It seems that languages vary parametrically as to what counts as a proper governor. In the case of (6.26) and (6.27) it can be suggested that in English both categories V° and P° count as proper governors, and therefore license empty categories which result from wh- movement, whereas in French only V° counts as a proper governor, and not P°. (6.26) is therefore ungrammatical because the empty category left behind by the movement of *qui* is not licensed in that language and violates an invariant principle of UG known as the Empty Category Principle (Chomsky, 1981), which states that empty categories resulting from movement must be properly governed. For case of reference we shall call this parameter the 'licensing parameter'.[4]

Now consider what this parametric difference consists of. French allows only pied-piping: that is, only V° licenses an empty category resulting from movement in French. English allows both pied-piping and preposition stranding: both V° and P° license empty categories resulting from movement in English. The English setting of the 'licensing' parameter includes the French setting within it. This kind of parameter is different from the parameters with exclusive values discussed above. Parameters with inclusive values do not impose an 'either one or the other but not both' choice on a language. Where values are inclusive, a language may choose one or both values (or more if the parameter has more than two values).

Inclusive Parameter Values and the Problem they Pose for Learnability in First Language Acquisition

Imagine an infant born with an innate knowledge of UG, including a 'licensing' parameter with open values for heads like V° and P°; i.e. the values have not yet been fixed for whether V° , P° license empty categories resulting from movement or not. The child does not know in advance of exposure to a particular language whether both V° and P° or only one of them (or indeed neither of them) will or will not be proper governors in that language. The child exposed to English will get positive evidence from the language heard around him or her in the form of examples like those of (6.26a) and (6.27a) that V° and P° are both licensers of empty categories, and hence proper governors in English. The child exposed to French, by contrast, will hear only examples such as (6.26b), but not examples like (6.27b): native speakers do not normally go around uttering ungrammatical sentences, and even if they did it is not clear that the child can make use of any such negative evidence (see discussion in Chapter 5).

What prevents the child exposed to French from overgeneralising the licensing parameter to P°? After all, the possibility that P° is a proper governor is given in principle by UG; perhaps the child has been unlucky in not hearing examples that would confirm that P° is a proper governor. Yet clearly children exposed to French as their first language uniformly grow into mature adults with grammars for French which do not allow preposition stranding, so that they must be able to determine that it is not accidental that they have not come across examples of preposition stranding. This is an example of what is known as the logical problem of language acquisition: how can a child arrive at the right grammar on the basis of: (a) the range of possibilities allowed by innate UG, and (b) exposure to samples of the language being learned?

Various answers to this learnability problem have been proposed in the acquisition literature, only two of which will be retained for consideration here, because they have both been explored in SLA. One of them, *markedness*, which received a great deal of attention from SLA researchers in the late 1970s and early 1980s (for representative accounts see, for example, Eckman, 1977; Mazurkewich, 1984b; White, 1986b, 1989b) will be rejected almost immediately, in order to consider in some detail the other one, the *subset principle*, which has been the subject of more recent attention in SLA.

Markedness

One answer that has been offered for why, given a parameter with two or more inclusive values, children learning an L1 are able correctly to set those values, even if the language in question has set only one of them (as in the case of V°, but not P°, as a proper governor in French), is that one of the values of parameters with inclusive values is always more natural than the others. It is said that this value is unmarked, whereas the other value or values are more marked. Marked values of parameters are less frequent in the world's languages than unmarked values, and actual examples indicating that a language has set a marked value will need to be encountered by the child first language learner before he or she will set the marked parameter value. Thus, assuming that it is more marked for P° to be a proper governor in languages than V°, one could say that children learning French as an L1 do not set the 'licensing parameter' to allow P° to be a proper governor because they do not come across examples of preposition stranding, and the presence of positive evidence is necessary to set marked values for parameters.

This is an appealing notion. It suggests that where a parameter has inclusive values one of them, universally, will be the most natural, the unmarked case, and this will always be the child's first assumption. It also has the very strong implication that unmarked parameter values will be easier to acquire than marked ones, because if a language sets a parameter at all it will always minimally set the unmarked value, and the child will expect this, so that little learning will be involved. The marked values, however, will require special evidence which the child will need to notice specifically.

This strong implication that unmarked parameter values will be easier to set than marked ones has been found to raise a problem, however. Studies of children learning first languages which have set both unmarked and marked parameter values have found that they do not necessarily develop the unmarked value first. For example, a study by French (1985: 137) of the acquisition of pied-piping and preposition stranding in English by 3–5 year olds found 'no significant difference in the comprehension of stranding across the three age groups, suggesting that stranding is not late to emerge'.

Now, one interpretation that can be given to this finding in order to rescue the notion of markedness is that 'acquisition' of an L1 (in the sense of 'ultimate competence' in the language) is not the same thing as 'development' in an L1 (the stages learners go through to get to 'ultimate competence'). Markedness may be relevant to acquisition, but not necessarily to development, which is perhaps directly influenced by input, so that if input appropriate to the setting of a marked parameter value is encountered first, learners may set the marked value before the unmarked. (For discussion of this point see Cook, 1985.) While this position is perfectly defensible, it is not clear what explanatory interest remains for the notion of markedness. If child language learners are invariably able to set parameter values on the basis of positive evidence for those values, then all that is necessary is the idea that a parameter value will not be set by the child in the absence of positive evidence. The fact that some parameter values are less widely chosen by the world's languages than others is neither here nor there. If it were the case that the notion of markedness made correct predictions about what language learners learn first, then it would be an extremely interesting concept. But given that this kind of prediction is not made, to say that certain parameter settings are more natural than others becomes nothing more than stipulation: a particular parameter value is unmarked because language learners do not generalise beyond it if there is no evidence for doing so.

Moreover, Wexler & Manzini (1987) have demonstrated that, paradoxically, some parameter settings in particular languages have to be both marked and unmarked to make the right predictions. The example they give relates to the reference of pronouns — he, him, she, her, I, me, and so on — and anaphors — himself, herself, myself, and so on. Simplifying the issues considerably, in English, pronouns cannot refer to another noun phrase within the same clause, but may refer to a noun phrase either in another clause in the same sentence, or outside the sentence. Thus, in (6.28a), 'her' cannot refer to 'Mary', but it can refer to 'Kim', or to some other noun phrase outside the sentence and mentioned elsewhere in the discourse.

6.28a Kim thinks [that Mary likes her].

By contrast, anaphors in English must refer to a noun phrase within the same clause, so that in (6.28b) 'herself' must refer to 'Mary':

6.28b Kim thinks [that Mary likes herself].

The domain of reference in these cases — i.e. the clause, which determines the area within which pronouns cannot refer to noun phrases, and anaphors must refer to noun phrases — is known as the governing category for reference. Wexler & Manzini demonstrate that in different languages the governing category can vary. For example, in Japanese, the equivalent of 'herself', *zibun*, can refer either to 'Mary' or to 'Kim'. In other languages the equivalent of 'her' can refer neither to 'Kim' nor to 'Mary'. It appears, therefore, that the governing category for reference varies parametrically between languages.

Wexler & Manzini then go on to suggest that the unmarked value of the governing category parameter for anaphors is the clause, as it is in English. The marked value is a domain larger than the clause, like the sentence, as in Japanese. But the unmarked value of the governing category parameter for pronouns is the sentence; that is, pronouns should not be able to refer to noun phrases which appear within the same sentence, only to noun phrases mentioned elsewhere in the discourse, in the unmarked case. Languages which allow pronouns to refer to noun phrases within the sentence have selected a marked option of the parameter. English has selected such an option. Therefore, the value of the governing category parameter that English has chosen — the clause — is unmarked for anaphors, and marked for pronouns — a paradoxical result.

A second answer to the problem of accounting for how L1 learners fix the right parameter settings, without recourse to an assumption of the 'naturalness' of particular settings, has become known as the subset principle (Berwick, 1985; Wexler & Manzini, 1987).

The subset principle

The subset principle suggests that where a parameter has inclusive values the L1 learner will be conservative and will assume the least inclusive setting of the parameter compatible with the input data. For example, in the case where a learner encounters a language with wh-movement, but only encounters wh- movement which extracts phrases from the complement of $V°$, the learner will assume that only $V°$ can be a proper governor of the empty category left behind by the movement of the wh- phrase, even though in principle UG allows other heads to be proper governors. That is, the subset principle excludes the generalisation of proper government to other heads if only $V°$ has been encountered as a proper governor.

It seems that the subset principle, unlike markedness, is not a principle of UG but rather a learning principle associated with UG which restricts even further the child's initial choice from within the already restricted options offered by the parameters of UG. It tells the learner only to set parameter values on the basis of evidence directly available in the input. Thus the child learning French will set the value of the licensing parameter only to $V°$, because only evidence compatible with this assumption is ever encountered; the child learning English will set the value to $V°$ and $P°$ because there is evidence compatible with this assumption from English; and the child learning a language such as Korean, where there is no wh- movement at all (Schachter, 1990) will presumably not set the licensing parameter at all for the syntax of Korean, in the absence of any positive evidence for movement.

At this point we should recall the cognitive learning strategies explored in Pienemann (1989) and Wolfe Quintero (1992), among others, which were described in Chapter 4, and which were criticised at some length. One of the main problems with approaches which take cognitive learning strategies as the central source of explanation for phenomena in SLA is their ambivalence about the role that learners' knowledge of grammatical structure plays. Proponents of cognitive approaches generally exclude grammatical structure from consideration, preferring instead the idea that general perceptual dispositions like conservatism, continuity, saliency, and so on, can account entirely for the behaviour of L2 learners.

As we demonstrated in Chapter 4, however, the exclusion of a theory of grammatical structure within such accounts leads either to the wrong predictions being made (as in the case of Wolfe Quintero's account of wh- extraction) or to the surreptitious use of grammatical constructs in cases where the perceptual strategies are in danger of making the wrong predictions (as in the case of Pienemann's account of why verb-final structures in embedded clauses in German are acquired last by L2 learners).

The subset principle, although a proposed learning principle external to UG, is, it would seem, of a different order to the cognitive learning strategies. While it is outside UG, it is not necessarily outside the language faculty. In other words, there is no suggestion that it has to have wider perceptual application, in the sense that 'conservatism' would seem to require. It is a language-faculty-based learning principle which is associated directly with principles of grammatical structure in order to ensure that only those parameter values for which there is evidence in the input are set.

It should be stressed that most proponents of UG-based approaches to language acquisition would not suggest that everything in language acquisition can be explained by UG alone. Other constructs, such as associated learning principles, may well be required. We shall develop this idea in connection with SLA more fully in later chapters. As it turns out, recent developments in linguistic theory have raised the possibility that the subset principle may be eliminable. We shall briefly consider this trend and its implications for SLA in Chapter 7.

The subset principle is superior to the notion of markedness because it does not require appeal to an undefined concept of 'natural' parameter settings. As a result there is no implication that some parameter values are easier to learn than others, and there is no prediction that some settings will be learned before others. Learners will freely set parameter values as soon as they become aware of triggering evidence in the input. This seems to match much better what actually happens in development, where children like those in the study by French (1985) can be seen to develop constructions compatible with the superset setting simultaneously with or even before they develop constructions compatible with the subset setting, and it is unnecessary to stipulate that the subset principle is a constraint on 'ultimate competence' rather than development. It is a constraint on both.

Transfer, Inclusive Parameter Values, and the Resetting of Parameters in Second Language Acquisition

Earlier in this chapter we outlined studies of the acquisition of word order in L2 French by L1 Dutch speakers (Hulk, 1991), and in L2 German by L1 Italian, Spanish and Portuguese speakers (Clahsen & Muysken, 1986; duPlessis *et al.*, 1987; Schwartz & Tomaselli, 1988; Pienemann, 1989) and by L1 English speakers (Ellis, 1989). Those studies suggested that although L2 learners initially transfer the parameter settings of their L1s into their L2 grammars, with exposure to positive evidence from the L2 they rapidly move away from those settings and, it was assumed, reset the parameters to values appropriate to the L2.

In both of those cases, however, we were dealing with exclusive parameter values: one choice of parameter setting excludes the other. But what happens in SLA where parameter values are not exclusive but inclusive? If we continue to assume that L2 learners initially transfer the parameter values of their L1 into their L2 grammars, where the L1 parameter setting is the superset case and the L2 the subset case, learners will get no positive evidence that the parameter setting in the L2 is the subset. For example, take the case of pied-piping and preposition stranding, and L1 English speakers learning L2 French; these learners will encounter only cases of pied-piped wh- movement. But this is compatible both with the setting of the licensing parameter for empty categories to $V°$ or to both $V°$ and $P°$. If English speakers transfer their inclusive L1 parameter setting into their L2 grammars for French they will never encounter any positive evidence that French does not allow preposition stranding.

By contrast, L1 French speakers learning L2 English, and initially transferring the parameter setting from French (i.e. that only $V°$ is a licenser) into their grammars for English, will get positive evidence from preposition stranding that English has the more inclusive setting. French speakers will be moving from the subset case to the superset case and will get positive evidence to help them to reset the parameter.

This account makes the general prediction for SLA that, assuming initial transfer of L1 parameter settings, learners should be more successful in resetting exclusive parameter values and resetting the subset value of inclusive parameter values to the superset setting than they are at resetting the superset value of inclusive parameters to the subset value, because they will encounter positive evidence for the first two, but no positive evidence for the last case. Rather, in order to reset in the second case they will have 'to notice the *absence* of some construction in L2' (White, 1986: 314) before resetting can take place.

There have been a number of studies of parameters with inclusive values in the SLA literature whose findings conform broadly to these predictions. We shall consider only one representative example: the acquisition of adverb placement in L2 English and L2 French.

Adverb Placement in English and French

White (1989a) has observed a difference between L1 English speakers acquiring L2 French, and L1 French speakers acquiring L2 English in their ability to acquire certain placements of manner and frequency adverbs. In French, manner and frequency adverbs may appear both between a main verb and its complement, and at the end of a VP (as illustrated in (6.29a–b)), whereas in English, manner and frequency adverbs cannot normally appear between a main verb and its complement (illustrated in (6.30a–b), which are the translation equivalents of (6.29a–b)).[5]

6.29a *Jean boit rapidement son café.*
   b *Jean boit son café rapidement.*

6.30a *John drinks quickly his coffee.
   b John drinks his coffee quickly.

It seems that L1 French learners of L2 English continue to assume that English allows constructions such as (6.29a) into quite advanced stages of acquisition (White 1989a, 1991a, c, 1992), whereas L1 English learners of L2 French are more successful in acquiring the fact that sentences such as (6.29a) are possible in French, becoming 'aware of quite subtle restrictions on the kind of material permitted' to appear between a main verb and its complement (White, 1989a: 154).

White attributes this effect directly to the subset principle, and the fact that L1 English learners of L2 French are going from the subset setting to the superset setting, whereas the French learners of L2 English are going from the superset to the subset. She suggests that the parameter involved is a parameter of 'adjacency of case assignment' (Stowell, 1981), which determines the relative positions of case assigners and the phrases to which they assign case. In UG all NPs must receive an appropriate 'case': subjects require nominative case (assigned by Infl to its specifier position), direct objects receive objective (or accusative) case (assigned by $V°$ to its complement), and prepositional objects are assigned oblique case (in English and French) (assigned by $P°$ to its complement). In English and French, case-marking of NPs by case-assigners typically has no overt morphological realisation (although nominative and accusative case are marked on pronouns: I/me, he/him, she/her, je/moi, il/le, elle/la, and so on). Languages seem to vary in whether they require case assigners to be strictly adjacent to (i.e. right next to) the phrase to which they assign case (as English does and hence disallows an adverb to separate a verb from its direct object, as in (6.30a)), or whether they allow case assigners to be separated from the phrases to which they assign case (as French does, allowing an adverb to separate a verb from its direct object, as in (6.29a)). The 'adjacency of case assignment' parameter is held to be a parameter with two values: [+ strict adjacency] and [- strict adjacency], and these values are inclusive, because a language which has the [- strict adjacency] setting will allow constructions where case assigners can be both adjacent or non-adjacent to their case-assignees, whereas a language which has the [+ strict adjacency] setting will require case assigners and case assignees to be adjacent.

This being so, English represents the subset case because it observes strict adjacency, whereas French represents the superset case because it allows both adjacency and non-adjacency for case assignment. White's account of the different developmental behaviour between the two groups of learners is that although both groups initially transfer the parameter setting of their L1, only the L1 English learners of L2 French will encounter positive evidence that they should reset the parameter to [- strict adjacency]. The L1 French learners of L2 English will not encounter cases like (6.30a), but the fact that they will encounter only cases like (6.30b) does not provide them with any direct evidence that their L1 parameter setting is inappropriate for English, since such examples are compatible with the [- strict adjacency] setting. This accounts for the fact that they continue to allow examples like (6.30a) into advanced stages of acquisition.

(The issue of adverb placement and the observed differences between English and French L2 learners will be reconsidered from a different theoretical perspective in Chapter 7.)

Parameter Resetting Versus Parameter 'Activation' in Second Language Acquisition

We have suggested that while L1 learners approach the task of language acquisition with 'open' parameter values given by UG which will become fixed on the basis of evidence from the language encountered, L2 learners approach the task with parameter values already set by their L1. The L1 settings may either be appropriate or inappropriate to the L2, but in either case the fact of prior resetting leads to a qualitatively different learning task for L2 learners from L1 learners: maintaining or resetting values in the case of L2 learners, fixing for the first time in the case of L1 learners.

There is a third possibility, however, and that is that an L1 has not activated a particular parameter at all, so that when a speaker of an L1 where such a parameter is not activated encounters an L2 where it is activated, it might be predicted that the learning task is again different for the L2 learner, perhaps resembling more closely the task of 'fixing' parameter settings that faces the L1 learner (that is, assuming that a parameter not activated at the time of L1 acquisition can be activated in later L2 learning — for some discussion of this issue see Chapter 7).

Although there are, to our knowledge, few studies bearing on this question, there are some, and their results are suggestive. A study by Zobl (1990) adopts precisely this perspective with respect to an interesting observation concerning a developmental difference between L1 speakers of Japanese (a null subject pronoun language) and L1 speakers of Spanish (also a null subject pronoun language) learning an obligatory subject language such as English as an L2. Zobl found that Japanese speakers appear to be able to recognise the obligatory status of phonetically specified subjects in English much more rapidly than Spanish speakers. In his analysis of this observation Zobl suggests that the underlying cause of phonetically null pronouns in the two languages is different. Whereas in Spanish a subject *pro* is licensed by an Infl with a rich inflectional paradigm from which the reference of a null subject can be identified, in Japanese inflection of this sort is completely absent. This leads Zobl to suggest that the notion of 'subject' itself is not operative in Japanese. Rather, noun phrases which are the 'topic' of discourse are given the same kind of prominence in Japanese that subjects are in Spanish, English or French. This being the case, Japanese actually allows 'null topics' rather than 'null subjects', 'subject' not having been activated as a syntactic category in Japanese. Thus, when L1 Japanese speakers acquire an obligatory subject language such as English as an L2, they have to 'activate' the parameter involved, rather than reset it, as the Spanish speakers do. They will receive positive evidence from English for obligatory subject pronouns, and so acquire these from early stages of acquisition, unlike the L1 Spanish speakers.

Summary

Throughout Chapter 6 we have argued that the assumption that L1 parameter settings are initially transferred into L2 grammars is an important factor in explaining the learnability problem in SLA: that is, how L2 learners arrive at grammars for particular L2s on the basis of the interaction between what they know internally, and the samples of the L2 that they are exposed to. From this perspective the essential problem for L2 learners has three possible strands: (a) to confirm parameter settings already set in the L1 which are appropriate to the L2; (b) to reset parameter settings already set in the L1 which are inappropriate to the L2; and (c) to activate parameters necessary for the L2 which have not been activated in the L1.

This task is complicated, however, by the fact that not all parameters have mutually exclusive settings (i.e. where there is a choice between either one setting of the parameter or the other, but not both). Some parameters have one setting which includes the other setting(s), in the sense that it generates a language which is a superset to the subset language generated by the included setting(s).

The general effect of the interaction of these factors can be represented informally in tabular form, as in Table 6.4. As can be seen from the table, the prediction made is that the most difficult case for an L2 learner is (d), where lack of positive evidence will lead to ongoing problems for resetting. Cases (b), (e) and (f) should be the easiest, because they simply require the learner to confirm the appropriateness for the L2 of an already-set L1 parameter value from positive evidence. Cases (a), (c) and (g) involve (re)setting a parameter on the basis of positive evidence, and will constitute an easier task for the L2 learner than case (d); they may, however, take longer to establish than cases (b), (e) and (f) if confirmation of appropriateness of an already set parameter is an easier task than (re)setting. Some evidence was also cited in the last section to suggest that activation of a parameter which has not been set in the L1 takes place more rapidly than resetting of an already established parameter. A representative sample of studies were considered which seem to offer broad support for the predictions of this account: the L2 acquisition of German word order, French word order, and adverb placement in English and French.

Table 6.4 Effects in SLA of the interaction of L1 parameter settings, L2 parameter settings and the availability of positive evidence from the target language

	L1 parameter setting	L2 parameter setting	Positive evidence	Resetting
(a)	exclusive	different	yes	easy
(b)	exclusive	same	yes	not necessary
(c)	subset	superset	yes	easy
(d)	superset	subset	no	difficult
(e)	superset	superset	yes	not necessary
(f)	subset	subset	yes	not necessary
(g)	not activated	exclusive/ subset/superset	yes	easy

Some recent work in SLA has begun to look more closely at scenarios (a) and (c), where the prediction is that resetting of parameter values will proceed straightforwardly, given positive evidence. It turns out that in such cases L2 learners do not always find it easy to reset parameter settings which have been set in the L1s, even if there is positive evidence. We consider this development in the next chapter, in conjunction with discussion of another of the observations about SLA which is in need of explanation: incompleteness.

Notes

1. This is not, in fact, the position taken by Clahsen & Muysken, who propose that adult L2 learners of German adopt a perceptually based Canonical Order Strategy which determines SVO order in early stages of acquisition (see Chapter 4 for discussion). They adopt this proposal because among the L2 population that they studied were a group of L1 Turkish speakers. Although Turkish is an SOV language like German, the Turkish speakers also initially appear to adopt SVO word order in L2 German. This suggested to Clahsen & Muysken that L2 learners were initially adopting a language-independent strategy. However, we have seen that an alternative explanation for this behaviour involving transfer can be offered (White, 1991b; see Chapter 5 for discussion), and anyway the behaviour of the L1 Dutch learners of L2 French in early stages would be inexplicable if they were adopting a Canonical Order

Strategy. Furthermore, transfer of parameter settings seems to be clearly operative in the examples cited from Odlin (1989) subsequently in the text.

2. A third possibility is that a parameter relevant to the L2 is not activated in the L1. In this case it might be predicted that the learning process is the same for L2 learners as it is for L1 learners: 'open' values are set on the basis of evidence from the primary data. We consider this possibility later in Chapter 6.

3. Preposition stranding which results from extraction of a following wh-phrase must be distinguished from what might be called preposition 'dangling', which is possible in standard European French in expressions such as *Tu viens avec?*, (literally 'Are you coming with?'), 'Are you coming with us?' Such a possibility would seem to follow from the fact that French allows phonetically unspecified (null) pronouns under some conditions. Thus it is possible in French to say both *Tu viens avec nous?* and *Tu viens avec?*.

One also needs to distinguish between standard European French, which is at issue here, and other varieties of French which may allow preposition stranding.

4. There have been a number of different proposals to account for the fact that only some languages allow both pied-piping and preposition stranding, while others allow only pied-piping. For technical details, see, for example, van Riemsdijk (1978), Hornstein & Weinberg (1981), Chomsky (1981).

5. There are cases known as 'heavy NP shift' where particularly long direct object NPs are moved to the end of the sentence for stylistic balance, placing a VP-final adverb in between the main verb and its complement, as in:

John drank quickly the tea which had been sitting on the table for the last ten minutes.

These cases are the exception rather than the norm in English, whereas placement of manner/frequency adverbs between the main verb and its complement is the norm in French.

7 Parametric Variation and Incompleteness in Second Language Acquisition

'Incompleteness' (in the sense that L2 learners do not arrive at the same intuitions of grammaticality as native speakers) has long been recognised as an important feature of SLA, often going under the name of fossilisation (Selinker, 1972). Up to this point it has been implied that where SLA fails to be fully 'complete' this is the result of learners transferring a superset parameter setting from their L1 into their L2 grammars, from which they are unable to retreat. In such cases no direct positive evidence will be encountered in the L2 to enable learners to determine that the superset setting is inappropriate to the L2. It has similarly been implied that where learners encounter direct positive evidence for a difference in parameter setting between the L1 and the L2 (either in the case of exclusive parameter values, or in the case where the L1 has a subset setting of a parameter with inclusive values and the L2 has a superset setting) then parameter resetting will proceed straight-forwardly, and learning will be fully successful. This has been the general assumption of much work in SLA over the past ten years.

Recently, however, this view has been changing. Some researchers are now exploring the idea that while in the general case UG constrains the construction of L2 grammars, certain subcomponents of it, which are fully available to child L1 learners, become difficult to access for adolescent and adult L2 learners. If this approach is correct, then incompleteness will occur in SLA not only where an L1 superset parameter setting is transferred in the acquisition of a language which has the subset setting, but also even where positive evidence is available to tell the learner that the L2 grammar which has been constructed is inappropriate for the L2.

There are two reasons for thinking that this recent approach might be worth exploring. The first is that studies of the effect of 'age of first exposure' to an L2, or 'age of arrival' in a community where the L2 is spoken, as in the study by Johnson & Newport (1989) described in Chapter 1 (and below) find that incompleteness grows progressively with age, i.e. the older you are at first exposure to an L2, the more incomplete your grammar will be for that L2. If incompleteness resulted entirely from the lack of availability of positive evidence, as the view we have been outlining up to here would imply, this progressive decline across age would not be expected. For example, given sufficient exposure to an L2, 39-year-old beginning L2 learners should ultimately be as complete or incomplete in their knowledge of the L2 grammatical system as 17-year-old beginning learners, but this is not the case (see below). The second reason why the recent approach might be worth exploring is that a growing number of cases are coming to light where incompleteness appears to occur even where positive evidence for parameter resetting is readily available. We shall consider some cases shortly.

Johnson & Newport (1989) examined success in SLA across a range of grammatical phenomena in the L2 English of 46 L1 Chinese and L1 Korean speakers, and compared their performance with that of a group of 23 American-born native speakers of English. They gave their subjects a grammaticality judgement task testing phenomena such as noun and verb inflection, word order in questions and declaratives, the selection of

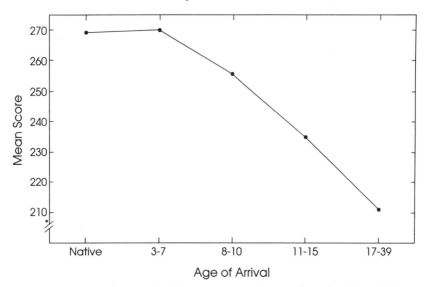

Figure 7.1 The relationship between age of arrival in the United States and total score correct on the test of English Grammar.

Source: Johnson & Newport, 1989

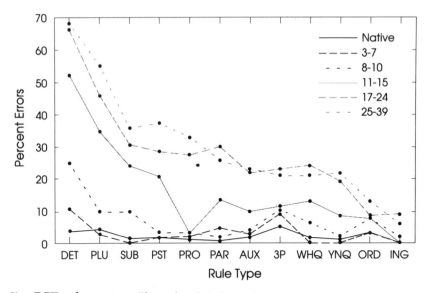

Key: DET = determiner, Plu = plural, Sub = subcategorisation, Pst = past, Pro = pronoun, Par = particle, Aux = auxiliary, 3P = 3rd person singular present, WHQ = wh-question, YNQ = yes/no question, Ord = word order, ING = present progressive inflection -ing.

Figure 7.2 Mean percentage of errors on 12 types of English rules

Source: Johnson & Newport, 1989

specifiers (determiners and pronoun subjects), and the selection of complements to verbs. Their L2 subjects had all had a minimum of five years' exposure to English in the United States, with at least three years' unbroken residence, and with some subjects having had considerably more exposure. The results are given in Figures 7.1 and 7.2.

Those subjects who had arrived in the United States as adolescents or adults showed marked differences in their intuitions about English from native speakers. Those, however, who had arrived between the ages of three and seven years performed like native speakers. In fact, from age 7 to age 39 there was a gradually increasing gap between the intuitions of the native speakers and the L2 speakers. Since length of exposure (minimum five years) remained a constant across the subjects, the conclusion must be that the critical factor determining whether an L2 learner will attain native-like intuitions is age of initial exposure to the target language.

Since the grammatical phenomena investigated by Johnson &

Newport are surface manifestations of particular underlying parameter values set in specific ways for English, the conclusion that we are forced to is that the ability of L2 learners to access and (re)set those values in their L2 grammars declines gradually with age. There must, then, be problems for L2 learners additional to the resetting of superset values in the absence of positive evidence.

This leads one naturally to look more closely at the extent to which resetting of parameter values in adolescent/adult SLA is possible even where positive evidence for resetting is available. Consider again the case of null subject languages and obligatory subject languages. Research findings suggest that native speakers of obligatory subject languages (such as English or French) acquiring null subject languages (such as Spanish, Italian or Greek) appear to acquire the null subject property more rapidly than native speakers of null subject languages (such as Spanish) acquire obligatory subjects in languages (such as English). One possible interpretation of these findings is that null subjects are determined by a superset setting of the null subject parameter (since both null and overt subjects are possible in null subject languages, while only overt subjects are possible in obligatory subject languages). Therefore, whereas English or French speakers learning Spanish are moving from the subset to the superset, Spanish speakers learning English are moving in the other direction, with no positive evidence available to them to tell them that English is the subset. Given the line of argument that has been pursued up to now, there is the assumption that native speakers of English or French *will* reset the parameter fairly easily, but Spanish speakers will perhaps never be able to fully reset it.

This has been called into question in studies by Tsimpli & Roussou (1991), and Tsimpli & Smith (1991), who argue that the performance of English speakers acquiring null subject languages such as Spanish, Italian and Greek is misleading. Such learners do not in fact reset from obligatory subjects to null subjects. Rather, they adopt strategies for organising the L2 data which makes it 'look as if' they had reset the parameter. To follow the line of argument they adopt it is necessary to expand on the nature of null subjects, and to consider a parameter which was one of the first to be proposed within the principles and parameters framework (Chomsky, 1981, 1982) and which is held to include null subjects as one of its corollaries: the pro-drop parameter.

The Pro-Drop Parameter

In most standard analyses of null subject languages such as Spanish, Italian and Greek, two other syntactic properties are held to be associated with null subjects. The first is the possibility of subject–verb inversion even in ordinary declarative clauses. For example, in the Italian equivalent of 'Gianni has telephoned', the subject can either appear to the left of the verb as in English, or to its right, as shown in (7.1a and 7.1b).

7.1a *Gianni ha telefonato.*
  b *Ha telefonato Gianni.*

According to Rizzi (1982, 1986) this possibility follows from the fact that Italian allows null *pro* subjects, because the structure of the (7.1b) example involves, in fact, a *pro* subject, as in (7.1c).

7.1c *pro*ᵢ *ha telefonato Gianni.*

Here *Gianni* is not the subject of the sentence, but a topic adjoined to IP which is co-referential with the subject *pro*, just as topics are adjoined to IPs in French, and to a much lesser extent English:

7.2a *Il a téléphoné, Jean.*
  b ?He has telephoned, John.

The second property associated with the null subject parameter is the possibility of extracting a wh- subject from the complement to a verb where there is an overt complementiser present. Compare the Italian and English equivalent sentences in (7.3).

7.3a *Chi credi* [*che* [___ *abbia telefonato*]]?
  b *Who do you think [that [___ has telephoned]]?

In Italian it seems that a wh- subject (*chi*) can be extracted from the subordinate clause across the complementiser *che* to produce a perfectly grammatical sentence. By contrast, in English the wh- subject ('who') cannot be extracted across the complementiser 'that'. Rizzi (1982, 1986, 1990) has argued that the possibility of extraction of *chi* in Italian also follows from the fact that Italian allows null subject *pro*, because *chi* is not extracted from subject position in (7.3a), but from the adjoined position it occupies in verb–subject inversion structures. That is, the structure of (7.3a) is rather (7.4).

7.4 *Chi credi* [*che* [*pro abbia telefonato* ___]]?

Extraction from postverbal position is generally available in all languages that allow extraction, as it is in English (7.5).

7.5 Who do you think [that [George has telephoned ___]]?

Thus the grammaticality of sentences like (7.1b) in Italian is the direct result of that language allowing *pro* subjects, and the absence of such a possibility in English is the direct result of that language not allowing *pro* subjects.

Exactly the same structural possibilities exist in Spanish (7.6a–c) and in Greek (7.6d–f). Alongside null subjects we find free subject–verb inversion and extraction of embedded wh- subjects across an overt complementiser.

7.6a pro *salieron a las ocho.*   (Spanish, examples
  '*pro* left at eight.'   from Liceras, 1989)

  b pro *han llegado mis estudiantes.*
    '*pro* have arrived my students.'

  c *Quién has dicho* [*que* [pro *va a venir* ___]]?
    'Who did you say that *pro* is going to come?'

  d pro *efige.*   (Greek, examples
    '*pro* left.'   from Tsimpli &
                                              Roussou, 1991)

  e pro *efige o Petros.*
    '*pro* left Peter.'

  f *Pjos ipes* [*oti* [pro *efige* ___]]?
    'Who did you say that *pro* left?'

One line of work in theoretical linguistics, then (since Chomsky, 1981), sees this clustering of properties to result from a single parametric difference between languages: the pro-drop parameter.

Now, studies of English/French speakers acquiring Spanish as an L2 report that learners appear rapidly to acquire the fact that null subjects are possible in Spanish (Phinney, 1987; Liceras, 1989). However, studies that report this finding also report that the other two associated properties are not necessarily acquired concurrently. Tsimpli & Smith (1991), studying the grammatical intuitions of a talented L2 learner (an L1 English-speaking 29-year-old who knows some 16 second languages including Italian, Greek and Spanish) about Italian, Greek and Spanish found that while he used null subjects appropriately, he did not accept free verb–subject inversion in declarative sentences in any of these languages (although he did accept it in questions), nor did he allow extraction of an embedded wh- subject across an overt complementiser in any of these languages. Liceras (1989), studying English and French learners of L2 Spanish found that only two very advanced subjects from her population allowed any cases of verb–subject inversion and wh-subject extraction across an overt complementiser.

In the other direction, although studies find that speakers of null subject languages have difficulty with obligatory subjects in English, they do not appear to have much difficulty recognising that free verb–subject inversion is not possible in English. White (1989b) reports that at the same time that her Spanish subjects were performing significantly worse than her French subjects on obligatory subjects in L2 English, they were performing at the same level (over 90% accurate) on obligatory subject–verb order. Tsimpli & Roussou (1991) in a study of Greek learners of English found that all their subjects recognised verb–subject order in English declaratives as ungrammatical. On the non-extractability of wh- subjects across 'that', however, subjects in these studies invariably performed poorly. Only 23% of White's subjects recognised the impossibility of such extraction, and only 5% of Tsimpli & Roussou's Greek speakers did.

To summarise the picture that emerges: adolescent/adult native speakers of pro-drop languages such as Spanish, Italian and Greek learning a non-pro-drop language such as English take time to acquire obligatory subjects, rapidly recognise that subject–verb inversion is not possible, but have great difficulty learning the constraint on wh- subject extraction, perhaps never acquiring it. Adolescent/adult native speakers of non-pro-drop languages such as English learning pro-drop languages rapidly acquire null subjects, but have considerable difficulty recognising the possibility of free verb–subject inversion and wh- subject extraction from embedded clauses.

There are two positions that could be taken by SLA researchers in the face of this differential L2 success on aspects of what is supposed to be the same parameter. One is to reanalyse the parameter and suggest that verb–subject inversion and wh- subject extraction are manifestations of a different parameter or parameters. It would then be possible to maintain that some parameter settings are being reset in SLA but not others. This is a line adopted by some (Liceras (1989) and White (1989b) seem to take this view). It loses some of the interest of the notion 'parameter' in this case. One of the justifications for the parametric approach should be the prediction that a single parameter setting will underlie a range of surface syntactic properties in a particular language.

An alternative, and radical, recent approach is to reappraise the idea that parameters are reset in SLA. Tsimpli & Roussou (1991) and Tsimpli & Smith (1991) argue that while L2 learner grammars are restructured after an initial stage where they are characterised by parameter settings transferred from the L1, this restructuring does not involve parameter resetting. Rather learners misanalyse the L2 data they are exposed to, in order to make it conform as far as possible to the parameter values imposed by the L1.

The argument runs (informally) as follows. The construction of mental grammars is constrained in both L1 and L2 acquisition by the invariant principles of UG (such as X-bar theory, and the Empty Category Principle). 'Open' parameter values, however, are available only for a limited period. (If we follow the findings of Johnson & Newport (1989), the 'critical period' during which they are available would be up to the age of around seven years.) The setting of parameter values takes place during this limited period, and is encoded in the lexical entries for grammatical items. Once the period ends (perhaps as the result of maturation) open parameters are no longer available to language learners. What is available is the invariant principles of UG, and the particular parameter settings of the L1, encoded in grammatical items stored in the lexicon. It is this which leads directly to transfer in the initial stages of subsequent L2 learning. However, on longer exposure to the L2 the learner will sometimes encounter L2 data which are in conflict with the parameter settings provided by the L1 (for example, null subjects if the learner's L1 is an obligatory subject language). In this case the learner will try to analyse the input (subconsciously, of course; we are still dealing with the subconscious language faculty) so that it conforms in some fashion with the L1 parameter setting. This results in development away from the initial-state L2 grammar, but involves the construction of grammatical representations which are not those of native speakers of the target language, and although restructuring of the grammar may lead to L2 learners 'performing like' native speakers in some areas, it almost invariably leads to them being distinctly 'non-native-like' in other areas. We shall illustrate with the concrete example of the pro-drop parameter.

Greek-speaking learners of L2 English, according to Tsimpli & Roussou, once they recognise that English has forms such as 'I', 'you', 'he', 'she', 'it', and so on, misanalyse these as 'agreement prefixes' to verbs. They therefore construct representations for English clause structure like that in (7.7), which are quite unlike the representations which native speakers have.

If Greek learners of L2 English were behaving in this way, then they

7.7

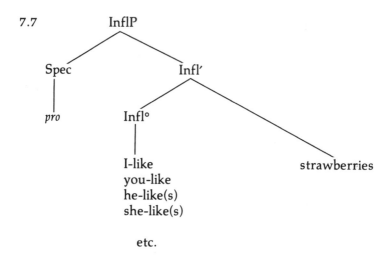

would 'appear' to have acquired obligatory subject pronouns; but in fact it would become clear that they have not reset the pro-drop parameter if they readily allowed wh- extraction across a complementiser in an embedded clause, which as we have seen they do. Tsimpli & Roussou also note that there are other aspects of their behaviour which would suggest that they are still operating in terms of a pro-drop representation: even advanced learners in the population they studied failed to acquire the so-called 'expletive' pronoun 'it' in sentences such as: 'It seems that Mary is happy', persistently preferring 'Seems that Mary is happy'. If they had reset the parameter this would not be expected. Subjects also produced a considerable number of what appear to be 'dislocated' subjects: 'John, he broke the plates', which are not common in native-speaker English. This would be expected if learners had constructed representations like the one in (7.7): the specifier of InflP would alternate between *pro* subjects and lexical subjects such as 'John', but the agreement marker on the verb would remain stable, leading to apparently dislocated main clauses. (It is not entirely clear, though, how speakers of pro-drop languages are able to recognise rapidly that free verb–subject inversion is not possible in non-pro-drop languages.)

Similarly, native speakers of English learning a pro-drop language might be expected to misanalyse agreement inflections on the verb in these languages as an obligatory subject which just happens to cliticise on to the end of the verb (Tsimpli & Smith, 1991). For example, Spanish *pro hablo*, 'I speak', *pro hablas*, 'you speak', *pro habla*, 'he, she, one speaks', and so on would be misanalysed as in (7.8).

7.8

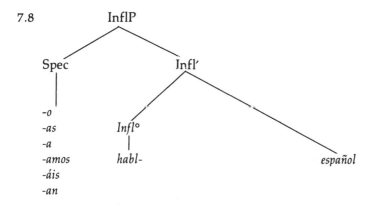

Cliticisation of pronouns to verbs is permissible within UG, and is arguably what occurs in the case of French subject pronouns (Kayne, 1975). If English speakers were analysing agreement markers in their L2 grammars for pro-drop languages in this way, it would readily explain learners' ability to acquire null subjects, but failure to acquire verb–subject inversion or extraction of wh- subjects across complementisers, because these properties are crucially dependent on a subject *pro*.

The approach of Tsimpli & Roussou, and Tsimpli & Smith to SLA makes the following predictions: first, SLA will essentially be like L1 acquisition because the construction of mental grammars is constrained in both cases by the invariant principles of UG. That is, both L1 and L2 grammars will be possible grammars for human languages. Secondly, in SLA 'success' will arise in two areas: (1) where an L1-set parameter value is the same in the L2; (2) where an L2 parameter setting is different from the setting in the L1, but where a learner is able to misanalyse L2 input data so that it is compatible with the L1 parameter setting. A third prediction is that incompleteness will arise where an L2 parameter setting is different from an L1 parameter setting, but where the L2 learner is unable to misanalyse L2 input data to make it compatible with the L1 parameter setting (for reasons to do with the limitations imposed by the principles of UG). In this case the L2 learner will display persistent differences from native speakers of the target language.

This approach is innovative and radical, in the context of previous work in SLA, because it suggests that 'incompleteness' is a property of SLA which can receive a definition within UG itself. Up to this point in our discussion of the UG-based approach to SLA we have been suggesting that incompleteness and differential development between different L1-speaking populations of L2 learners is the result of a language-faculty-external learning principle: the subset principle. The argument has been that L2 learners have difficulty where their L1 has fixed a superset parameter setting and positive evidence is not available to enable them to reset it. Now Tsimpli & Roussou's, and Tsimpli & Smith's accounts allow us to dispense with the UG-external principle while still capturing the relevant generalisations.

Verb Movement in French and English

Interestingly, the trend to eliminate the subset principle as an explanatory factor in SLA is paralleled by a trend within linguistic theory itself towards more abstract structural representations which would make the subset–superset distinction unnecessary in considering the learnability problem for language learners. The idea is best illustrated by example. For this we shall consider proposals concerning the clause structure of French and English.

We have already referred to a study by White (1989a) of the different placement of manner and frequency adverbs in English and French, and the acquisition of these placements in SLA. Typical cases are those in (7.9) and (7.10).

7.9a John often eats doughnuts.
  b *John eats often doughnuts.

7.10a *Jean mange souvent des beignets.*
  b **Jean souvent mange des beignets.*

White's study was conducted within a theoretical framework (that of Stowell, 1981) which assumed a parameter of [± strict adjacency] for case assignment. If a language selects the [± strictly adjacent] setting of the parameter then case assigners must be directly adjacent to the phrases to which they assign case; if a language selects the [– strictly adjacent] setting then case assigners may, but need not, be adjacent to the phrases to which they assign case. In the case of verbs, which assign objective (accusative) case to their object noun phrases, English has fixed the parameter to [+ strictly adjacent], while French has fixed it to [– strictly adjacent], hence the pattern illustrated in (7.9) and (7.10).

Within this framework, given the fact that children acquiring English as an L1 do not mistakenly fix the parameter value to [– strictly adjacent], it has to be assumed that some learning principle like the subset principle is involved which prevents learners from setting parameter values for phenomena which are not positively present in the samples of language they are exposed to. White's study extended this idea to SLA, by suggesting that the subset principle was not available to L2 learners. The result of this was that although L1 English-speaking learners of L2 French find it relatively easy to acquire the [– strictly adjacent] setting for French, because they have positive evidence for it in the input, L1 French-speaking learners of L2 English find it difficult to lose their native [– strictly adjacent] parameter setting, because there is nothing about English to tell them that it is a [+ strictly adjacent] language, and they do not have access to the subset principle.

More recent work by Pollock (1989), however, and an extension of it by Rizzi (1990), has argued that the different placement of manner and frequency adverbs in French and English is just one element of a range of distributional phenomena which reflect a deeper structural difference between the two languages. Pollock observes, for example, that it is not just the placement of adverbs which differs, but also the placement of the negators *pas*/'not' and the placement of quantifiers such as *tous*/'all' which have 'floated' off the subject into the middle of the sentence, as in examples (7.11)–(7.14).

7.11a John doesn't eat doughnuts.
    b *John eats *not* doughnuts.

7.12a *Jean ne mange* pas *de beignets.*
    b **Jean ne* pas *mange de beignets.*

7.13a The boys *all* eat doughnuts.
    b *The boys eat *all* doughnuts.

7.14a *Les garçons mangent* tous *des beignets.*
    b **Les garçons* tous *mangent des beignets.*

Notice that in these cases 'not'/'n't' and 'all' must appear to the left of the lexical verb 'eat', while *pas* and *tous* must appear to the right of the lexical verb *manger*. (Lexical verbs are verbs with semantic content, such as 'eat', 'read', 'kiss', and so on. They are opposed to auxiliary verbs such as 'do', 'have', 'be', and modal verbs like 'must', 'may'.)

A further related property is that, in questions, French lexical verbs are able to move into C°, whereas in English they are not, and an auxiliary verb 'do' must be moved into C° instead.

7.15 [CP *Mange-t-[il des beignets]*]?

7.16a [CP Does [he eat doughnuts]]?
   b *[CP Eats [he doughnuts]]?

Furthermore, distribution of some of these phenomena varies between finite clauses (as in the examples given above) and infinitive clauses. For example, in infinitive clauses in both French and English negators must appear to the left of the lexical verb.

7.17a To not eat doughnuts would be a torture for him.
   b *To eat not doughnuts would be a torture for him.

7.18a *Ne pas manger de beignets lui serait un supplice.*
   b **Ne manger pas de beignets lui serait un supplice.*

Adverbs and quantifiers must also appear to the left of infinitive lexical verbs in English, but they may appear either to the right or the left of the infinitive in French.

7.19a To often eat doughnuts would be fun.
   b *To eat often doughnuts would be fun.

7.20a *Souvent manger des beignets serait marrant.*
   b *Manger souvent des beignets serait marrant.*

7.21a To all eat doughnuts would be fun for the boys.
   b *To eat all doughnuts would be fun for the boys.

7.22a *Tous manger des beignets serait marrant pour les garçons.*
   b *Manger tous des beignets serait marrant pour les garçons.*

All of these distributional differences, Pollock argues, can be seen as the reflection of a single parametric difference between the two languages if it is assumed that clause structure is more abstract than it was originally assumed to be. In particular, if it is assumed that Infl° (see Chapter 5) is not in fact a single category but is a conflation of two distinct categories: T° (tense) and Agr° (agreement). If it is also assumed that verbs in French tensed clauses raise to 'pick up' tense and agreement-with-subject features, but in English tense and agreement features lower on to the verb, then a range of the distributional phenomena described above automatically follow. Consider the structure of the English and French clause from this point of view illustrated in (7.23) (following Rizzi, 1990).

If, given this underlying structure (D-structure), French verbs raise to T° and then to Agr° to pick up tense and agreement inflections, the appropriate location of negation, adverbs and floated quantifiers, to the right of the verb, will follow automatically. Moreover, if question

7.23

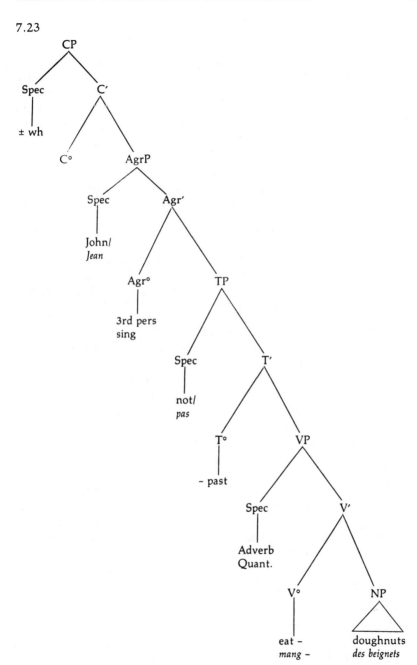

formation is characterised by the movement of Agr° into a CP marked with the feature [+ wh], lexical verbs will move with that Agr° in French. On the other hand, if agreement and tense inflections lower to the verb in English, then it will automatically follow that adverbs and floated quantifiers will appear to the left of the verb. In the case of negation, it appears that it is not possible for the agreement inflection to lower when a negator is present (for technical reasons which are not of concern here), and the insertion of the auxiliary verb 'do' is forced. Similarly in questions, because the lexical verb cannot raise, the insertion of 'do' is forced which picks up the tense and agreement inflections and moves into CP. In infinitive clauses the same D-structure obtains, but verb movement is more restricted in French: verbs can raise to T°, but not beyond T°. This gives the difference between the location of the negator in French in finite and infinitive clauses.

Given the abstract and highly articulated structure of the clause illustrated in (7.23), all of the observed distributional facts can be taken to follow from a single parametric difference between French and English: whether the verb is able to raise or not.[1]

The implication of this account for learnability in language acquisition is quite different from the implication of Stowell's 'adjacency' parameter. Whereas the adjacency parameter has inclusive values (the [- strict adjacency] value allows case assigners to be both adjacent and non-adjacent to the phrases to which they assign case, and this includes the property of adjacent case assigners and assignees allowed by the [+ strict adjacency] value), the verb movement parameter has exclusive values: selection by a language of verb raising excludes the option of inflectional affix lowering, and vice versa. In other words it does *not* display the subset–superset relation. This means that language learners will always find positive evidence for one or the other setting in the samples of language they are exposed to. And indeed in this case there should be a considerable amount of positive evidence for a French-speaking learner of English, or an English-speaking learner of French, from the cluster of distributional properties related to the parameter: adverb placement, negative placement, floated quantifer placement, and question formation.

With regard to SLA, however, recall that White (1989a) found a clear difference between L1 French-speaking learners of L2 English, and L1 English-speaking learners of L2 French in their performance on adverb placement. The French learners of L2 English had greater problems losing the property that adverbs may appear between verbs and their complements than the English learners of L2 French did in acquiring it.

We have, then, something of a problem for explanation if positive evidence is available to both groups of L2 learners, but one group seems to be more successful in acquiring the property than the other. This specific problem was investigated in a study by Hawkins, Towell & Bazergui (1993) in a detailed consideration of the development of intuitions of grammaticality between high intermediate and advanced L1 English-speaking learners of L2 French (104 university students with at least seven years of largely classroom exposure to French, and the advanced learners having spent at least six months resident in a French-speaking country).

The general conclusions of this study were that although the high intermediate learners displayed what appeared to be target-like intuitions in their judgements of the grammatical placement of negation and adverbs in French finite clauses, they performed poorly in judging the grammatical placement of floated quantifiers. Further inspection of their judgements of ungrammatical placement of negation, adverbs and quantifiers, and their judgements of the placement of these phenomena in infinitive clauses revealed that their intuitions were unlike those of native speakers in these areas. The analysis suggested for these findings followed the work of Tsimpli & Roussou (1991) and Tsimpli & Smith (1991): it was suggested that learners had misanalysed the input to make it conform with the L1-transferred parameter setting for the lowering of tense and agreement inflections. In particular, they had misanalysed the negator *pas* as an affix generated under Agr° which could then be lowered, with Agr°, to the verb. The effect of this is to produce an acceptable French negative surface structure in finite clauses, while retaining the operation of affix lowering.

Similarly, it was proposed that the appropriate surface placement of manner and frequency adverbs in finite clauses is achieved by learners not through verb movement, but through moving the complement of a verb to the right across a clause-final adverb: [*Jean* [*mange des beignets souvent*]] → [*Jean* [*mange t_i souvent*] *des beignets$_i$*]], in a manner analogous to what is known as 'heavy NP shift' in English. In heavy NP shift particularly long complements to verbs can be moved to the right across other items for stylistic reasons (e.g. to avoid having a 'light' item like an adverb at the end of a sentence), for example: '[John [drank the beer which his friend said was made by one of the best breweries in Suffolk quickly]]' → '[John [drank t_i quickly] the beer which his friend said was made by one of the best breweries in Suffolk$_i$]'. Both of these operations — analysis of Agr° as containing the feature [+ negation] and rightward adjunction to VP — are permissible operations within UG. At the same time they are both *ad hoc* strategies which allow the L2 learners to retain L1 parameter settings in the face of conflicting evidence in the L2 input. This account allowed us to explain why learners had performed poorly on grammatical floated quantifier placement, in judging the ungrammaticality of certain ungrammatical placements of the phenomena in question, and on certain aspects of placement in infinitive clauses (see Hawkins, Towell & Bazergui (1993) for details).

At the same time, it was found that the advanced subjects (who had had three years' more classroom exposure to French than the high intermediate learners, and who in addition had spent at least six months resident in France) were considerably more native-like than the high intermediate learners. Their performance led us to conclude that they had indeed reset the verb movement parameter. If this is the case, it is in conflict with the strong view held by Tsimpli & Roussou and Tsimpli & Smith that parameter values are in principle inaccessible to resetting by L2 learners. But given the length of exposure these learners had had before resetting took place, it might suggest that parameter values are highly resistant to resetting, although not in principle unresettable.

This view has some appeal, for two reasons. First recall that Johnson & Newport (1989) found that incompleteness in SLA correlates progressively with age; that is, the older you are at first exposure to the L2, the more incomplete your grammar is likely to be, relative to native speakers. One interpretation of this might be that parameter values become progressively resistant to resetting with age, following the critical period. Secondly, there are cases reported in the SLA literature involving what are standardly regarded as cases of parametric variation, but which seem to be rather more easily acquirable than, say, the pro-drop parameter or the verb movement parameter. Word order in German is a case in point. Recall that Romance-language-speaking and English-speaking learners of L2 German have to reset parameters for both head position, with respect to IP and VP (in German I° and V° follow their complements), and the status of C°. (Recall that the C° of German root clauses attracts the tense-marked verb.) While they do so through developmental stages, it nevertheless seems to be the case that, given sufficient exposure to German, they do reset the parameters.

Work along these lines is at the forefront of current research within UG-based approaches to SLA. As a result, many questions remain open. Nevertheless, it is a promising area for characterising the nature of incompleteness in SLA.

Summary

'Incompleteness' in SLA is a failure on the part of L2 learners to acquire the same grammatical representations for phenomena in the target language as native speakers. At the beginning of the chapter we suggested that incompleteness resulted from the lack of positive evidence to reset parameters already set in the L1. Then we described a recent refinement in the perception of the nature of incompleteness: that it also results from certain subcomponents of UG becoming difficult to access for adolescent and adult L2 learners. There are two reasons for thinking that there is also this further dimension to incompleteness. The first is that incompleteness is progressive with age: the older you are at first exposure to an L2, the more incomplete your L2 grammar will be. The second is that incompleteness seems to occur even in the presence of positive evidence. The pro-drop parameter was considered in this connection. The pro-drop parameter is held to affect three phenomena in languages: null subjects versus obligatory subjects, free subject–verb inversion versus restricted subject–verb inversion, and the possibility of extracting a wh- subject across an overt complementiser versus the impossibility of doing so. In studies of English and French speakers acquiring pro-drop second languages it has been found that although subjects acquire null subjects rapidly, the other properties are not acquired concurrently. And in studies of Spanish, Italian and Greek speakers learning English (a non-pro-drop language) it has been found that although learners rapidly recognise that free subject–verb inversion is not possible, they take time to acquire obligatory subjects, and have persistent difficulty with the impossibility of extracting wh- subjects across overt complementisers.

Two positions have been taken by researchers in the face of these observations. The first is to suggest that each of the three phenomena follow from separate parameters, and therefore simultaneous acquisition is not to be expected. The second, adopted by Tsimpli & Roussou (1991) and Tsimpli & Smith (1991), is to suggest that L2 learners do not reset parameters at all, but rather 'look as if' they do, because they misanalyse L2 input to make it conform, where possible, to the parameter settings of their L1.

Three predictions follow from the non-resetting approach. The first is that L2 grammars still fall within the class of grammars defined by UG. The second is that success in SLA will arise either where parameter settings are the same in the L1 and the L2, or where L2 learners are able to misanalyse L2 data to make them fit with their L1 parameter settings.

The third is that incompleteness will arise where learners are unable to misanalyse L2 data within the limits defined by UG.

The latter approach opens up the possibility of accounting for incompleteness in SLA as a property directly associated with UG: the fossilisation of certain subcomponents after the critical period for language acquisition. This does not require recourse to language-faculty-external learning principles, like the subset principle, yet still captures the relevant generalisations.

It is not entirely clear, however, that all parameters are unresettable for all time. In a detailed study of the acquisition of French verb movement by L1 English speakers, Hawkins, Towell & Bazergui (1993) found that learners seemed to persist with misanalysis of French data in conformity with the English parameter setting for non-verb movement into quite advanced stages, but there was evidence that learners were beginning to reset the parameter in very advanced stages. This suggests that parameters may be highly resistant to resetting, rather than unresettable in principle. This would be compatible with the findings of Johnson & Newport (1989), in the sense that it could be said that parameters become more resistant to resetting the older one is on first exposure to an L2.

Note

1. The technical details of the parameter are complex and beyond the scope of this book. Refer to the sources already cited, and additionally to Chomsky (1989), Iatridou (1990) for discussion.

8 Parametric Variation, Staged Development and Cross-learner Systematicity in Second Language Acquisition

The Logical and Developmental Problems in Language Acquisition

In Chapter 6 we examined the effect that parameter settings transferred from the L1 into the L2 have on the development of grammatical knowledge in SLA. The effects of the availability and non-availability of positive evidence for parameter resetting were considered, and the more general question of whether parameter resetting is in principle a possibility for post-seven-year-old L2 learners was broached. The effects of transfer and the possibility or not of parameter resetting are factors which are crucial in determining the eventual knowledge which L2 learners attain in the L2. We have seen that post-seven-year-old L2 learners are typically 'incomplete' in their eventual knowledge, by contrast with L1 learners, even given large amounts of exposure to the L2. And we have argued that this is the direct result of the fixing of parameter values in the L1 and the difficulties that L2 learners experience in resetting those values. We now need to consider in more detail what happens in SLA on the route from no knowledge of the L2 to advanced knowledge of the L2, and consider why there might be stages of development towards advanced knowledge which are systematic across learners.

Two problems are standardly recognised in the study of language acquisition. One is the logical problem of language acquisition, the other is the developmental problem in language acquisition. In the study of L1 acquisition, the logical problem is to explain how children eventually come to know as much as they do about their native language on the basis of limited exposure to often fragmentary samples of language. This eventual knowledge is typically neither overgeneral nor undergeneral: that is, it broadly corresponds to the knowledge that other native speakers of the same variety have. As we have seen, the principles and parameters view of language acquisition suggests that children are able to acquire such rich linguistic knowledge because they are innately equipped with a 'language faculty' made up of invariant principles of Universal Grammar and specified parameters of variation with open values. This biologically endowed mental architecture greatly reduces the learning task for the child, which is to fix the settings of the parameters on the basis of positive evidence from the language the child is exposed to.

The developmental problem in L1 acquisition is to explain why children take time to fix the appropriate settings for parameters, and why they appear to go through stages of development on their way to fixing those settings. In principle, just one piece of evidence should be sufficient to enable a child to fix a given parameter. For example, take a child learning English as an L1, and assume that the child knows the meaning of the words 'biscuit' and 'want'. In principle, one hearing of a native speaker saying: '(do you) want (a) biscuit?' — because it involves a head (a verb) followed by its complement (a noun phrase) — should be sufficient for the child's language faculty to generalise and fix the appropriate setting of the parameter for head position in English — head first, complement last.

But in reality it is sometimes the case that even with quantities of apparent triggering evidence in the input for the fixing of a given parameter value, children will not appear to fix that value until late on into the acquisition process. Recall that in the case of children acquiring the parameter for obligatorily specified subjects in English, there is an early phase where they allow null subjects. And yet for the most part they will be exposed to samples of language where there is considerable evidence for obligatory subjects.

Various approaches have been adopted to the developmental problem in L1 acquisition research (cf. Hyams, 1991: 72–3). Some of these attempt to explain developmental phenomena on the basis of the organisation of the components of the language faculty alone. Others make appeal to non-linguistic factors. For example, one language-faculty-internal approach to L1 development argues that different components of UG become available to the child at different points of physical development. This links the problem to general maturation: the child cannot set parameter values until parameters themselves come 'on-line' in the language faculty. On this scenario there is a biologically determined timetable of development within the language faculty such that some components of knowledge are made available before others. This is a position argued for at length in Radford (1990), who provides considerable evidence to support the idea that functional categories (the categories dealing with strictly grammatical phenomena such as agreement, tense, definiteness, case marking, and so on) become available to the child only several months after the lexical categories (noun, verb, preposition, adjective) have come on stream.

By contrast, one approach which appeals to non-linguistic factors suggests that children's early perceptual mechanisms (i.e. the mental devices through which they perceive and segment continuous speech) are not sufficiently developed to enable them to take in all the relevant data, in one go, that would allow them to fix parameters. For example, in the early stages of language acquisition the child's short-term memory may be just too short to allow the processing of more than two or three words at a time, and this will considerably restrict the amount of primary linguistic data that can be made available to UG. This kind of approach is adopted in the work of Slobin (1985), who proposes a set of 'operating principles', which direct the child to focus on particular aspects of the samples of language he or she is exposed to. For example, Slobin (1985: 1,251–6) suggests that the child operates in terms of operating principles such as: 'Pay attention to the last syllable of an extracted speech unit. Store it separately and also in relation to the unit with which it occurs'; or 'Determine whether a newly extracted stretch of speech seems to be the same as or different from anything you have already stored. If it is different, store it separately . . .'. He cites many such operating principles in the work cited. Their interaction, it would be claimed, will produce the developmental orders that are observed in L1 acquisition.

An important issue in constructing a theory about the developmental problem — i.e. the route that learners follow to attain their eventual knowledge of the language — is the extent to which it is necessary to 'step outside' the language faculty in order to provide explanations. A parsimonious view would be that, where all other things are equal, a language-faculty-internal account of the developmental problem would be preferred over one which requires the postulation of other factors, simply because the language faculty is required anyway, and appeal to non-linguistic factors requires two sets of constructs rather than one. Thus, in L1 acquisition Radford's account of the cause of developmental stages would be preferred over Slobin's on the grounds of theoretical simplicity. But at the same time, there may be developmental phenomena which simply fall outside the scope of UG, and which necessarily require appeal to other mechanisms. In that case, the task is to determine where the explanatory power of UG stops, and where explanations from other areas of cognition begin.

The Logical and Developmental Problems in Second Language Acquisition

The same two problems exist in the study of SLA. The logical problem involves explaining the nature of the eventual knowledge that L2 learners ultimately attain on the basis of the samples of the L2 that they are exposed to. As we have seen, in one way L2 learners are like L1 learners in that the knowledge which constitutes their mental grammars goes well beyond any evidence they may have received in the input, and falls within the class of grammars defined by UG. In another way they are unlike L1 learners because they rarely develop the same kinds of mental representations for grammatical phenomena as L1 learners: their grammars remain incomplete, relative to those of native speakers. We discussed this issue of 'incompleteness' in SLA at some length in the preceding chapter.

The developmental problem, on the other hand, involves providing an explanation for the routes which L2 learners take in moving, over time, from no knowledge of the L2 to the eventual mental representations that they construct. For example, why do speakers of non-preposition-stranding languages learning an L2 with preposition stranding, like English, go through a stage of deleting the preposition before they acquire stranding (Bardovi-Harlig, 1987) as in:

Stage 1 She talked to whom?
Stage 2 Who did she talk Ø?
Stage 3 Who did she talk to?

Why do L1 Romance-language-speakers and L1 English-speakers learning L2 German go through the following stages, in the order that they do, in acquiring German word order?

Stage 1 Non-separation of verb and participle: *Ich bin gegangen ins Kino.*
Stage 2 Separation of verb and participle: *Ich bin ins Kino gegangen.*
Stage 3 Verb-second: *Gestern bin ich ins Kino gegangen.*
Stage 4 Verb-final in subordinate clauses: *Er glaubt, dass ich gestern ins Kino gegangen bin.*

One could put this question another way and ask why learners do not go through the stages: verb-second → verb separation → verb-final, or verb-second → verb-final → verb separation instead.

Why do English-speakers learning L2 French go through the following stages in acquiring unstressed object pronouns?

Stage 1 *J'ai reconnu le.*
Stage 2 *J'ai reconnu Ø*
Stage 3 *J'ai le reconnu.*
Stage 4 *Je l'ai reconnu.*

and so on.

In addressing this problem, the same issue about the extent to which it is necessary to 'step outside' UG to provide an account exists as it does in L1 acquisition. On the grounds of simplicity, one would prefer a theory which attributed learner development to the nature of the language faculty, over a theory which appealed to factors in addition to the language faculty, all other things being equal. But at the same time, there may well be phenomena which simply cannot be accounted for adequately by UG.

In what follows we shall reconsider a number of the cases of staged development that have already been described, and attempt to offer an account within the limits offered by UG. Much of this is speculative in nature. At the same time, areas of SLA development which are difficult to bring within the orbit of the explanatory power of UG begin to emerge, a matter which we shall take up in connection with 'variability' in Chapter 9.

Take a first case where it seems that a UG-based account is central to an understanding of a particular example of staged development, but where some language-faculty-external factor also seems to be involved. Languages which have obligatorily phonetically specified subjects (like English, and in contrast to null subject languages such as Italian, Spanish and Greek) appear to have three types of pronoun subject:

- *referential* pronouns, which, as their name implies, refer to people or things mentioned elsewhere in the discourse, or to the speaker or listener involved in the speech act (i.e.: I, you, he, she, it, they, and so on)
- *quasi argument* pronouns, as in the English 'it' which occurs with 'atmospheric' verbs such as 'it's snowing', 'it rained today'
- *expletive* pronouns such as English 'it' or 'there' in 'it is difficult to explain his behaviour', 'there are three boats in the harbour'.

Null subject languages apparently have no overt phonetic realisation for quasi argument or expletive pronouns, although they do have phonetically specified variants of referential pronouns which are generally used instead of *pro* for emphasis.

Speakers of null subject languages (such as Italian, Spanish and Greek) learning obligatory subject languages (such as English), acquire obligatory phonetically specified pronouns, but they do so slowly. Tsimpli & Roussou (1991) have found that the way that L1 Greek-speaking learners of L2 English acquire them is in three developmental stages: (1) referential pronouns → (2) quasi argument pronouns → (3) expletive pronouns. Since neither quasi argument nor expletive pronouns are overt in null subject languages, this suggests that the three-way distinction in pronoun type must form part of UG, and guides the construction of the learners' L2 grammars. Why else would such a distinction show up in development? The result is particularly telling in the case of English as an L2, because 'it' has the same overt phonetic form in all three functions: referential ('it is in the drawer'), quasi argument ('it is raining') and expletive ('it is difficult to explain his behaviour'), so that it cannot simply be its non-salience as an unstressed pronoun which is causing the acquisitional problem. In any non-UG-based account it might be expected that once learners had acquired the form 'it', they would be able to use it in any context in which it appears, and yet this seems not to be the case.

At the same time, it is not clear why obligatory pronouns are acquired in this particular order. When a learner begins to recognise obligatory subject pronouns, why is this recognition initially limited to referential pronouns? Why is the recognition extended next to quasi argument pronouns and not expletives? Possibly this is related to input frequency: L2 learners may encounter more examples of referential than quasi argument or expletive pronouns, and not be in a position to use quasi argument and expletive constructions until they have encountered sufficient quantities of them. But 'input frequency' has nothing to do with UG. It is a factor involved in language use. And it may be that we begin to see here the limits of UG in explaining aspects of L2 development.

As a second example consider preposition stranding again, as in English: 'Who did she speak to?'. As we noted above, Bardovi-Harlig (1987) has observed that learners of L2 English, speaking native languages which do not have preposition stranding, in early stages of proficiency, display a kind of half-way position between the non-stranding of prepositions and full stranding. They front a wh- phrase and simultaneously delete the preposition, as in (8.1).

8.1 Who did she speak Ø?

How might this intermediate stage between non-stranding and stranding be accounted for? If we were to adopt a non-linguistic factors approach we might follow Wolfe Quintero (1992) and suggest that the problem for learners at this stage is one of perceptual discontinuity. Recall that Wolfe Quintero suggests that language learners are perceptually predisposed to prefer continuous constituents over discontinuous constituents. Preposition stranding involves a discontinuous prepositional phrase, for example in (8.1) 'Who . . . to?', so in early stages of L2 learning learners will avoid, or perhaps be unable to process, such structures. Nevertheless, spoken English provides many examples of the fronting of wh- phrases, to the extent that one could imagine an L2 learner who had become aware that question formation involved wh- phrase fronting, while at the same time was unable to process discontinuous constituents. In this situation perhaps learners adopt a strategy to avoid discontinuity: the deletion of the preposition.

While this account might seem plausible, it is no less plausible to offer a similar account on the basis of properties internal to the language faculty, and thereby avoid appeal to an outside and rather vague notion of 'perceptual continuity'. In Chapter 6 it was suggested that empty categories left behind by movement must be properly governed by another head category, in order not to violate an invariant universal principle: the Empty Category Principle (ECP). Languages vary, however, as to which head categories are able to properly govern, or license, empty categories. In languages which allow preposition stranding (such as English) P° is a licenser; in languages which have prepositions but do not have preposition stranding (such as French) P° is not a licenser. Native speakers of languages which do not allow preposition stranding have not set the parameter value of P° to [+ licenser], and in learning English must do so. Another task for them is to acquire, in questions, wh- phrase fronting to the specifier of CP. Suppose that learners acquire the fronting of wh- phrases before they set the parametric value for P° to [+ licenser]. If this is the case, then sentences like (8.2) will be ungrammatical for them, even though they are perfectly grammatical for native speakers.

8.2 Who$_i$ did she speak [to [ec$_i$]]?

The reason why they are ungrammatical is because ec$_i$ is not properly governed by 'to' in the grammar of the L2 learner, and by the ECP the sentence is therefore ruled out. In other words, an invariant, innately determined principle of UG — that empty categories must be properly governed by a governing head — constrains learners' early L2 grammars to exclude preposition stranding, while allowing wh- fronting in prepositionless environments. Suppose that in this circumstance learners adopt a strategy to circumvent the ECP: they delete the preposition. With no preposition present the verb, which in many languages is normally a proper governor, properly governs the empty category, and the sentence is grammatical.

How the deletion of the preposition is to be understood is not entirely clear on either scenario, but one possibility is that in the lexical representations for verbs (their dictionary entries) the specification of which complements they take is not clearly determined by L2 learners in early stages of acquisition. For example, an early L2 learner of English may not yet be entirely sure whether a verb such as 'speak' is an indirectly transitive verb selecting a prepositional phrase complement: 'She spoke to John', or a transitive verb selecting a noun phrase complement: *'She spoke John', but in the case of wh- fronting of the complement, one possibility only is forced on the learner: the prepositionless NP complement, because he or she has grammatical representations constrained by invariant principles of UG.

Although both the 'perceptual disposition' and 'language-faculty-internal' accounts are speculative, the latter is to be preferred because staged development follows from constructs required anyway to account for the properties of the world's languages: the ECP and the notion that certain head categories may or may not be licensers of empty categories. Only one construct is required (the language faculty) rather than two (the language faculty and more general cognition).

At the same time, this account begs at least two questions. One has to assume that wh- fronting is acquired here before the acquisition of P° as a licenser of empty categories. Why? And why did Bardovi-Harlig find that extraction of the whole prepositional phrase (i.e. pied-piping) was acquired later than both deletion and preposition stranding, when extraction of the whole PP would have the same effect as preposition deletion, as far as the ECP is concerned? These are questions to which we do not have answers, but which seem not to be of the order which fall easily under UG-based explanations. They appear to fall more readily within the domain of a theory of language use.

The stages of development found in the acquisition of French preverbal unstressed pronouns by English speakers could also be treated along similar lines. Here we need to account for why learners, after initially assuming the postverbal location of object pronouns, as in *J'ai reconnu le*, 'I recognised him', first delete the pronoun — *J'ai reconnu Ø* — and then hypothesise that it attaches to the first element of the verbal complex (a participle in this case) — *J'ai le reconnu* — before arriving at the appropriate hypothesis for French, which is that unstressed object pronouns attach to the tense-marked element in the verbal complex, i.e. *Je l'ui reconnu*.[1]

A language-faculty-external approach to the developmental stages displayed in this case might cite 'perceptual saliency' as the determining causal factor. Recall that clause-final position is held by proponents of such accounts to be perceptually more salient than clause-internal positions (see Chapter 4). Learners therefore find it difficult initially to handle elements which are clause-internal, as unstressed object pronouns are. They soon notice, however, that in the samples of language they are exposed to, pronouns do not occur after verbs. They are therefore in a situation where they are not perceiving clause-internal pronouns because this is a perceptually non-salient position, but they are perceiving the absence of pronouns in post verbal, clause-final position. This will lead them, perhaps, to assume that unstressed object pronouns are not represented overtly in French, and will lead to the second stage of development. In the next phase of development, learners begin to be able to perceive that pronouns occur clause-internally, but perhaps under some notion of continuity they prefer at first to place them directly next to the verb which governs them. This will give rise to the third stage of development. In the final stage, learners attach them appropriately to the tense-marked verb.

Again, however, it is no less plausible to offer a similar account on the basis of properties of UG. Following an initial stage where learners assume that the order of unstressed object pronouns in French follows the canonical 'head first–complement last' parameter setting for French word order, they notice that in the samples of language they are exposed to pronouns do not in fact appear to the right of verbal heads. In the face of this conflict between presumed parameter setting and input, one possibility is that learners initially hypothesise, on the basis of the absence of phonetically specified pronouns in this position, that French has object *pro*: recall from Chapter 7 that *pro* is a normal referential pronoun with all the properties of referential pronouns except phonetic content: i.e. it is a null pronoun. Null object pronouns are permissible within UG, and languages vary parametrically as to whether V° licenses object *pro* or does not license object *pro* (Rizzi, 1986). Although in English V° does not license *pro*, it is possible that English-speaking learners of L2

French assume that French V° has been set to license *pro* on the basis of the absence of postverbal pronouns. Indeed, French does license object *pro* in the restricted environment of an object pronoun with arbitrary reference (that is, where it refers to unspecified persons or things, in the way that English 'one' or 'you' do sometimes) as in (8.3).

8.3 *Cet entraîneur force* pro *à se lever tôt.* (Example from Authier, 1991.)
   This coach forces you to get up early.

Subsequently learners begin to notice clause-internal affixes in just those contexts where they have assumed that there are *pro* object pronouns. They may initially treat these as some kind of agreement affix, agreeing with object *pro*, just as forms like -s agree with a third person singular subject in English: 'she eat -s'. This leads them to construct sentences such as those in (8.4).

8.4a *Je [le + reconnais]* pro.
   b *J'ai [le + reconnu]* pro.

Eventually, however, they come to realise that the affix is in fact a pronoun which has moved from the canonical post-head position for complements in French to adjoin to the tense-marked verb in the clause.

Again there is little to decide between these two stories of what happens in so far as they provide some account for the facts. They are both rather informal and speculative. However, the UG-based approach is considerably more interesting on the level of theoretical simplicity, because it is based on constructs such as 'the head position parameter' and 'object *pro*', which are independently required in the description of the world's languages. In the case of the perceptually based account appeal has to be made additionally to poorly understood notions such as saliency, and the continuity of perceptual material.

Again, though, the UG-based account begs at least one question: why aren't learners able to recognise the preverbal location of pronouns in French as soon as they notice that they are absent postverbally? It is not clear whether this hiatus between the initial hypothesis, and the eventual acquisition of preverbal pronouns in French can appropriately be explained within UG.

As a final example, consider again the developmental stages that L1 Romance-language-speaking and English-speaking learners of L2 German go through in the acquisition of German word order. In Chapter 4 we described a cognitive account of this development. Consider now how a UG-based account might handle the same phenomena.[2]

The phenomena in need of explanation are:

(a) why, following an initial SVO stage where the tense-marked verb and any participle, infinitive or particle are adjacent, the first stage is the separation of the tense-marked verb from this latter item, and its placement at the end of the clause, for example:

8.5a *Ich bin gegangen ins Kino* → *Ich bin ins Kino gegangen*

(b) why verb second (V2) comes next, for example:

b *Gestern ich bin ins Kino gegangen* → *Gestern bin ich ins Kino gegangen*

(c) why verb final in subordinate clauses is the last property to be acquired.

As was argued in Chapter 6, all three properties would appear to follow from the interaction of two parameter settings: the first is that the German VP is head-final, i.e. OV (unlike Romance languages and English in which the VP is head-first (VO)); the second is that the value of C° in German is fixed to attract the tensed verb in all root clauses, unlike the Romance languages and English, in which the value of C° is fixed to attract the tensed verb only in questions (and with certain specific adverbial items in some of these languages, e.g. English: 'Never would I have believed it'; French: *Sans doute sera-t-elle heureuse*, 'Doubtless she will be happy', and so on).

Romance-language-speaking and English-speaking learners of L2 German therefore have to reset parameters in order to get German word order right. But recall that it was argued in Chapter 7 that L2 learners have considerable difficulty in accessing parameters in order to reset them. Suppose that learners are initially not able to reset either the head position or C° parameters. At the same time they become aware that, in the samples of language they are exposed to, non-tense-marked verbal elements appear at the end of the clause. To deal with this conflict between the setting of the head position parameter in their L2 grammars and a surface ordering of participles/infinitives/particles, they reorder the verbal complex by a non-parametric adjunction operation. This operation moves a participle/infinite/particle from its D-structure position to the right across the complement to the verb, adjoining it to the VP, as in (8.6).

8.6 *Ich bin gegangen ins Kino.*

↓

Ich [[bin ec$_i$ ins Kino] gegangen$_i$].

This is an operation which is permissible within UG (it is an adjunction to a maximal projection — VP in this case), it does not involve the resetting of the head parameter and is analogous to the operation known as heavy NP shift, described in Chapter 7. In that case a complement to a V° was moved across a clause final constituent for stylistic purposes (to avoid a 'light' constituent like an adverb following a 'heavier' complement to a verb). We also argued that the same adjunction to VP operation was what English-speaking learners of L2 French used to accommodate French adverb placement between verbs and their complements without having to reset the verb movement parameter from its English to its French value. By using adjunction to VP, L2 learners of German would be able to produce verb separation without having to reset the head position parameter. The fact that verb separation emerges as the first stage of development would then follow because it is the one operation in the acquisition of German word order which does not require parameter resetting.

In a subsequent phase learners do appear to reset both the value for C°, so that it attracts the tense-marked verb, and the head position parameter, so that the D-structure position of V° is clause final. It might be suggested that the reason why C° is reset before the head position parameter is reset has to do with frequency of positive evidence in the input that learners receive. If parameters are difficult to reset for L2 learners, one might expect that a considerable amount of positive evidence is necessary before they are in a position to reset. In the case of verb-second, which is a root clause phenomenon, there will be evidence from very many samples of language that learners are exposed to. By contrast, subordinate clauses are generally less frequent than root clauses, and in the spoken varieties of most languages are very infrequent indeed. The order verb-second → verb-final could, then, be an effect of input frequency.

The latter is clearly a language-faculty-external factor, however. Input frequency has nothing to do with the structure of UG. And again, an area of development in SLA emerges which is likely to be beyond the explanatory power of UG.

Summary

We have been arguing in this chapter that attempts to explain the developmental problem in SLA on the basis of the role that UG plays in the construction of L2 grammars are to be preferred over attempts at explanations which cite other cognitive factors. This is on the grounds of theoretical simplicity: it is beyond doubt that a theory of linguistic structure (Universal Grammar) will be necessary in a theory of language acquisition anyway. If accounts of the developmental problem in SLA can be given as consequences of UG, then only one, rather than more than one, theoretical construct need be invoked.

At the same time, in the consideration of concrete examples of staged development in SLA, certain areas begin to emerge where it is not at all clear that UG will be able to offer an explanation: as for example where input frequency plays a role. In the next chapter we shall consider a pervasive factor in SLA development — variability — which seems to fall wholly outside of the explanatory possibilities of UG. This will lead us into a more general consideration of the interaction of linguistic knowledge and language use in SLA.

Notes

1. A more likely account is that unstressed object pronouns attach not to a verbal element *per se*, but either to T°, or perhaps to Agr°. Although this shows up at the surface in French as an apparent attachment to a verbal element, because T° and Agr° inflections are 'picked up' by a verb, in a language such as Italian there appear to be cases where unstressed object pronouns are not attached to a verbal element even at the surface:

   Parlar [*gli* + Agr°] *sarebbe un errore.*
   To speak to-him   would be an error.

   See Kayne (1989: 241) for discussion.
2. For alternative UG-based accounts of the developmental stages in the acquisition of German word order see duPlessis *et al.* (1987), and Schwartz & Tomaselli (1988).

9 Parametric Variation, Variability and the Limits of the Explanatory Power of Universal Grammar in Second Language Acquisition

Throughout their development, and even into advanced stages, L2 learners are characteristically variable in their performance in the L2. By 'variable' we mean specifically that they use two or more variants of a particular grammatical property where native speakers of the target variety use only one, and where the samples of language that the L2 learners are exposed to display only one version of the grammatical property. For example, the cases given in (9.1) illustrate variability of this sort in the English of L2 learners.

9.1 *Non-native variability*

	Native speaker invariance
I *no* like it/I *don't* like it.	I *don't* like it.
Where *you are* going?/Where *are you* going?	Where *are you* going?
I read Ø book/I read *a* book.	I'm reading *a* book.
He eat-Ø in restaurant/He eats in restaurant	He eats at the restaurant.

Variability of this sort seems to take the same form across learners generally: that is, many L2 learners of English go through a phase where they alternate between 'no' and 'don't' to mark sentence negation, many go through a phase where they alternate subject-auxiliary verb inversion and non-inversion in questions, and so on. A number of the grammatical constructions that we have previously considered in this part of the book are also subject to variability in SLA. For example, in the acquisition of the unstressed preverbal object pronouns of standard European French, intermediate level English-speaking learners typically go through a phase where they alternate target-language placement as in *je l'ai reconnu*, 'I recognised him', and non-target language attachment of the pronoun to the past participle, as in: *J'ai le reconnu*.

Hulk (1991) in her study of the acquisition of L2 French by native speakers of Dutch also notes a stage when learners are variable. Dutch is a strict verb-second language, as is German, which means that whatever appears in the specifier of CP in root clauses — the subject, adverbials or other constituents — the verb must appear in second position under C°, for example, as in (9.2).

9.2a *Jan heeft aardbeien gegeten.*
   John has strawberries eaten.
   b *Gisteren heeft Jan aardbeien gegeten.*
   Yesterday has John strawberries eaten.

and so on. By contrast, French, like English, allows only verb-second in wh- questions, and not in declarative root clauses; in most declarative root sentences the verb appears to the right of the subject, whether adverbials or other categories are fronted or not; see (9.3).

9.3a *Jean a mangé des fraises.*
   b *Hier Jean a mangé des fraises.*

Hulk found that at one stage of development and 'for quite a long time' (p. 28) her subjects allowed, variably, both verb-second and non-verb-second in root sentences in their L2 French, where native speakers allow only non-verb-second constructions.

Following the line of argument adopted in the preceding chapters, ideally one would want to account for such variability as a function of the constraints imposed on language acquisition by UG. The reason for this is theoretical simplicity. UG is required independently of variability to account for the structural properties of the world's languages. If it can be shown that variability in SLA follows as a consequence of the particular way that UG operates in SLA, such an account would be preferred over one which has to invoke a theory additional to UG.

Can UG be deployed in this way to give an account of variability in SLA? We think it is implausible, in view of what is known about variability (described below). More plausible is the possibility that variability arises at the point where L2 grammatical knowledge becomes involved with real-time language comprehension and production (i.e. in language use).

Consider some of the characteristics of variability which need to be taken into account in exploring this issue. It seems that variability in SLA can take two forms: systematic and non-systematic. Systematic variability occurs where one variant of a grammatical property used by a learner is consistently found in one set of environments, and the other variant(s) in a different set of environments. For example, suppose that a learner of L2 French consistently writes *je l'ai reconnu*, where the pronoun *le* appears before the tense-marked verb, but equally consistently says *j'ai le reconnu*, where the pronoun appears to the left of the participle. This would be a case of systematic variability.

Ellis (1988) has observed a subject who marked third person, singular, present tense verbs with the affix -s when the subject of the clause was a pronoun, e.g. 'He eat-s turkey', but tended not to add the -s inflection when the subject was a noun phrase, e.g. 'John eat-ø turkey'. This is a case of systematic variability.

Hulstijn & Hulstijn (1984) in their study of learners of L2 Dutch, which we described in Chapter 2, found that their subjects, when asked to retell stories while focusing on the grammatical accuracy of what they were saying, were significantly more likely to produce embedded clauses in which the tense-marked verb was clause final (correct for Dutch) than they were when they were asked to retell stories and focus on the accuracy of the information in what they were saying. In the latter condition they would place the tense-marked verb in non-final position in embedded clauses. This, too, is a case of systematic variability.

On the other hand, non-systematic variability occurs where a learner uses two or more variants apparently interchangeably in a given context under the same conditions. Ellis (1985b) observed an L1 Portuguese-speaking learner of L2 English who, during a game of cards, produced both 'No look my card' and 'Don't look my card' under exactly the same conditions. Here the alternation 'no'/'don't' would appear to be free, i.e. non-systematic.

Second, it has been found that systematic variability correlates with two factors: context of utterance and linguistic context. In the case of context of utterance, one variant is used by the L2 learner when performing one kind of task in the L2, and another when the learner is performing a different kind of task. The example of variability in the production of verb final in Dutch embedded clauses observed by Hulstijn & Hulstijn falls into this category.

In the case of linguistic context, one variant appears in one linguistic environment, and another in a different linguistic environment. An example of this is Ellis's observation that in the grammar of one learner of L2 English, third person, present singular -s appears in the context of a pronominal subject, while -Ø appears in the context of a nominal subject.

Another example is provided in a study undertaken by Roger Hawkins (1990). A grammaticality judgement task was administered to a group of nine English-speaking learners of L2 French. The test contained tokens of unstressed object pronouns occupying both grammatical and ungrammatical positions in sentences, and in a range of different linguistic contexts, along with a number of other sentences displaying different grammatical phenomena. It was found that 100% of subjects accepted grammatical pronoun placement in simple declarative sentences such as (9.4a). At the same time, 100% of subjects rejected ungrammatical pronoun placement in the same simple declarative sentence type (9.4b), suggesting that they were performing in a native-like way on pronoun placement.

9.4a *Il l'a consulté au moins une fois par semaine.*
   He consulted him at least once a week.

   b **Il a le consulté au moins une fois par semaine.*

But when the pronoun subject of the sentence was replaced by a clause (a sentential subject), the proportion of subjects who accepted the object pronoun in its grammatical position preceding a tense-marked verb fell to 55.6%, and the proportion of subjects who rejected the object pronoun in an ungrammatical position preceding a past participle also fell to 44.6%. This suggests that around half of the subjects studied have a grammar for French which allows both [*le* + *avoir* + past participle], and [*avoir* + *le* + past participle], where the first variant appears in the context of 'simple' subjects such as pronouns, and the second variant in the context of 'heavy' subjects such as clauses.

9.5a *[Que sa femme ait arrangé pour lui une visite au théâtre] l'a vexé énormément.*
   That his wife had arranged a visit to the theatre for him annoyed him enormously.

   b **[Que sa femme ait arrangé pour lui une visite au théâtre] a le vexé énormément.*

Few studies have attempted to offer an account of variability from a UG-based perspective. One exception is duPlessis *et al.* (1987) in their consideration of the development of word order in L2 German. They investigated the L2 German of 28 third level (advanced) English-speaking German language students (average age 19–20 years) at McGill University.

Data were collected from essays written by the subjects. DuPlessis *et al.* found that in root clauses some of their subjects varied between the two types of sentence illustrated in (9.6) (via examples which will by now be familiar).

9.6a *Gestern bin ich ins Kino gegangen.* (Correct in target German.)
      Yesterday have I to the cinema gone.

  b *Gestern ich bin ins Kino gegangen.* (Incorrect in target German.)
      Yesterday I have to the cinema gone.

When using adverbs at the front of a clause these subjects were alternating between: (a) the verb second construction of (9.6a) in which the I° constituent (*bin*) moves from its D-structure position in the IP into the position under C°, and the adverb *gestern* moves into the specifier of

9.7a

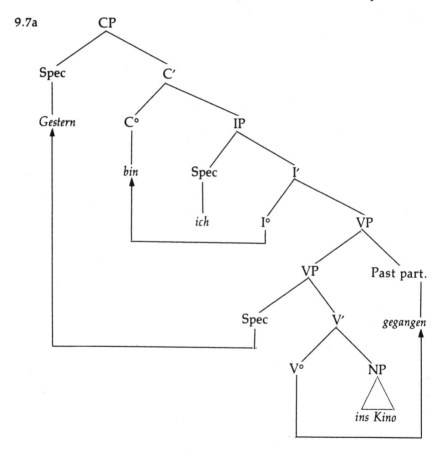

9.7b

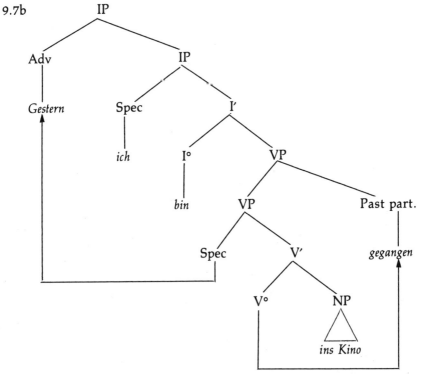

CP position, and (b) an SVO construction of the kind used in English where an adverb is adjoined to the IP, without any movement into a CP. These structural differences between the two constructions are illustrated in the tree diagrams of (9.7), where, following our previous analysis of English speakers' early grammatical representations for German word order, the D-structure of the clause is SVO, and the past participle is moved to clause final position by an adjunction to VP operation (see Chapter 8).

Subjects also varied between the two types of embedded clause structure illustrated in (9.8).

9.8a *Er glaubt, dass ich ins Kino gegangen bin.* (Correct in target German.)
  He thinks that I to the cinema gone have.

  b *Er glaubt, dass ich bin ins Kino gegangen.* (Incorrect in target German.)
  He thinks that I have to the cinema gone.

The structural differences between these two sentence types are illustrated in (9.9).

9.9a

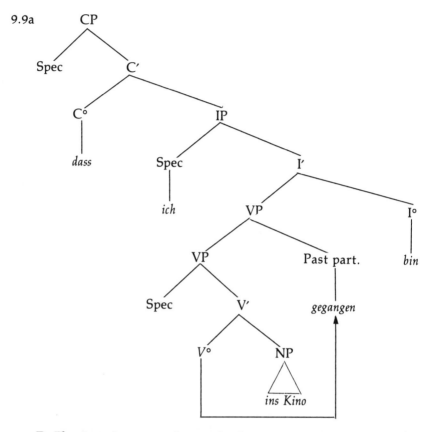

DuPlessis *et al.* suggest that in the first case, (9.6), the possibility of having both adverb fronting with verb-second, and adverb fronting with SVO, is allowed within UG, and can be found in particular languages: they cite Spanish as a language which allows both possibilities. As it happens, neither German nor English allow them to co-occur, each language having chosen a different option. At the same time, English-speaking learners of L2 German develop an L2 grammar which allows both. One explanation that might be given for this is that learners initially transfer the SVO option from English, but when they encounter evidence in German for verb-second, they are conservative about abandoning their initial hypothesis, and since UG allows a language to have both possibilities, this is the option they select. We therefore have a UG-based account of the variation involved, without apparently having to appeal to factors beyond the language faculty.

At the same time, however, the second case, (9.8), is considerably

9.9b

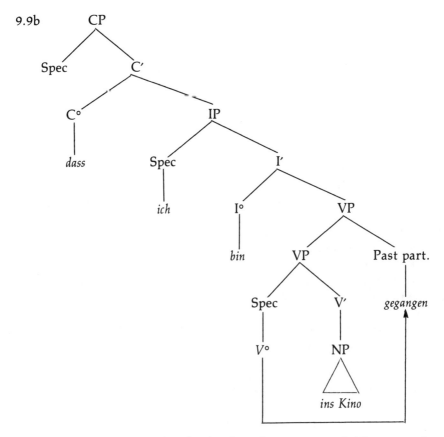

more problematic for this kind of explanation, as duPlessis *et al.* themselves note. In (9.8), as the structural representation in (9.9) shows, subjects are alternating between an SVOI word order (9.9a) and an SIVO word order (9.9b). That is, they are varying on the head position for the same category, I°. Now, the parameter which determines head position is standardly assumed to have exclusive values (either head first or head last, but not both). Even in languages with mixed orders, if there is a head which goes in a direction opposite to the canonical ordering, for example if a language has predominantly head last but has, say, prepositions which are head first (i.e. [P° complement]), this ordering difference seems to affect the whole class of items belonging to the category in question. One would not expect the same category to be able to display both head first and head last options. In the case of (9.8), however, the L2 learners seem to be alternating on head position within the category I°. To account for their behaviour on the basis of UG, one would have to claim that learners' grammars simultaneously allow both settings of the same parameter, a messy result, as duPlessis *et al.* (1987: 71) note: 'although theoretically messy, we may have to assume a period of transition between parameter settings'. Similar patterns of variability were found in a study by duPlessis (1986) of the L2 acquisition of Afrikaans (also a verb-second language) by English speakers, and in Hulk's (1991) study of Dutch learners of French referred to above.

We have, then, something of a problem here for UG-based explanations in the form of variability where learners would be expected to have grammars which instantiate either one parameter setting or the other, but not both. This seems to require appeal to a notion of 'period of transition' between one parameter setting and another in development in SLA. But period of transition is rather more a notion relating to cognitive development than to UG. Even the account of duPlessis *et al.* of the alternation in root clauses illustrated in (9.6) is not very convincing. While UG might allow both possibilities to occur in principle, why should English-speaking learners of L2 German opt to retain both possibilities in their L2 grammars? It is dubious to argue that they might get conflicting evidence from German, since German categorically requires verb second in root clauses. Again learners seem to have grammars which are in a period of transition. One possibility is to suggest that learners are conservative, preferring not to abandon an earlier grammatical represen-tation unless they have to. They do not have to in this case because UG allows them to retain the old and the new within the same grammar. But conservatism of this type leading to a period of transition would again seem to be a factor of more general cognition rather than a notion of UG.

Similarly, it is difficult to see how a UG-based account could provide an explanation of the kind of correlation between alternating variants and the linguistic task that the subject is undertaking, as found in the study by Hulstijn & Hulstijn (1984), or the correlation between alternating variants and linguistic context, as found in the studies of Hawkins (1990) and Ellis (1988). Variability of this sort is not isolated. It is a pervasive feature of L2 grammars. Tarone (1988) has devoted a book to the topic. It seems that while UG allows us to characterise the structural properties of the variants which enter into such variable relationships in SLA, in many cases it does not seem to be in a position to offer an explanation for the source of such variability.

Variability goes together with certain other aspects of development in SLA that were beginning to emerge in our discussion in Chapter 8: for example strategies used by L2 learners to avoid the violation of invariant principles of UG (e.g. the deletion of prepositions in wh- constructions in L2 English to avoid violating the Empty Category Principle), and certain kinds of staged development which seem to be an effect of input frequency (e.g. the order in which speakers of null subject languages acquire referential, quasi argument and expletive pronouns in L2 English). Strategies used by learners and frequency of input are not factors which fall within the domain of UG.

There is a cluster of phenomena of this sort which are part and parcel of SLA, but which do not appear to be readily amenable to an explanation which treats them as consequences of the organisation of UG. Another case is formulaic language as used by L2 learners. Formulae are apparently unanalysed, or only partially analysed, chunks of language which L2 learners use in a range of functions. For example, Huebner (1980) (cited in Larsen-Freeman & Long, 1991) studied a learner who used the chunk *waduyu* as a generalised wh- word, as in (9.10).

9.10 Waduyu kam from? (Where are you from?)
      Waduyu kam? (Why did you come?)
      Waduyu sei? (What did you say?)

Formulae are in some sense a use of language prior to the development of UG-guided grammatical representations, and some account is needed of their role in SLA. The general clustering of variability, strategies, input frequency and formulaic language would appear to fall most readily within the domain of theories of language use, a topic which we consider next.

Summary

Variability occurs in L2 development where there is no evidence for it in the target language. The most parsimonious account of such variability would suggest that it follows from the interaction of UG with the primary linguistic data that the learner encounters. However, this line of account seems implausible in that many cases of variability involve variation between exclusive values of a parameter within the mental grammar of the same learner, for example between verb-second and non-verb-second in the case of L2 German. To admit that speakers can freely alternate between the two exclusive values of a parameter goes against the spirit of the principles and parameters approach to language. It is theoretically 'messy'.

More plausible is that variability arises at the point where L2 grammatical knowledge becomes involved in language use, and this idea is compatible with the fact that variability correlates with performance factors like the type of linguistic task the learner is engaged in, or the complexity of the surrounding linguistic context. There are also other features of development in SLA which appear to fall outside the explanatory power of UG, and require a different kind of explanation: features such as hypothesis-creation in those areas where UG is inaccessible or inapplicable, the effects of different kinds of input, the effect of language processing, the use by learners of formulaic language, and learner strategies.

10 Explanations of Variability

In Chapters 2–4 we described a number of approaches which have been adopted to explain SLA: the contrastive analysis hypothesis, Krashen's (1985) hypotheses including the monitor theory, models with a strong sociolinguistic dimension such as Tarone's (1983) capability continuum and Ellis's (1985b) variable competence model, and models with a strong cognitive bias such as that illustrated by Wolfe Quintero's (1992) treatment of the acquisition of wh-questions based on learning principles. We argued that, for a number of reasons, these approaches were 'incomplete' or 'mysterious' or 'circular'. The argument was based largely on the view that they neglected to take into account what is known about the nature of language structure and therefore deprived themselves of information which is essential for any explanation of SLA.

In Chapters 5–9 we set out to show the critical importance of linguistic structure in understanding the issues. We argued that transfer, staged development, cross-learner systematicity and incompleteness can be explained to quite a large extent in relation to the influence of UG and the transfer of L1 parameter settings.

These two factors will not, however, provide a sufficient basis to enable us to understand how the learner might acquire the totality of the L2 and the ability to use it consistently in real-time in communicative situations. UG, in essence, prevents the learner from entertaining hypotheses which are not part of human language and prompts the learner to expect specific relationships to be operating within that part of the system to which it relates. The L1 parameter settings may be transferred and perhaps reset with greater or lesser success (see Chapters 6 and 7).

Beyond these (considerable) resources, the learner may make use of general cognitive skills to construct a knowledge of and an ability to use a working L2 on the basis of the empirical data provided by the environment in which the learner is placed. To look at these processes we have to examine those dimensions of the SLA process which fall mainly outside the domain of linguistic theory. In terms of our five initial 'observable phenomena of second language acquisition', we will be concerned here with a broadly defined concept of variability.

In the first part of this chapter we will critically discuss five approaches to the explanation of variability. We will propose that these can be reduced to three main questions for further investigation. That investigation requires a number of concepts from psychology and studies of human information processing: these will be introduced in the second part of the chapter. Chapters 11, 12 and 13 will then deal with each of the main questions in turn. In Chapter 14 we will seek to bring together the threads of the argument in a single model.

Variability is a Pervasive Phenomenon

In contrast to studies of L1 acquisition, variability is a recurrent theme in L2 acquisition studies, even those usually associated with the demonstration of systematicity. The morpheme order research is usually cited in the literature in order to demonstrate the existence of the natural order. The evidence is based on the use of large groups and on the use of statistics to state group averages. The raw data has had little exposure but Rosansky (1976) showed that the performance of individuals on the tests was extremely variable. Subsequent responses (Krashen, 1977b; J. Anderson, 1978) have perhaps resolved Rosansky's initial doubts about the statistical validity of the group means but the examination of individual data demonstrates that group means can conceal individual variability. Work by Larsen-Freeman (1975) compared the morpheme orders in data gathered from adults with different linguistic backgrounds on the basis of the Bilingual Syntax Measure (Burt, Dulay & Hernandez-Chavez, 1975) with the morpheme order in data from the same adults gathered using other tasks (notably in reading and writing tasks). The results showed that there were different orders on the different tasks. Both contributions demonstrate that even in the evidence most associated with the natural order hypothesis, variability is present at the level of individual learners either within the single task (BSM) or across tasks. The difficulty lies in assessing the contribution of each of the many potential causal factors which could give rise to such evidence. We will now examine five of these.

Variability caused by differences in cognitive abilities and learning environments

One main potential causal factor is the fact that learners come to L2 learning at different ages and therefore with different cognitive abilities. It is obvious that older learners have greater general cognitive capacities than very young children and it would be surprising if that fact in itself did not modify the learning process (Bley-Vroman, 1989). As was mentioned in Chapters 5 and 8, arguments have been sustained which suggest that young children may have very special mental capacities which are specifically attuned to language learning and that once these have been applied to the learning of the L1, they are not available in the same way for the L2 (Felix, 1987; Felix & Weigl, 1991).

Equally obvious are the environmental differences applicable to L1 and L2 learning: a baby learning L1 is typically surrounded by adults, one or more of whom is likely to be constantly attending to the baby's needs. The baby can devote unlimited amounts of time to language learning. L2 learners may be exposed to the L2 in very different ways, none of which is as rich as the L1 environment. They range from simple exposure to the language in the country with no explicit instruction, to a total lack of contact with the language in the country where it is spoken and a complete reliance on instruction in a classroom setting. Time devoted to language learning is likely to be quite limited and will compete with other activities.

Differences in general cognitive capacities and in learning environment are bound to lead to significant differences between L1 and L2 learning. L2 learners have several knowledge sources on which they may call. Variability may thus be a product of the interaction of language which has been constructed on the basis of different kinds of underlying knowledge. A particular phrase for a particular learner, for example, may be a remembered whole taken directly from the authentic situation or the classroom where it was first heard. The same phrase for another learner, or for the same learner at a later stage, may be a product of developed generative mechanisms.

Variability caused by the demands of different tasks

Variability across tasks has been demonstrated in work by Lococo (1976) in comparative tests using free composition, picture description and translation to examine a variety of syntactic structures. Hyltenstam (1983) studied the learning of pronominal copies in relative clauses (e.g.

*'The man *who* I met *him* yesterday comes here'), of sentence negation and subject–verb inversion in declarative main clauses by learners of Swedish as a second language. He elicited data through grammaticality judgement tests, picture identification, oral production, written compositions and imitation. The results showed considerable variation under the different elicitation conditions. Hyltenstam suggests that there probably is no single cause for this variation but allows for the possibilities of 'stylistic variation', 'degrees of formality' or 'mode of linguistic processing' (Hyltenstam, 1983: 60) as possible causal factors. He notes (p. 72), however, 'that there is a great deal of individual variation regarding what tasks a given learner can handle'. As noted in Chapter 3, Ellis (1987b) examined the use of tenses in written narrative. He asked the same learners to undertake three separate tasks: to write a narrative story based on a picture composition, to relate the same story orally in a language laboratory with the benefit of having already undertaken the written task and to relate a different story in the language laboratory with only a few minutes' warning. The ability to maintain continuity of tenses was shown to vary consistently with the circumstances of the task.

The evidence for task-based variability is well-established. The causes of it are not, however, well understood. Bialystok (1982, 1990a) has stressed the different demands called for by different tasks and attempted to plot them on charts according to the extent to which they call for 'analysed' knowledge or 'controlled' knowledge (see Chapters 11 and 13). Others have indicated the important differences between activities where the learner is focused on form as opposed to meaning (Krashen, 1988; Hulstijn & Hulstijn, 1984). Further task-based issues concern time and medium. A learner with time can select and plan an utterance; a learner required to produce language quickly cannot. Written language is normally the result of a certain amount of reflection, oral language has to be produced without time to reflect. Tasks which demand real-time comprehension and production require that linguistic knowledge should be available in such a way as to permit fast access and not all of a learner's language may be stored in an appropriate manner. Differences in this storage may give rise to significantly variable performance on different tasks.

Variability caused by variable focus of attention

Other studies have stressed the importance of the focus of attention of the learner. It is claimed that the more the learner is paying attention to the form of the language, the more likely he or she is to use the correct form and vice versa (always assuming, of course, that the correct form is known). Early studies of oral production building on the evidence of L1 differences provided by Labov (1970) showed this to be the case: some of the clearest evidence came from phonological or phonetic studies. Dickerson (1975) and Dickerson & Dickerson (1977) showed that Japanese learners of English pronounce /r/ much better in word lists than they do in reading dialogues and better in reading dialogues than they do in free speech. R.W. Schmidt (1977) working with native Arabic speakers similarly showed a systematically declining progression going from minimal pairs to word lists to reading a passage. Researchers interested in this area suggest that the learner's attention is focused on the form of the language in exercises such as minimal pairs whereas less concentrated activities permit more diffuse attention or allow it to be focused elsewhere. The more the learner's attention is focused on the form, the more likely he or she is to get it right. This simple explanation has, however, not always been confirmed by experimental results.

Tarone (1985), who was initially attracted by the Labovian concept of 'attention to form' as an explanation for the variability found in learner language, decided, on the basis of empirical evidence, that this alone was insufficient. Her results using grammaticality judgement tests, oral interview and oral narrative did not reveal for each of the four items tested the expected progression from the grammaticality judgement tests, where considerable attention was presumably being paid to form, to the spontaneous oral narrative. In some cases, the order was exactly the opposite with the weakest performance coming on the grammaticality judgement test. In addition, the same pattern of variability was not present for each of the forms tested. Using evidence from Huebner (1985) as a guide, Tarone then examined the data in more detail in order to establish exactly which forms were being used differentially. She discovered that the differences were attributable in large part to those forms which performed a particularly important role in maintaining the communicative flow and cohesion in the narrative task. She therefore felt that, in addition to 'attention to form', the 'communicative pressure to be clear' (Tarone, 1985) played a functional role in determining the pattern of variability.

Variability caused by the use of formulaic language

Ellis (1984a) refers to another way in which learners' language can vary. He notes the ability of learners to produce certain utterances which go beyond the set of rules which they hold at a given time. Examples which he cites (Ellis, 1984a: 69) include stylistic formulas such as 'Can I have rubber/colour/etc., please' to request goods from a teacher or another pupil and gambits such as 'This one or this one?' when asked to identify the nature of a classroom task. When a learner produces utterances of this kind, he or she may not be creating the structure of the utterance on the basis of productive grammatical rules but instead producing a complete unit which is more or less fixed in its form.

Most researchers into L1 and L2 acquisition have indicated that they are aware of the presence in their data of a number of utterances which cannot be explained in terms of the generative potential which the speakers have at that stage. Brown & Hanlon (1970: 50–51) studying English L1 acquisition state:

> We suggest that any form that is produced with very high frequency by parents will be somehow represented in the child's performance even if its structure is far beyond him. He will find a way to render a version of it and will also form a notion of the circumstances in which it is used. The construction will become lodged in his speech as an unassimilated fragment. Extensive use of such a fragment probably protects it, for a time, from a reanalysis when the structure relevant to it is finally learned.

Peters (1977), who set out to study what she calls the 'analytic' speech development of a learner, found that the density of these 'ready-made sentences' or formulaic constructions was such that she had to revise her whole research strategy to cope with what she calls 'Gestalt' language. L.W. Fillmore (1976, 1979) working on the learning of five individuals felt that their use of formulaic language was probably the most important element in the growth of linguistic knowledge. Hakuta (1976), Huang & Hatch (1978) and Hanania & Gradman (1977) have also stressed the importance of these forms. Pawley & Hodgetts-Syder (1983) have even suggested that memorised sequences require a special place in any grammar, native and non-native. Ellis (1956) shows formulaic language as a continuing contributor to all levels of his Variable Competence Model. Krashen (1988) thinks of these formulas as the learner's way of 'outperforming his competence'. There seems little room for doubt, therefore, that formulaic language exists in all kinds of learner language.

The difficulty is in assessing its significance in SLA and its contribution to an explanation of variability.

Variability caused by the use of strategies

The notion that learners may find ways of outperforming their competence introduces a final element into this presentation of the evidence related to variability. Krashen and Ellis suggest that learners do so by learning formulaic utterances: others suggest that they also do so by a series of communication or compensatory strategies. These are means by which learners resort to a variety of devices to convey a message when that message is beyond what can immediately be communicated by their existing interlanguage. Tarone, Cohen & Dumas (1976: 6–7) show how transfer from the native language, overgeneralisation, the use of prefabricated patterns, overelaboration, avoidance, appeal to authority, paraphrase, message abandonment and language switch can all be seen to be used at the phonological, morphological, syntactic and lexical levels of linguistic organisation to overcome a communication 'gap'. Faerch & Kasper (1983) provide a similar set of examples and classify them into 'reduction' and 'achievement' strategies. Bialystok (1990a), O'Malley & Chamot (1990) and Poulisse (1990) have each provided book-length treatments of the use of strategies. As we shall see in Chapter 13, many early approaches to strategies showed a tendency to be satisfied with classifications which were often subsequently found to be arbitrary. In recent years, however, rather better theoretical foundations have been provided and have rendered the area worthy of serious consideration once again.

Three explanations for variability

As can be seen from this brief review of approaches to the understanding of variability, it is a complex phenomenon which can variously be attributed to differences in cognitive ability among learners of different ages, differences in the knowledge sources provided by different learning environments, differences in the demands of various tasks, the learner's variable focus of attention, the learner's ability to learn formulaic utterances and to invent ingenious ways of compensating for lack of knowledge.

Rather than pursue each of these avenues, we shall argue in the rest of this book that variability can best be understood in relation to three separable but interrelated aspects of SLA. Briefly, these are the learner's need to:

- use data from multiple sources of knowledge to construct and revise hypotheses, especially about those aspects of the L2 system which are not directly guided by UG nor provided by the successful transfer of the L1 parameter-settings
- turn the knowledge of the L2 into procedures which will allow the processing of language in real-time comprehension and production
- communicate adequately with other users of the L2 despite the inadequacies of the second linguistic system possessed at any given time.

As indicated in Chapter 9, these three aspects can be seen to operate mainly in areas not covered by the scope of UG-based linguistic theory.

They can be expressed initially here in the form of three questions. These questions will form the starting point for each of chapters 11, 12 and 13 respectively and they are:

1. In addition to hypotheses about the L2 provided by UG and successful transfer from the L1, how can learners construct and revise hypotheses on the basis of data provided by different learning environments? What effect does this have on language acquisition and variability?
2. Given the need to process language in real-time, how do learners develop a real-time production and comprehension ability and what effect does this have on language acquisition and variability?
3. Given the need to communicate with inadequate resources, how do learners develop strategies to enable them to overcome difficulties and what effect does this have on language acquisition and variability?

In Chapter 11 we shall seek to address issues which are essential to the understanding of the process of hypothesis construction and revision. We will look to this area to provide an account of that kind of variability which might be attributable to different knowledge sources and differences in cognitive ability. The main issue will be the extent to which learners can derive hypotheses akin to those of native speakers from internal and external knowledge sources (see Zobl, 1992). The principal internal knowledge sources will be Universal Grammar and transfer of parameter settings from the L1. The principal external knowledge sources will be formal instruction and negative feedback on the one hand and exposure to formulaic language in authentic data on the other.

Our second major question, addressed in Chapter 12, concerns the consequences of the learner's need to develop an ability to process language in real-time comprehension and production. Kees de Bot (1992: 11) points out that given an average rate of speech of 150 words per minute, and a peak rate of 300 words per minute, we have 200 to 400 milliseconds to choose a word when we are speaking. We are choosing, at a conservative estimate of an active lexicon, one out of 30,000 items. We very rarely get it wrong and we are not at all aware of what we are doing. It is argued that for this to be possible the speech production system must rely on highly efficient automatised systems. How this ability is created is a matter for some debate. We will argue in Chapter 12 that the automatisation of linguistic knowledge takes place in a way which is related to but different from the creation of the linguistic system. Since Miller & McKean's (1964) early research showed that different numbers of the transformational rules proposed by linguists failed to produce a difference in the time needed to process sentences of different complexity, linguists have tended to insist on a separation between mental knowledge of the linguistic system and the mental mechanisms needed for processing language.

Building on that separation, we will argue that the mechanisms for processing language and the methods used to create those mechanisms in the mind may be different in kind from the processes used in the creation of linguistic systems. For example, while movement rules are posited as part of syntax, it does not follow that the learner actually 'moves' the syntactic element as part of language production or comprehension. Instead, the fluent speaker will possess what is called a 'procedure' or a 'production' (see below and Chapter 12) which will automatically be activated when the message the speaker wishes to convey calls for it. Learners have to develop this capability, which is separable from the knowledge of the L2 system, and learn to make use of it in different circumstances. This ability may be an application of a more general learning capability which relates to the learning of other kinds of knowledge, some of which has to be integrated with linguistic knowledge to permit language use. The issues discussed here will encompass the kinds of variability so far attributed to the demands of different tasks and will provide a different perspective on formulaic language. The main question will be the method by which learners automatise their linguistic knowledge so that it becomes available to them in a variety of circumstances.

The third question, addressed in Chapter 13, concerns the learner's need to communicate adequately with other users of the L2 despite the inadequacies of the linguistic system possessed at any given time. L2 users are confronted with a well-documented problem: certain elements of the language necessary for the expression of the meaning they can conceptualise and wish to convey are missing and yet they still have to get the message across as best they can. As a result they have recourse to a series of compensatory mechanisms. We will discuss that part of variability attributable to such strategies. We will also assess the extent to which these strategies can be deemed to contribute to the SLA process.

Our answers to the three questions depend to a considerable extent on an understanding of certain psychological concepts and models used in discussing human information processing and, before we can proceed further, these need to be introduced in the second part of this chapter.

Psychological Mechanisms

The arguments developed in Chapters 11, 12 and 13 depend on a certain number of concepts which are used in psychology when dealing with human information processing. In the second part of this chapter we wish to introduce these concepts and explain their potential relevance to this part of the acquisition process.

Two sets of important distinctions are widely accepted by psychologists. These have been outlined in papers by Shiffrin & Schneider (1977) and drawn to the attention of SLA researchers by writers such as McLaughlin (1987: 134). The first of these is that there are two memory stores, a short-term memory store (STM) and a long-term memory store (LTM). The second is that there are two kinds of processing, controlled and automatic. Learning, storage and production take place within this framework. Memory itself is 'conceived to be a large and permanent collection of nodes, which become complexly and increasingly inter-associated and interrelated through learning' (Shiffrin & Schneider, 1977: 155).

Short-term and long term memory, controlled and automatic processing

The short-term memory store consists of the set of nodes which are activated in memory at the same time. It is largely predetermined in its capacity; it can treat only a limited amount of information for a limited amount of time. The STM therefore allows the organism to carry out certain operations on relatively small amounts of information for a given time. Shiffrin & Schneider (1977: 157) call this: 'the provision of a work space for decision making, thinking and control processes in general'. Learning is essentially the transfer of patterns of activation from the short-term memory store to the long-term memory store in such a way that new associations are formed between information structures or nodes not previously associated.

The processes which govern these operations can be either controlled or automatic. Controlled processing requires that the subject pay attention to the processing while it is happening; automatic processing is carried out without that attention. Both offer certain advantages and disadvantages.

The advantage of controlled processing lies in the fact that processes may be created easily and quickly. They are under control and therefore may be adapted to fit any novel aspect of a situation. The disadvantage is that, because it requires subjects to pay attention to processing through the STM and consequently not to pay attention to other matters 'controlled processes are tightly capacity limited' (Shiffrin & Schneider, 1977: 156).

Automatic processing has the advantage of not being limited by the capacity limitations of STM and of not requiring the attention of the subject. The disadvantages of automatic processing lie in the fact that once initiated all processes will run to completion, that they require a lot of training to set up and that once learned they are difficult to modify. The kind of learning which is associated with improvement over a number of trials would normally be thought of as being linked to the development of automatic processes.

It can be seen that the two kinds of processing are complementary and can be productively combined. Sensory inputs are first encoded within the automatic processing system; they may subsequently be treated via controlled processing during which the subject will pay attention to them, thus enabling learning to take place before the knowledge can be stored as an automatic process. Shiffrin & Schneider (1977: 161) express the benefits of the two systems thus:

> In novel situations or in situations requiring moment-to-moment decisions, controlled processing may be adopted and used to perform accurately, though slowly. Then, as the situations become familiar,

always requiring the same sequence of processing operations, automatic processing will develop, attention demands will be eased, and controlled operations can be carried out in parallel with the automatic processing, and performance will improve.

The argument is that in this way efficient use is made of the limited capacity system. The limited attentional capacity is oriented to those aspects of processing which most need it when they most need it. Once aspects of the processing have been automatised, this 'allows the limited capacity system to be cleared and devoted to other types of processing necessary for new tasks' (Shiffrin & Schneider, 1977: 161). In particular: 'it allows the organism to learn increasingly complex modes of processing by building upon automatically learned sub-systems' (p. 162).

This conceptualisation of the processes is appealing when searching for an explanation of variability in SLA, as has been indicated by McLaughlin (1987: 136). It suggests that there might be a link between processing abilities and certain aspects of acquisition which could indirectly or directly contribute to various kinds of variability. The argument put forward here and developed later, especially in Chapter 12, is that the limited-capacity nature of working memory may influence both comprehension and production of an L2. Learners who continually have to rely to a large extent on controlled processes for comprehension and production, because they have not automatised some of their knowledge, may be limited in what they can achieve. Conversely, in so far as learners are able to make use of a large stock of automatised procedures for comprehension and production, they may have a greater potential for language acquisition.

As far as comprehension is concerned, the argument is that a learner who has to use up all the available space in working memory to extract meaning from data will not be able to pay attention to language form. In this sense the limitations imposed by short-term memory contribute indirectly to possible variability. Until the learner has made comprehension processes automatic, the ability to develop new hypotheses on the basis of empirical evidence will be reduced. Only when the learner can listen to the message and extract the meaning by a series of cost-free automatic processes will he or she be free to attend to the other information which is contained in the message, notably information about the form in which it is expressed. In Chapter 11 we shall discuss the need to create linguistic hypotheses from empirical data in certain areas of linguistic structure. It will be suggested that learners do this only when they are 'familiar' with the language in context. One of the reasons why this may be so is because only when 'familiarity' is achieved is the language 'automatised'. Only when it is automatised can learners find enough short-term memory space to explore aspects of the internal structure of the message. This is likely to be a continuing phenomenon which persists throughout L2 learning. However advanced the learner, there will always be parts of the system which have not been automatised. Because of this, learners will not be able to perceive the structures which may be visible to an outsider.

The argument about the potential significance of automatisation applies also on the production side. The ability of a speaker to make use of the language apparently 'known' in a variety of situations may depend on the extent to which that knowledge has been converted into automatised productions. Even when a learner knows a great deal 'about' the language, whether or not he or she is able to produce it in a situation where other cognitive demands have to be met will depend to a significant degree on whether or not that language knowledge is available in an appropriate form.

Pienemann (1985: 37) has suggested a relationship between processing ability and staged learning but it has been difficult to pin down exactly what is understood in his theory by processing ability. Harrington & Sawyer (1992) have stressed the importance of working memory in the development of L2 reading skills. Crookes (1991) and Schmidt (1992) have reviewed the potential significance of psychological mechanisms.

Before we are able to discuss this in detail in Chapter 12, we need to place the concepts of controlled and automatic processing within a more complete model of language production.

A model of language production

Automatised structures play a key role in the workings of a recent model of language production provided by Levelt (1989). His model is designed to provide a framework to account for language production by a mature, monolingual native speaker with a steady state grammar. However, with the help of de Bot (1992) it can be adapted to allow us to consider bilingual developmental aspects (see below). It is presented in Figure 10.1.

The model assumes the existence of two kinds of knowledge: procedural and declarative. In terms of our discussions so far, procedural knowledge is similar to automatised knowledge.

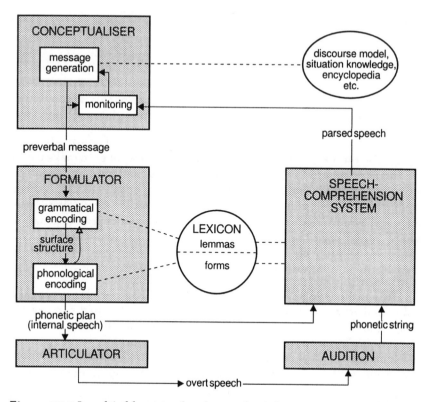

Figure 10.1 Levelt's 'blueprint for the speaker' showing major components of the 'Speaking' model.

Square boxes represent processing components and contain automatised productions, circle and ellipse represent declarative knowledge stores.

Source: Levelt, 1989: 9

Procedural knowledge is contained in the square boxes in the diagram and it is to do with 'how' something happens. In detailed specifications, it can be formulated as a series of condition/action pairs. These specify in detail the different stages which are gone through in achieving a certain goal. They take the form of statements, the first one of which begins IF (e.g. IF the intention is to commit oneself to the truth of 'p' . . .) and the second one of which begins THEN (e.g. THEN assert 'p'). The IF statement indicates the conditions under which the action is appropriate in relation to the goal; IF they apply, THEN the specified action is taken. The value of these pairs is that they enable goals and subgoals to be specified and combined in very detailed ways, thus breaking behaviour down into sequences of actions, none of which individually would overload the system (see Chapter 12 for examples).

In the case of language production and language comprehension by mature native speakers, these procedures are fully automatised. They are the mechanisms which ensure the speed of operation described above as being essential for fluent speech. They also determine the extent to which speakers have to pay attention to ('control') the speech: the more automatised the procedures, the less the need to devote attention to the form of language. In the course of speech, the procedures are activated and called into short-term memory. Because they are fully automatised they do not represent a cost on the memory space in STM: if they had to be controlled (as may be the case for a learner) then they would take up more of the limited space. Mature native speakers, Levelt argues, use their controlled knowledge ('executive control' in his terminology) to construct the message — i.e. in the conceptualiser — and not to formulate the syntax — i.e. in the formulator.

This brings us to the other kind of knowledge: declarative knowledge. This is knowledge 'that' and is shown in circles in the diagram. It is information about the world (encyclopedic knowledge), about the specific nature of a given situation (situation knowledge), about the style of speech which is appropriate for a particular set of circumstances (discourse model). It is also the dictionary-type knowledge of the words in the language, the lexicon. The lexicon in this model contains what Levelt calls lemmas. These are specifications of the meaning of the lexical item together with all relevant information about the syntax, i.e. the syntactic category to which it belongs, its conceptual argument structure, its grammatical functions (such as whether it takes an object and whether or not it can be used with a dependent clause (relation to COMP)), and those parameters along which it may vary in context, such as tense, aspect, number etc. It also includes the 'address' (lexical pointer) in the 'form' part of the lexicon where the morphological and the phonological information about the item may be found.

The lemma for 'give' is shown as follows (Levelt, 1989: 191):

give: conceptual specification:
    CAUSE (X, (GOposs(Y, (FROM/TO (X, Z)))))
    conceptual arguments: (X, Y, Z)
    syntactic category: V
    grammatical functions: (SUBJ, DO, IO)
    relations to COMP: none
    lexical pointer: 713

diacritic parameters: tense
                      aspect
                      mood
                      person
                      number
                      pitch accent

The speaker generates the message by calling on declarative knowledge and combines this with procedural knowledge in the conceptualiser to construct a preverbal message as shown in Figure 10.1. The preverbal message expresses in propositional form the meaning to be conveyed. This enables the appropriate lemma to be activated and called into short-term memory, bringing with it all the information indicated above. The 'formulator' then automatically processes the message to give it a surface syntactic form, calling up other forms to meet the requirements of the initial forms. At the surface structure stage it will be necessary to provide the exact information about the form required for phonological encoding: a message is sent to the address specified and the appropriate form supplied.

The production process is thought of as composed of relatively autonomous stages as specified by the boxes in the diagram. Processing has to be both incremental and parallel to allow for the speed at which it must take place. Together this means that different parts of the message may be being processed at the same time (parallel), different parts of the message may be at different stages of the production process (incremental) and that these will not interfere with one another. In order to ensure that the message can nonetheless be delivered in the right order despite this flexibility there are buffer areas between the units which can delay delivery until the order is correct.

It may be helpful to provide a simple, but reasonably detailed, example of how this process would take place. The production of an utterance (e.g. 'The train arriving at platform 6 is the 9.15 for London') begins with the conceptualiser where the message is generated in the form of a proposition. This is called macroplanning and is likely to be under attentional control. Given this attentional control, feedback by a monitoring process is possible within the conceptualiser. The message may still be modified at this stage ('Oh sorry!, platform 7!'). In the second part of the conceptualiser, not shown in the diagram, is a process called microplanning. Here are determined matters such as where the emphasis should lie in the utterance (topic and focus) so that it can correctly be interpreted by the receiver, what tense it should have, the degree of politeness with which it should be expressed. In this example, we are presumably dealing with an announcement to a wide audience, suggesting a degree of formality in the speech. It is addressed to an audience of people in a railway station and they are aware of the presence of 'trains' in general. They are interested in not missing 'the' one which interests them. The message therefore identifies one train from many possible trains. Microplanning decrees that 'The train arriving at platform 6' should be stated as the defined topic. The audience is interested in whether this train is the one they want. Therefore, the rest of the message must provide this information. The tense is the present, the verb is a copula verb and certain consequences will follow from these choices (e.g. the verb will require a following noun phrase and the second noun phrase must also be definite).

The conceptualiser thus provides an output containing all the propositional information necessary to act as input to the formulator and call up the appropriate lemmas. The 'preverbal message' has to contain all the information which the formulator needs because the formulator is an automatic processor of the language. It has within it a set of procedures which act according to the cues given by the preverbal message and the items selected from the lexicon. As this utterance contains 'train', for example, then the preverbal message will have to specify a definition of this means of locomotion so that the word can be selected from the lexicon. It will also have to specify the relationship between the two nouns and therefore the fact that a subject and an object will be required but that there cannot be a dependent clause.

The formulator, having selected 'train' and 'third person singular of the verb "to be"' for the meaning will then have to seek from the lexicon whatever other lexical items are available to fill the required slots with lexical items expressing the message specified by the preverbal message.

The generation of the message then depends on a very rapid to and fro movement by means of which in a few milliseconds the correct items are selected and ordered by the grammatical encoding procedures within the formulator. The output of that stage is the surface structure. This acts as the input to the phonological encoder. Among the information conveyed will be the particular morphological form which is required, for example, the present tense 'is' as the third person present singular form of the irregular verb 'be' and the address where that may be found in the form part of the lexicon. It will immediately be called up and passed with the rest of the message, suitably ordered, to the articulator. The articulator then articulates the speech that can be monitored by means of the reverse set of procedures linked to the comprehension side of the diagram. Note that in the model there is no opportunity for monitoring between the preverbal stage and the overt speech stage. This has to be so because of the automatic nature of the procedures in the formulator.

The significance of such a model for SLA is at least twofold. On the comprehension side, fluent comprehension will depend on developing procedures for decoding the message in real-time. On the production side, if language is to be creative (i.e. other than set phrases) the procedures for processing syntax in real-time will have to be developed. These are unlikely to be the same as 'sentence generation' within the mental grammar: the generative processes operative within the mental grammar will have to have been transformed into productions suitable for processing. The mechanisms by which this may be done will be discussed in Chapter 12. In the meantime we must examine the consequence of wishing to adapt the model for the purposes of discussing bilingual development.

De Bot (1992) has suggested that the model may be adapted for use in relation to the development of language in bilinguals with little difficulty. Relying on arguments from Paradis (1987) and Green (1986) he proposes that for bilingual speakers the L2 lexicon should be added to the L1 lexicon in such a way that it evolves as a separate subset. The advantage of this proposal is that where meanings are common the items could be stored together and where meanings are different they would automatically be stored apart. As the knowledge of the language grows and as the forms are used more frequently a mechanism would strengthen the ties between the items in the subset so that when one is called there is an increasing probability that other members of the subset will be activated. This enables interaction between the items within a subset to be more probable (and quicker) than interaction between the two subsets. In the case of the formulator and of the microplanning unit, however, there would be a more urgent need for separate units because these will necessarily contain quite different syntax and rules for the formulation of items, such as rules for topicalisation. They may, however, begin as insertions into the existing formulator and grow apart, as suggested for the lexicon.

De Bot views these issues as a continuum based on language distance and language proficiency. He argues that between similar languages and at a level of low proficiency, there will be a tendency to simply add the L2 forms to the existing language system but that, as the proficiency increases, autonomous subsystems will be created within the lexicon and within the formulator. They will naturally evolve as the mechanism for the creation of the subset will lead to a strengthening of the activation of the forms as they are used more and more in the L2. As a result, the L2 processing mechanisms will gradually grow out of the L1 mechanisms and establish their own autonomy. A learner acquiring *donner*, for example, as a French form alongside the English 'give' might well begin by setting up equivalent entries for both terms in the lexicon. This would result in the activation of both terms whenever the appropriate propositional entry appeared in the preverbal message. Only the stronger would be produced. Strength, however, would be relative to the situation, i.e. the English term would be more likely in response to an English utterance, the French term more likely in response to a French utterance. This notion is developed by Green (1986) who suggests that for bilinguals (or multilinguals) all automatised forms will be activated to some degree in response to an appropriate preverbal message. The language which is not being used is nonetheless present at quite a high level of activation and can be called on if desired. Such a view would explain how code-switching can take place with virtually no loss of rhythm in speech and frequently entirely without hesitation.

The advantage of a model such as this in the discussion of SLA is that all the interacting features necessary for the successful acquisition and use of the language are brought together in a meaningful relationship. It is clear that fluent and accurate production of L2 utterances will depend on the possession and use of appropriate declarative knowledge of the language in relation to appropriately automatised, procedural knowledge of the syntax, allowing room for the presence of the L1 and for the need to compensate for inadequacies in any of the component elements. In the next three chapters we shall explore further the difficulties of constructing an L2 system, the difficulties of turning that system into automatised procedures and the difficulties of using that system before it is complete. In each case we shall be seeking to understand the influence of these factors on acquisition.

Summary

In the first part of this chapter we reviewed the evidence and the theories concerning variability in SLA. There were many of these and we decided that most of them could be best understood in relation to three main questions: How do learners formulate and revise hypotheses? How do learners transform linguistic knowledge into procedures for comprehension and production? How do learners cope with the need to communicate with an inadequate system? An attempt to answer these questions and to delimit the role of variability in L2 acquisition will form the substance of Chapters 11, 12, and 13.

These questions clearly go beyond the domain of linguistic theory and we therefore needed a framework which included psychological mechanisms. In the second part of this chapter we introduced the concepts of long-term and short-term memory, controlled and automatic processing, declarative and procedural knowledge and a model of language production.

Human information processing depends on the appropriate allocation of information to long-term and short-term memory stores. Short-term memory is tightly capacity limited, long-term memory is not. When information is activated in the short-term memory it takes up memory space. In order to ensure that processing is rapid, a great deal of information must be automatised. Automatised information can be processed without occupying space in short-term memory, thus allowing the memory space to be used for paying attention to what is deemed important. We have argued that the possession of a certain degree of automatised knowledge may be a necessary precondition for the learner to be able to construct new hypotheses on the basis of externally available data.

In a model of language production, we need to distinguish between two further types of knowledge: declarative knowledge and procedural knowledge. Declarative knowledge is knowledge 'that', procedural knowledge is knowledge 'how'. Declarative knowledge is knowledge about the facts of the world and the facts of a language, procedural knowledge is knowledge of the mechanisms which make language work in production and comprehension. In mature language production, it is clear that most attention will be paid to what is being said (declarative knowledge) and not to how it is to be said (procedural knowledge). In the model of the mature speaker, therefore, the conceptualiser uses declarative knowledge in a controlled manner and the formulator uses procedural knowledge in an automatised manner. The speaker is thought likely to control (in the sense of 'pay attention to') only the conceptualisation, not the processing of the message.

In the case of learning to know and use a second language, however, it is clear that fluent use will depend on the degree to which the learner has been able to construct the complete linguistic system of the second language, the degree to which that system has been stored as an automatised set of mechanisms within the formulator and the degree to which the learner has been able to make the system work as a whole for the purposes of communication.

In Chapter 11 we shall examine how the learner may construct and revise hypotheses about the language system, especially for those areas where the L1 may not have provided a UG-based or transferred hypothesis, bearing in mind the fact that hypothesis creation may not be possible unless the memory space is freed for that purpose through a degree of automatisation. In Chapter 12 we shall examine how the learner turns hypotheses into the mechanisms of language production. In Chapter 13 we shall examine how communication is maintained while the whole system is constructed and what effect that may have on the learning process. In each of the chapters we shall call on the concepts developed here in Chapter 10.

11 Hypothesis Creation and Revision

In this chapter we are concerned with the processes of linguistic hypothesis creation from different knowledge sources and with the revision of these hypotheses in the light of further data. We have taken the view that L2 learners (after the age of seven years) may draw on a variety of sources for hypotheses about how the L2 works (for a related view, see Zobl, 1992). In Chapter 10 we referred to these as internal and external sources. By internal sources we mean Universal Grammar and transfer from L1. The contribution of these sources has been examined in some detail in Chapters 5–9. We now need to examine the contribution of external sources of knowledge. We shall deal with explicit instruction about the L2, negative feedback by correction and the role of formulaic language.

The position we adopt is close to that of Schwartz (1993), although in the later part of this chapter we shall propose that the dichotomy she puts forward may not be quite as radical as it first appears. She distinguishes between two types of knowledge of language: competence and learned linguistic knowledge. Competence underlies performance. Learned linguistic knowledge finds its expression in learned linguistic behaviour. Both are present in L1 and L2. Both make a significant and important contribution to fluent and accurate language production. They are, however, quite separate and learned linguistic knowledge cannot feed competence, for reasons explained below.

According to Schwartz (1993), competence can be acquired in only one way. It is the product of the triggering of innately determined parameters through exposure to positive evidence. Those parts of the language system which are determined by parameters can be learnt only in this way. This is because the innate knowledge which gives rise to those parameters is held in what Fodor (1983) has called an encapsulated module of the brain. This language specific entity is attuned only to positive evidence. Because of its nature, it cannot, for example, be modified by explicit instruction about language or by negative evidence.

To attempt to do so would be akin to trying to make a petrol engine run on diesel. This view is strongly supported in relation to L1 acquisition and evidence for it seems to be growing. Competence gives rise in a fairly direct manner (but see Chapters 12 and 14) to performance.

Learned linguistic knowledge is what learners come to know about language by virtue of explicit instruction and/or negative feedback. In the L1 the most obvious examples are the conventions which govern language use: prescriptive forms such as 'whom', the prohibition of prepositions in final position in written sentences, stylistic norms such as those associated with letter-writing or speech-giving and the written form of language as determined by arbitrary spellings are all learned linguistic knowledge. Arguably, all the knowledge of language which was described as declarative knowledge, including the lexicon, in our presentation of the Levelt model could be learned linguistic knowledge.

In the case of SLA by post-seven year old learners it is possible that learned linguistic knowledge will have a greater role to play. This is in part because there may be less direct access to UG (see discussion in Chapter 7) but also because adult memory capacity is a much more powerful instrument. Learned linguistic knowledge may over time give rise to automatised behaviour (learned linguistic behaviour) which may be difficult to distinguish from performance, but its source is different. Its mental representation in the mind has been created via general cognitive abilities and not via the language specific module which deals only with parameters.

Schwartz (1993) claims that this view of two separate mechanisms has considerable theoretical and empirical backing. It is supported by linguistic theory associated with UG and by Fodor's (1983) concept of modularity. It explains how learners can know more than the surface structure provides evidence for (the logical problem of language acquisition), it explains how learners learn in a systematic way through parameter (re-)setting and it explains why learners (especially L1 learners) are impervious to instruction in areas related to parameters.

This position makes an important prediction about hypothesis creation and revision in SLA: it claims that those areas of the language which are determined by parameter setting can be reset only by positive evidence. It follows that these areas will be difficult, probably impossible, to teach through explicit instruction and negative feedback. It is possible that they may be reached via exposure to extensive positive data. But if the parameters cannot be reset, then they will either give rise to systematic errors or the learner will have to find other means of producing utterances which appear to be governed by the appropriate parameter settings (see Chapters 6 and 7 for discussion of mimicking etc.). One of these means may be learned linguistic behaviour encoded in productions (see Chapter 12) derived from learned linguistic knowledge.

In order to discover what empirical justification there may be for this view, we will first look at studies which have set out to examine the effect of teaching which makes use of explicit instruction and negative feedback. In the main these will confirm the view taken here. Some evidence of effective learning will be put forward but there is little evidence to support the idea that genuine parameter resetting can result from this kind of input.

In the second part of this chapter we will look at the contribution of another kind of input: formulaic language both in authentic situations and in classrooms. We will examine evidence about learning which takes as its source authentic language embedded in situations. It is argued by some, particularly L1 researchers (to whom it appears self-evident), that learners must begin with natural language perceived initially largely as unanalysed wholes. Children begin with utterances which they cannot initially decompose. The question is whether and how language of this kind, sometimes called semantic or formulaic language, can be unpackaged to become the basis for language learning.

It has been argued by some researchers that it is, in principle, impossible to derive what they have called 'creative' speech from language initially encountered as a formulaic utterance embedded in a situation. The proponents of this view argue that the form will be 'acquired' only when it is encountered at the right time as part of the natural order, a position very close to the concept of triggering. Other researchers argue, on the contrary, that formulaic utterances must be an important starting point for learners and that the process of learning involves analysing and unpackaging these formulaic utterances. Evidence will be cited from the work of Karmiloff-Smith (1986a, b) to exemplify a process of mental restructuring which might make it possible for these forms to interact with 'competence'. We will argue that where Karmiloff-Smith (1986a) sees 'metaprocedures' at work, there could be an interaction with linguistic competence. Subsequent detailed analysis of the best evidence of learning from formulaic utterances fails, however, to provide totally convincing evidence of 'unpackaging'.

Explicit Instruction and Negative Feedback

For many learners exposure to the L2 in a classroom environment means exposure to explicit instruction with negative feedback. This provides more or less accurate information about certain aspects of the L2, usually an account of the surface structure regularities of the language plus some semantically based generalisations. Intelligent learners will be able to assimilate this explicit knowledge but, as explained above, there are serious doubts about whether they can turn this into linguistic competence (i.e. knowledge equivalent to that of a native speaker).

There are a number of studies which examine this issue, many of which are presented in Long (1983, 1988) and Ellis (1990). Long came to the conclusion that instructed learners did, on balance, do 'better' than non-instructed learners. However, the evidence was based on a rather unsatisfactory majority of the studies examined and the definition of 'better' is not related specifically to issues of parameter resetting. Ellis (1990) concludes on the basis of the studies he has examined that 'there are constraints on the effects that instruction can have on acquisition' and, more precisely, 'spontaneous speech may be impervious to instruction'.

The evidence which backs up these assertions comes mainly from four studies. Schumann's (1978) well-known study showed that a Costa Rican learner, Alberto, did not improve on his spontaneous speech despite targeted instruction on areas where he clearly had basic problems, such as negatives and interrogatives. Schumann does report, however, an improvement in a test situation. A study by Lightbown, Spada & Wallace (1980) revealed that whilst instruction was immediately effective when a grammaticality test was readministered, there was much less effect when a follow-up test was used five months later. Ellis's (1984b) own study on wh- pronouns showed no improvement when a spontaneous game was played. A study by Kadia (1988) suggested that only controlled production (i.e. in a test situation) was affected by explicit teaching but not spontaneous speech. Ellis (1990: 151) concludes that 'three of these studies support the claim that instruction can improve accuracy in careful, planned speech production but that this improvement may disappear over time as more "natural" processes take over'. All these findings are compatible with the suggestion that instruction has an effect on learned linguistic knowledge but not on parameter resetting. None of them, however, sets out to study the learning of forms which could specifically be interpreted in relation to parameter resetting. This is not the case with three more recent studies.

Doughty (1991) claims that L2 instruction does make a positive difference. She worked on the teaching and learning of relative clauses in English with groups of learners from many different language backgrounds. As in most other research in this area, the format was one of using pre-tests, a teaching method ('treatment period' in Doughty's terms) and post-tests. The tests were both written and oral and involved grammaticality judgement and sentence combination.

Doughty's study was different from most others in several ways. First, the learners were selected as being 'ready' for the particular teaching provided. By examining previous work by potential subjects Doughty was able to exclude those whose performance was too distant from being able to learn the relatives she wished to teach or whose performance revealed that they were too advanced. Second, Doughty was able to provide two different instruction methods for each of two groups, one 'meaning related' and one 'rule-related' and to have a control group. All three groups were given instruction via computers and careful differences were inserted into the teaching methods used: the control group were presented with texts which contained a large number of relative clauses but had no physical means of highlighting those clauses. For the 'meaning' group the relevant relative clauses were highlighted by typographical means on the screen. For the 'rule' group, in addition to this highlighted presentation, there were explicit rules and graphics which transformed nouns into pronouns and moved clauses around.

The results showed that all three groups improved their performance on the post-test as a result of the 'treatment' but the 'instructed' groups (whether meaning or rule based) improved twice as much as the control group. In addition, Doughty claims that the learners were able to generalise their new knowledge to other kinds of relative clause higher up on the Noun Phrase Accessibility Hierarchy proposed by Keenan & Comrie (1977), a consequence similar to the concept of generalising within a parameter.

Doughty accepts that no long-term effect has been demonstrated because no follow-up test after the post-test was possible. It is also true that the oral tests which she described do not equate with the kind of spontaneous language which was required in the Ellis (1984b) study. The study does, however, provide evidence that instruction has an immediate positive effect and the generalisation to other structures within the hierarchy argues in favour of an effect beyond the learning of the structure taught.

A second study which is relevant was that undertaken by Felix & Weigl (1991). The conclusions, particularly in relation to parameter resetting, were not so positive. The focus of the study was the investigation of whether UG could be seen to influence a group of learners who had been exposed only to the L2 in a structured classroom environment.

The subjects of the study were high school learners of English in Germany. The researchers devised a set of grammaticality judgement tests based on UG principles, using examples where transfer between German and English could not operate and which had not been directly taught as part of the teaching. The view was that, if these learners had access to UG, their performance would be similar to that of learners in other environments (e.g. exposure only) because access to UG is determined by biological and not environmental factors.

The tests were then taken by different groups of pupils in their second, fourth and seventh year of instruction. On the face of it, the results were a disaster. Pupils scored very low on the tests, much worse than random and there was virtually no difference in the global scores between pupils at each of the three levels. Looking in more detail at some aspects of the test scores revealed that the learners at the highest level were considerably worse in certain areas than those at the lowest level. This discovery, and the fact that the results were so much worse than random, indicated that, although it was clear that UG principles were not operative, some other factors must be guiding the choices made. More detailed examination of the results led Felix & Weigl to suggest that these learners were: (a) assuming that what was permitted in German was also permitted in English wherever this was possible, and (b) refusing to generalise beyond the specific structures which had been taught.

The first case can be illustrated by passivisation. Subjects accepted both sentences such as: 'It was expected that John would win the race' and *'It was expected a letter'. The second sentence, unacceptable in English, is possible in German. The difference between the two languages is attributed to a difference in parameter setting within case theory. Clearly, the learners had not reset the parameter. The second case is illustrated by preposition stranding: learners accepted as grammatical 'What does John look at?' because, suggest Felix & Weigl, this is similar to examples chosen in text books, but reject 'Who did he see pictures of?' because these particular forms are neither taught in class nor mentioned in the text books. Again, if they had reset the parameter all examples of such forms would have been acceptable, not just those which resembled directly what they had previously seen.

Felix & Weigl use the evidence presented here and evidence from earlier studies, such as Felix (1987), to put forward arguments similar to those of Schwartz (1993). They argue that the different hypothesis construction capabilities evidenced between L1 and L2 learners are attributable to the fact that humans have two distinct cognitive systems for dealing with the kind of abstract symbol manipulation required by language and that these come into play in language learning at different times. A first system, akin to UG, operates for L1 learning only. It is available when children are very young and it is specific to the learning of the first language(s). It controls the kind of systematic linguistic development visible in L1 learning. The second system, of the kind described by Piaget (1923) for general cognitive skills, develops much later (around puberty) and functions as a general problem solver. It is not specific to language. Adults, therefore, tend to use the general problem solver when attempting to learn language. Thus, these classroom learners are learning language in the way they would learn any subject. They have conscious knowledge of the forms they have been taught and they apply only that knowledge; they do not generalise beyond it; where they have not been taught, they deal with the problem as best they can by transferring their knowledge of the L1 system. They are always conservative about generalising into new areas, and the more advanced they are, the more wary of generalisations they become. Felix & Weigl (1991: 178) are understandably pessimistic about classroom language learning beyond the age of around seven ever being successful:

As is well known, the major problem in learning a language is to internalize a rich and highly structured system of knowledge on the basis of extremely limited evidence. This holds true not only for naturalistic, but also for classroom learning. What is being taught in the classroom represents only a small portion of the structural complexities and intricacies of natural language; and typically, most of the deeper properties are not taught. If the results of our study are not merely accidental, then it is precisely these deeper properties that our students failed to acquire.

A third set of studies which are also directly related to parameter resetting have been carried out by White (1991a, d) and Trahey & White (1993). These studies are particularly interesting because they examine the effect of various approaches to instruction on the learning of the same structure.

The studies focus on the learning of some of the consequences of differences in the verb movement parameter between French and English (see Chapter 6, under 'Adverb placement in English and French'). In English it is forbidden to place an adverb between the lexical verb and its direct object: SVAO *'Mary watches often television', whereas in French it is permissible: *Marie regarde souvent la télévision*. French speakers tend to infringe this rule in English and to produce sentences like the unacceptable English example. On the other hand, in English it is legitimate to produce sentences on a subject–adverb–verb (SAV) pattern: 'Marie often watches television', while the French equivalent: *'Marie souvent regarde la télévision'* is not acceptable. From the perspective of the French learner of English, it is necessary to learn both that SAV is possible and that SVAO is not. According to the analysis of Pollock (1989), resetting the parameter correctly would produce correct behaviour on both patterns. The problem provides a particularly good test-bed for the influence of different kinds of evidence on parameter resetting because learners learning English have to 'retreat' from an overgeneralisation when there is no positive evidence to help.

White (1991a) set out to examine whether French-speaking children, average age 11 and 12 years (82 children in all) could be taught the relevant aspects of adverb placement by using explicit instruction complete with negative feedback. In order to assess the effect of specific instruction, while the experimental group were being taught about adverbs, another group was being taught question formation. Both groups were given the same tests. The effect of the teaching would show up only in the 'adverb' group but both would be familiar with the test situation.

In this case a first post-test took place at the end of the intensive teaching programme, a second one after five weeks and, in the case of some learners, a follow-up test a year later. The tests were all written: one grammaticality judgement test in the form of a cartoon story, one written preference test in which pupils had to choose whether only one of a pair of sentences was right, whether both or neither were right and a manipulation task in which sentences had to be made up using word cards.

The results of the experiment showed that the children who had been explicitly taught adverb forms scored significantly higher on all of the post-tests and maintained that improvement for the time separating the post-tests. It did not, however, carry through to the follow-up tests. White (1991a: 151–2) comments: '. . . it is quite possible that the knowledge gained here was conscious rather than unconscious, and that it never became part of the learner's underlying interlanguage grammar.' We cannot know this for certain because there was no means of eliciting this kind of data in spontaneous speech. White (1991a: 158) states:

> The results from the main study here suggest that negative evidence is effective in helping L2 learners to master the fact that SVAO is ungrammatical in English, while positive evidence is insufficient. However, the follow-up study suggests that the structured classroom input did not, in this case, have lasting effects, that it did not, in fact, result in significant changes in the learners' underlying competence.

An additional study (Trahey & White, 1993) looked at the learning of the same structure by a similar group of subjects, but this time provided only positive evidence. Over a period of two weeks, experimental classes were provided with an 'input flood' of sentences containing adverbs within specially prepared teaching materials. The test instruments were the same, although an oral test was added. This time the learners performed well on the area where positive evidence could be provided, i.e. the correct SAV forms, as in 'Marie often watches television', which would not be allowed in French. However, for it to be possible for the researchers to claim that the parameter had been reset, the subjects would also have had to reject the SVAO forms *'Marie watches often television' which is unacceptable in English but acceptable in French. In fact, learners continued to accept sentences like this. They were significantly worse at judging the incorrectness of these sentences than the learners who had had explicit instruction and negative evidence.

Trahey & White conclude that the learners did not reset the parameter even on the basis of the positive evidence, although they did learn the SAV form. It seems that we must conclude that this positive evidence also led only to learned linguistic knowledge rather than parameter resetting.

In their interpretation of the evidence, Trahey & White (1993: 201) suggest that learners may behave in ways which indicate that they are entertaining two parameter settings at the same time. It is perhaps more likely, however, that the parameter setting has not changed. The parameter is still as it was in the L1. But the learner has acquired learned linguistic knowledge which enables him or her to behave in one context as if the parameter had been reset. The result may produce the kind of behaviour which has been called nonsystematic variability. We will return to this question when we consider hypothesis revision later in this chapter.

The evidence presented in this section suggests that parameter resetting is unlikely to take place with L2 learners whose exposure to the L2 is through explicit instruction and negative feedback in the classroom. Even a flood of positive evidence appears not to have enabled a parameter to be reset. On the other hand, instruction, negative feedback and a 'flood' of positive evidence are all ways in which learners' language can be modified, even if the results are less than permanent. At least for a time, learned linguistic behaviour enables the learner to appear to produce native-like language.

Exposure to Authentic Data

A debate which has been going on for many years (see the review article of Towell, 1987c) concerns the extent to which it is possible for learners to derive awareness of the linguistic system from formulaic utterances which are closely embedded in situations and first experienced as unanalysed wholes. It is fairly clear that L1 learners must begin with utterances which are unanalysed wholes. It follows that at some point these must be analysed. However, some researchers have objected most strongly to this idea in an SLA context.

Krashen & Scarcella (1978) and Krashen (1988: 86) argue that '. . . routines are part of a system that is separate from the process generating rule-governed, propositional language . . . automatic speech does not "turn into" creative constructions'. They use evidence from neurolinguistic research into language loss to claim that 'automatic' speech is stored in a different part of the brain and therefore fundamentally different to creative speech.

However, not everyone takes this view, particularly in relation to first language acquisition. Clark (1974) considered 'the child's speech becomes creative predominantly through gradual analysis of the internal structure of sequences which start out as patterns' and cited the following examples of sequences which have been combined after having begun as independent units:

I want *you get biscuit for me*
I don't know *where's Emma gone*
I want *I eat apple*

L.W. Fillmore (1976, 1979), having carried out a detailed longitudinal study of five L2 learners was convinced that the unpackaging of these formulas is one of the most important ways in which L2 acquisition occurs:

The point that has been missed so far is that the strategy of acquisition of formulaic language is central to the learning of language: indeed it is this step that puts the learner in a position to perform the analysis which is necessary for language learning. (L.W. Fillmore 1979: 212).

Ellis (1984a) attempted to resolve this debate by studying three classroom learners and seeking to examine in particular whether an utterance which appeared to be initially formulaic 'I don't know' (i.e. a routine used monomorphemically to cope with a situation) evolved into other forms over time. The question could be answered by finding out whether the subject 'I' was replaced by other subjects (e.g. 'You don't know'), whether 'know' would be released for use without 'don't' or whether additional constituents would be combined with this utterance. Ellis found (see Tables 11.1a and 11.1b) that during the period of the study only one of the subjects developed the ability to replace 'I' with an alternative pronoun ('You don't know where it is' — week 21), that all three children used 'don't' with other verbs before releasing 'know' for independent use, and that all the learners used 'I don't know' with juxtaposed structures at certain points (indicated by the weeks when they did so in Table 11.1b) (Ellis 1984a: 74/5).

Table 11.1(a) The development of the formula 'I don't know' in the speech of three classroom learners

Developmental feature	Portuguese speaker	R	T
'don't' used in similar but different expressions	I don't understand. (14)	I don't like holiday. (22)	I don't like this book. (26)
Alternative subject to 'I'	You don't know where it is. (21)	Ø	Ø
'know' used without 'don't'	I know this (18)	I know 'five'. (26)	I know this one. (28)
Additional constituent	I don't know that big one. (18)	I don't know this one. (24)	I don't know this. (18)

Table 11.1(b) Combinations used by learners based on 'I don't know' specifying in which weeks of the study they were used

(1) *That one* I don't know. (Portuguese boy — week 21)
(2) You don't know *where it is.* (Portuguese boy — week 25)
(3) I don't know *how to play.* (Portuguese boy — week 27)
(4) I don't know *what is squirrel.* (R — week 24)
(5) I don't know *what's this.* (R — week 26)
(6) I don't know *'holiday' spelling.* (T — week 22)
(7) I don't know *what's this.* (T — week 25)
(8) I don't know *making.* (T — week 30)

Source: Ellis, 1984a: 74–5

Ellis comments:

> Although considerable development in the three children's use of 'I don't know' has taken place it is not clear how much of the grammatical information contained in the formula has been 'unpackaged' and made available for productive use . . . much of the apparent development can be explained either in terms of additional routines or by the conversion of routines to patterns. If such an analysis is correct, little real analysis has taken place . . . It is, in fact, quite likely that many of the new forms (e.g. 'I don't understand' and 'I don't like') are also formulas and that only when the learners are able to perceive the syntactic similarity between the two routines will completely productive use result.' (Ellis, 1984a: 75)

In terms of Schwartz's division, it is therefore questionable whether this kind of positive evidence is sufficient to enable learners to develop competence. It would seem important, however, to establish whether anything other than the rather under-described process of 'triggering' may be involved in the creation of competence.

Mental representation

One researcher who has repeatedly stressed the importance of the way in which child L1 learners derive hypotheses from authentic naturalistic speech is Karmiloff-Smith (1979, 1985, 1986a, b). Her arguments may also apply to L2 learning. Key issues are levels of mental representation, the phases operating within levels and the motivation for restructuring.

Karmiloff-Smith is concerned to make a clear distinction between behavioural change and changes in mental representation. She argues that it is essential to be able to give an account of development in mental representation which may or may not give rise to immediately visible behavioural change. At the level of mental representation she claims that there is a process of 'restructuring' which enables the learner to pass from a level of implicit knowledge of the language (knowledge of the meaning of the language in context, possibly as unanalysed wholes) to different levels of explicit knowledge (going from no awareness of relationships between linguistic forms to an unconscious awareness and then (possibly) on to a conscious awareness). She also argues that these changes are the result of positive evidence ('success') and not negative evidence.

In addition, Karmiloff-Smith sees a role for innate linguistic structures alongside psychologically determined representations: 'I consider language acquisition to be in part determined by innately given linguistic constraints and subsequently in part by general processes of representational explicitation, particularly with respect to lexico-morphology' (1986a: 100). A central question, however, is whether the two may interact through changes of mental representation or whether, as Schwartz claims, they must remain separate and give rise to two different kinds of L2 knowledge.

Karmiloff-Smith (1986a) posits the existence of four levels:

- implicit (I)
- primary explicitation (E-i)
- secondary explicitation (E-ii)
- tertiary explicitation (E-iii).

Knowledge is differently represented at each of the levels: the actual linguistic forms may be the same, but the learner's perceptions of them will have changed and in consequence so will the situations in which the learner can make use of them. The movement is accomplished in phases. Here we shall discuss only the phases which enable the learner to move from the lowest, implicit, level to that of primary explicitation. We believe that these may correspond to 'formulaic language in situations' (implicit) and to 'available for input into competence' (primary explicitation). Higher levels are to do with bringing what is known to levels of consciousness and do not interest us here.

In the case of the child L1 learner, the process must begin with implicit knowledge. When knowledge is implicit it has no representational definition. It consists of what others would call semantic or formulaic utterances which are retained because of their communicative effect in defined situations. The language is a means to an end: it is the mechanism by which desired objects may be obtained, unwanted threats removed, and so on. It is argued that language of this kind will not initially be represented internally and the fact that different procedures may have common components will be ignored. The utterances which make up implicit knowledge cannot be defined as a system: they could only exist as a list, i.e. implicit language is only potentially definable over the totality of 'procedures' in which it occurs.

Thus, in phase 1, the child acquires the surface output for a particular linguistic form. The reason for that acquisition derives from external forces: the child learns the form because it is a means to a communicative end. The form is stored in such a way that it can be recalled for use in that situation and is not stored in a way which would establish links with any other forms. It is stored independently. At this stage 'the child's goal is to attain one-to-one mapping between the specific linguistic form and the particular extralinguistic/pragmatic context for which it is used in the output of the adult model' (Karmiloff-Smith, 1986a: 105). This process may be communicatively quite successful as it establishes a series of useful, independent form/function pairs embedded in a situation. At this stage any 'patterns' of linguistic structure which are visible to an outsider are not visible to the child.

In phase 2 language is worked on in a different way:

Phase 2 is characterised by the fact that the child now ignores to a great extent the external stimulus and concentrates on gaining control over the organisation of those internal representations which had hitherto been stored independently. (Karmiloff-Smith, 1986a: 107)

As this is carried out the forms become available for a greater degree of access (although at this stage such access is still totally unconscious) and in this way relationships are perceived: 'any form/function analogies and differences can be explicitly defined' (Karmiloff-Smith, 1986a: 107). As a result of this 'scanning' the learner comes to accept that the same form which may have initially appeared in several procedures may actually possess more than one function and that several functions can be fulfilled by the same form.

From phase 2 subjects will move on to phase 3 which, in this example, will lead to access to the primary explicitation (E-1) level. At phase 3 the child can operate on the internal structure of a procedure in ways which would not previously have been possible. In phase 3 the child has both the 'bottom-up' information initially provided by phase 1 implicit language and the 'top-down' mental representation provided by phase 2 linked representations. In terms of the actual forms which the child will produce at phase 3 there will be no observable difference from those produced in phase 1: the difference lies in the (invisible) changes in mental representation. The child thus has greater understanding and greater flexibility, but not yet conscious access to the representations which would require rewriting into further levels.

A concrete example of the phases is offered in relation to the learning of the indefinite article: in French a single form distinguished for gender (*un/une*) will perform several functions e.g. non-specific reference (*je voudrais un crayon*, 'I would like a pencil' — our illustrative examples), a numerical function (*il n'y a qu'un crayon*, 'There is only one pencil') and an 'appellative' function (*c'est un crayon*, 'It's (called) a pencil'). Karmiloff-Smith first observed that children 'automatise' and 'use' these forms efficiently in context. Subsequently they introduce a new form, which happens not to correspond to the adult forms, to indicate the numerical function. They add *de* to give *un de mouchoir* to indicate 'one handkerchief'. This is similar to another distinction which Karmiloff-Smith (1986b) has observed by means of which children distinguish *même* meaning 'same one' and *même de* meaning 'same kind', again using non-adult forms. For Karmiloff-Smith these changes in form are a demonstration that the children have entered phase 2. They have changed the forms because they now see that the same form has more than one function. They seek to preserve the relationship 'one form one meaning', and therefore invent a new form for one of the meanings. Previously there was no need to do this because the forms were so embedded in their context that the 'problem' was invisible. The progression towards phase 3 is seen when the children stop introducing the additional *de* forms and revert to the utterances visible in phase 1. There is, as indicated above, no difference in the output in phase 1 and phase 3 but the passage through phase 2 indicates that the mental representation has now changed. Karmiloff-Smith (1986a: 114) comments:

> The very fact that phase 2 differentiated marking occurs *after* the developmentally prior consistently correct output at phase 1 is, I would argue, a clear indication that new internal representational links have become explicitly defined by phase 2.

A discussion of how and why such changes should come about gives rise to some disagreement between the approach taken by Karmiloff-Smith and the more linguistic approach taken throughout this book.

Karmiloff-Smith notes that the 'implicit' behaviour of the child is successful in communicative terms. If that is so, the question arises of why the child should seek to reorganise the data and to seek different kinds of mental representation:

> By the end of the first phase for a particular linguistic form, children have achieved a correct mapping between their output and the adult output . . . Now, if children were merely driven by the goal of successful mapping between their output and the output of the adult model . . . no further development should occur (Karmiloff-Smith, 1986a: 106).

One of Karmiloff-Smith's main arguments is that children are not simply driven by the desire to obtain successful output but that they go beyond it. Nor, she argues, are they driven purely by economy. It is not conflict within the system which makes the children reorganise their mental representation but 'internal stability':

> . . . the final stability of phase 1, which cues the passage beyond success to phase 2 and its representational changes, is based on repeated positive feedback, i.e. it is internal stability, rather than conflict/disequilibrium, which functions as a cue for the onset of representational change. And it is internal stability that enables the child to become sensitive at phase 2 to conflict between potentially competing/inconsistent representations, a conflict ignored for some time developmentally during phase 1. Indeed, the isolated nature of phase 1 representations allows different, potentially conflicting entries to live in 'peaceful coexistence'. Thus the stability and 'success' of independently stored representations is a prerequisite for real representational change, not in the form of mere adjunctions to memory, but in the explicit defining of relationships across redescribed existing representations. (Karmiloff-Smith, 1986a: 106/7)

To explain this process, Karmiloff-Smith (1986a) proposes a mechanism which is called into play by positive feedback to move the system into phase 2. 'At the end of phase 1 when procedural success has been attained, a metaprocess is called into play, which has the function of evaluating the internal state of any part of the organism.' What this metaprocess is, where it comes from, what its status is, what formalism it belongs to is not stated. The metaprocess and other 'metaprocedural operations' are as 'mysterious' as the learning principles of Wolfe Quintero or the constructs of Krashen mentioned in Chapters 2–4. From the linguists' point of view this is a matter for some regret when the principles and parameters of UG could be seen to be guiding the learning process. Their essential capacity is precisely to establish the relations between forms.

Karmiloff-Smith, however, argues that it is a 'metaprocess', which enables the child to re-evaluate the forms learnt so far. She argues that factors internal to the child (presumably maturational) are causing the mental representation of the linguistic system to be reorganised. The question which arises is: how does the child know how to do this? What kind of knowledge could lead the child to carry out this reorganisation in such a way that it does not lead to the many possible overgeneralisations, 'wild' grammars or other potential aberrations which we do not see in child language? Instead we see an ordered acquisition of linguistic forms in staged development and we see this to some extent also in L2 acquisition. Karmiloff-Smith says:

> Once the 3-phase cycle has been completed for a particular part of the developing linguistic system, a specifically linguistic operation evaluates the phase-3 representations with respect to their appropriateness for systemic restructuring for the needs of on-line discourse computation" (Karmiloff-Smith, 1986a: 110).

No doubt on-line discourse processing does play a significant role in language development but in L1 learning the syntactic system must be put into place along guidelines offered by UG.

It seems that our understanding of the language learning process would be greatly enhanced if the kind of developmental framework outlined by Karmiloff-Smith were placed together with the insights of UG. Karmiloff-Smith (1986a: 112) does agree that 'Clearly there are innately given linguistic universals which constrain the child's processing of the input during the initial stages of language acquisition' but emphasises:

> However, with respect to some of the processes at work in the subsequent representational change regarding the specific relationships to be established in the lexico-morphology part of the child's particular mother tongue, I believe that this 3-phase model of representational change via progressive explicitation provides a plausible theoretical framework. (Karmiloff-Smith, 1986a: 112–13)

The UG suggestion would, of course, be that the learners already have an innate ability which constrains the possibilities which they may entertain and that this lessens or even eliminates the need for metaprocesses or metaprocedural operators. The learners know what the possibilities are: they simply take time to develop them in situ. It is possible that Karmiloff-Smith is describing in detail the processes associated with 'triggering' which are rarely made explicit in the UG literature. In the case of L1 learning, it is plausible (Atkinson, 1992; Radford, 1990) that processes of maturation explain the developmental process, but this is not an explanation available for L2 learners. If this view is correct, however, it opens up the possibility that the dichotomy presented by Schwartz might not be absolute in the case of SLA. In cases where internal hypotheses (originating in UG and transfer) are present in the encapsulated module of the L2 learner's mind, the kind of changes in mental representation described above in the various phases might result in positive evidence which permits restructuring of linguistic knowledge guided by internal hypotheses. This is, however, only a possibility and empirical proof is difficult to establish.

In a series of articles and books another researcher into L1 and L2 acquisition, Ellen Bialystok (Bialystok 1978, 1982, 1988, 1990a, b, 1991; Bialystok & Sharwood Smith, 1985) has put forward a very similar set of ideas to those of Karmiloff-Smith. She works with twin concepts 'analysis' and 'control'. Both are qualities of the mental representation a speaker can give to the symbol system which is language. A more 'analysed' representation means that the speaker can perceive relationships between the symbols. This seems exactly to parallel the movement from 'implicit' to 'explicit' via 'restructuring' which has just been described in some detail in relation to Karmiloff-Smith's work. A more 'controlled' representation means that the speaker can select information from a representation. By such a process of selective attention the speaker is able to perform in a wider range of contexts. Bialystok argues that L2 learners progress along these two relatively independent but interacting axes of development.

Building on the ideas of Karmiloff-Smith and Bialystok, we are arguing here that, especially in those areas of the linguistic system where empirical hypothesis creation on the basis of exposure to data is the only option, i.e. if it is shown that the internal sources of UG and transfer from L1 cannot supply hypotheses, there may be a process of progressively evolving mental representation which allows learners to reach a stage where the principles and parameters underlying competence can, in some instances, provide the basis on which linguistic relationships can be established. It is not entirely clear whether by doing so, we are questioning the absolute nature of Schwartz's (1993) dichotomy or merely describing in more detail a form of the triggering process in SLA for learners post age seven years. However, if we maintain the rigid separation which she has psoposed, in those cases where UG has not provided guidance and where either the L1 is no help or has provided an 'incorrect or overgeneralised' hypothesis about the L2, it is difficult to see how learners can ever recover unless there is a possible point of contact through mental restructuring with linguistic competence. If it is the case that L2 learners cannot recover, then they will have to find means of using the language without an awareness of its internal structure. While this may indeed be what happens, it remains difficult to accept the notion that human beings will perform a reiteration of a task on a completely different basis.

Let us now return to some of the specific evidence related to the unpackaging of formulaic utterances which was seen to be contentious at the beginning of this section and examine it in the light of the evidence just presented.

Formulaic language seen in the light of changes in mental representation

As we have seen above, Krashen & Scarcella (1978) in particular are reluctant to believe that formulaic language can feed into what they call 'creative' language, but it is worth looking in more detail at the data from Fillmore's study in the light of the Karmiloff-Smith account to see whether it provides more support for the view that such a developmental pattern is possible.

L.W. Fillmore (1976, 1979) studied five child L2 learners, aged between five and just over seven years, who were native speakers of Spanish newly arrived in the USA from Mexico. Each child was paired with an English child native speaker (with one exception for a child who preferred a bilingual) and Fillmore studied the language produced by the children in one-hour play sessions once a week for one school year.

From her observations she derived a set of cognitive and social strategies that the children deployed each to a greater or lesser extent and each with greater or lesser success. These strategies are listed in informal terms. As cognitive strategy 2, for example, Fillmore (1979: 211) lists: 'Get some expressions and start talking'. By this she means that the children picked up formulaic expressions which were acquired and used as unanalysed wholes. She notes (p. 211) 'There was a striking similarity among the five subjects in the acquisition and use of formulaic expressions'. Examples of these formulaic utterances were:

I wanna play Do you wanna play?
Whaddya wanna do?
I gotta hurry up.
Shaddup your mouth.
OK, you be the X, I'll be the Y, etc.
(L.W. Fillmore, 1979: 211)

These structures are presumably exactly the kinds of linguistic forms which Karmiloff-Smith (1986a) has in mind when talking about the language to which initial learners are exposed. They are closely embedded in situations, although — because we are talking here not about babies but about young children — the forms are correspondingly longer and more complex than the initial utterances of infants.

Fillmore is convinced that these forms are the essential starting point for language learning:

> Formulaic speech in this study turned out to be important not only because it permitted the children to begin speaking the language long before they knew how it was structured, but also because the formulas the children learned and used constituted the linguistic material on which a large part of the analytical activities involved in language learning could be carried out. (L.W. Fillmore, 1979: 212)

In the case of these learners it is quite probable, given that they had emigrated with their parents who were taking up farm work in the area, that the home language would continue to be Spanish and therefore the data from which the children had to work would be present in the school and the classroom.

Fillmore maintains indeed that, as Karmiloff-Smith (1986a) suggests, it was once the learners became confident in the use of these forms (the forms became 'familiar') that they were in a position to begin analysing them:

> Once in the learner's speech repertory, they became familiar, and therefore could be compared with other utterances in the repertory as well as with those produced by other speakers. Their function in the language learning process, then is not only social, but cognitive too, since they provided the data on which the children were to perform their analytical activities in figuring out the structure of the language. (L.W. Fillmore, 1979: 212)

Fillmore suggests that this next stage of analysis merits the title of another cognitive strategy: '3rd strategy: Look for recurring parts in the formulas you know.' According to Fillmore, the learner can either use the changes in the speech situation to spot variations in parts of the formulaic expressions, thus becoming aware of which parts can vary and how; or the learner may identify recurrent parts of the formulas already known, noting how they resemble the utterances used by others.

The most telling example quoted by Fillmore is that of Nora.

> She had in her speech repertory two related formulas: 'I wanna play wi' dese' and 'I don'wanna do dese'. No doubt the similarity of these expressions allowed her to discover that the constituents following 'wanna' were interchangeable, and that she could also say 'I don'wanna play wi' dese' and 'I wanna do dese . . . At that point these formulas became formulaic frames with analysed slots: 'I wanna X/X' = VP and 'I don' wanna X/X'=VP, that is, where other verb phrases (VP) can be inserted into the slot represented by X. (L.W. Fillmore, 1979: 212–3)

This is not exactly what is described by Karmiloff-Smith (1986a) who thinks more in terms of the child using the information given to discover the rules underlying the linguistic system. But Fillmore argues that this first stage of 'slot creation' is a first step on the way to breaking down the structure of complete utterances so that the structure is revealed:

> Thus the analytical process carried out on formulas yielded formulaic frames with abstract slots representing constituent types which could substitute in them, and it also freed constituent parts of the formulas to function in other constructions either as formulaic units or as wholly analysed items. (L.W. Fillmore, 1979: 213)

The process is illustrated by the table provided by Fillmore which shows the development of the speech of Nora, labelled by Fillmore 'From formula to productive speech' — see Table 11.2.

Fillmore comments:

> Looking at this data without the time periods specified, we might have guessed that the developmental course went the opposite direction — from the less well-formed versions to the well-formed ones at the top. Indeed this would have been the case if the acquisitional procedure had been a gradual sorting out of the rules whereby the learner was able to structure the utterances herself. Instead the procedure was one which might be described as 'speak now, learn later'. (L.W. Fillmore, 1979: 215)

Table 11.2 How do you do dese? — from formula to productive speech (Nora).

Structure	Examples
Time 2	
Wh[F]: How do you do dese?	How do you do dese?
Time 3–4	
Wh[Fx]¹: How do you do dese (X)/ X = NP,PP	How do you do dese? How do you do dese September *por mañana?* How do you do dese flower power? How do you do dese little *tortillas?* How do you do dese in English?
Wh[Fx]²: How do you How did you X/X = VP	How do you make a little *gallenas?* (= ballenas) How do you like to be a cookie cutter? (= How would you . . .) How do you like to be a shrarks? How do you make the flower? How do you gonna make dese? How do you gonna do dese in English? How did you make it? How did you lost it?
Time 4	
Wh[Fx]³: How do How does X/X = Clause How did	How do cut it? How do make it? How does this color is? How did dese work? (= How does this work?)
Wh[S]: HOW is freed, preposed	Because when I call him, how I put the number? (= How will I dial his number?) How you make it? How will take off paste?

Source: Fillmore, 1979: 214

Fillmore puts forward two more cognitive strategies (p. 218): 'C-4 make the most of what you've got', by which she means that the children did not always limit the use of their formulas to contexts where they were entirely appropriate; 'C-5 Work on big things: save the details for later', by which she means that 'they were apparently working dealing with major constituents first, and leaving the grammatical details to be worked out later (although only two of the five learners got to the second part by the end of the year)'.

At this latter point, Fillmore's presentation of the way the learners' language is developing certainly falls short of what might be expected from the Karmiloff-Smith account. Karmiloff-Smith argues that the learners will move towards an understanding of the linguistic system and indeed in other articles she cites examples of the learners' ability to make use of the absence of forms as well as the presence of forms functioning within a single system. Fillmore, however, is not actually able to show that these learners progressed to the learning of the language system in the way suggested. This is perhaps not surprising given that she was writing at a time when parameter setting was not proposed as essential to language learning. It is to be hoped that new research can be carried out in ways similar to Fillmore's but informed by more recent views of language structure.

Even in Karmiloff-Smith's (1986a, b) accounts, convincing though they are, the question of where the learners acquire the knowledge which will enable them to derive the linguistic patterns without passing through 'wild' grammars or the kinds of overgeneralisations which are never, in fact, present in learner language remains unanswered and will remain unanswered until it is seen how the developmental patterns described in this part of the book can be integrated with the linguistic insights presented in Chapters 5-9.

The arguments have been developed here at some length because of the importance of the issue, given recent trends in language teaching. More and more the early stages of language teaching rely on 'authentic' language of a formulaic nature embedded in the context. Whether or not a language system can be built on evidence of that kind is a crucial question for these pedagogical methods. As can be seen from this discussion, the issue is not yet resolved.

Hypothesis Revision

The accounts presented in this chapter have dealt with the ways in which internal hypotheses and external evidence interact. As a result of this interaction, learners establish hypotheses. In those cases where simple triggering has taken place on the basis of appropriate innate UG information, the result will be linguistic knowledge which can be swiftly automatised as performance. In many cases, however, simple triggering will not happen. The L1, for example, may have a different parameter setting and incorrect information will be hypothesised. Also the evidence available may mislead the learner into overgeneralisations. As learners progress they acquire more information about the language from their various sources and data. They are constantly required to revise their hypotheses. In this section, we shall briefly examine some of the consequences of this requirement.

As was first indicated in Chapter 3, it has been argued that hypothesis revision may lead to the presence in learner language of nonsystematic variability. Ellis (1985b: 124) claims that this exists when two forms occur in the same situational context, they perform the same illocutionary meaning, they occur in the same linguistic and discourse context and there is, in their manner of production, no evidence of any difference in the amount of attention paid to the form of the utterance. Despite these stringent requirements it is surprising how often, especially in spontaneous language, nonsystematic variability can be observed. The evidence from the recent Trahey & White (1993) experiment quoted above has led to the proposal that, given that in grammaticality judgement tests learners accept sentences which illustrate contradictory settings, it may be possible for learners to entertain two parameter settings at the same time.

Ellis argued that nonsystematic variability is a natural development: the learner initially learns a single form to convey a given meaning, such as 'no' for negation, but subsequently realises on the basis of positive evidence that other possibilities exist, e.g. 'don't' also for negation. Ellis (1985b) cites a learner 'J' who used these two forms in the same context in rapid succession (playing bingo, he said 'No look my card', closely followed by 'Don't look my card'). Ellis (1985b) suggests that these two forms must have been in free variation in that learner's language at that time and, following Gatbonton (1978) claims that free variation is a stage in the diffusion of knowledge. The other stages of the diffusion model are the acquisition phase during which the learner acquires the competing form and the replacement or reorganisational phase during which the learner sorts the forms into their correct functions or contexts. In this particular example, Ellis (1985b) believes that J sorted the forms into commands (eventually expressed by 'don't') and statements (eventually expressed by 'no') but that the process went through stages when the two coexisted in the system, as illustrated by Table 11.3.

Table 11.3 The diffusion model applied to form-function relationships

	Meaning	
	Commands	Statements
Acquisition phase		
Time 1	(1)	(1)
Time 2	(1), (2)	(1)
Time 3	(1), (2)	(1), (2)
Reorganisational phase		
Time 4	(2)	(1), (2)
Time 5	(2)	(1)

(1) = 'no' + V rule
(2) = 'don't' + V rule.
Source: Based on Gatbonton, 1978, from Ellis, 1985b, by permission of OUP.

Schachter (1986) contests the position adopted by Ellis (1985b) in relation to nonsystematic variability. Their differences of opinion (summarised by Tarone, 1988: 108ff) centre on competing reanalyses of data from a Cazden *et al.* (1975) study. Cazden *et al.* had proposed that their data, again related to the acquisition of negation, displayed free variation in learner language. Schachter's (1986) reanalysis of the data suggests that two forms which had been shown to co-occur at the same time in the data of another learner, Jorge, were, in fact, used for functions which could be pragmatically separated: in her view one form ('(I) don't V', e.g. 'know') was used to express the idea that the learner did not have the required information while the other (no V) was used to express denial. For Schachter, therefore, variability can be attributed to the ability of learners to keep apart linguistic forms which they use for a definable purpose. McLaughlin (1987, 1990) has provided some support to the Ellis view in his discussions of 'restructuring'. He argues that, as the interlanguage system grows, the arrival in the system of new data will provoke continual internal reorganisation. This is bound to lead to restructuring and this will mean that it is quite probable that learners observed from 'outside' will seem to 'regress' or 'backslide' (Selinker, 1972).

Many of the examples cited here would, however, be compatible with the view that when two forms appear to be in nonsystematic variation as described, one of the forms may be the result of learned linguistic knowledge (a product of externally driven hypotheses) and one the result of transfer either of the form (borrowing) or a parameter setting from the L1 (a product of internally driven hypotheses). The important question is how such nonsystematic variability may be resolved. It may be that the tension between the two is either never resolved and different forms are used in different environments, as some of the evidence of variability presented in Chapter 10 showed. Or, more optimistically, perhaps the kinds of restructuring described by Karmiloff-Smith (1986a) would permit access to competence which could then guide the learner towards a resolution. If this is the case, it would again call into question the total impermeability of linguistic competence which has been suggested by Schwartz (1993).

There is no doubt that the processes of hypothesis creation and revision described here for L2 learners are quite different from the consistent processes observed for L1 learners. One may argue that with more input L2 learners will eventually acquire a native-like competence but it clearly takes a very long time. The evidence of 'incompleteness' from Johnson & Newport (1989) and from Coppieters (1987) suggests indeed that the process is rarely ever complete.

Summary

In this chapter we have examined the various ways in which the process of hypothesis construction can be viewed. We began with the separation proposed by Schwartz (1993) between, on the one hand, competence acquired by the triggering of innate parameters on the basis of positive evidence and, on the other hand, learned linguistic knowledge acquired through explicit instruction and negative feedback. Both have a role to play in L2 learning but, she argued, they had to remain separate.

We then looked at evidence relating to learning resulting from explicit instruction and negative feedback. We concluded that there was relatively little evidence that learners were able to derive long-term native-like competence in this way but that teaching did have a direct effect. There were more grounds for optimism in cases where the learners had been selected because they were 'ready' to learn a particular structure. However, none of the studies examined could demonstrate that parameters had successfully been re-set by means of negative feedback and explicit instruction, or even by an 'input flood'.

We then examined the effectiveness of learning through exposure to authentic data in the form of situationally embedded utterances. This process was not seen as straightforward by all researchers. Krashen & Scarcella (1978) maintained that formulaic language could not develop into 'creative' language. However, Karmiloff-Smith (1986a) for L1, and Bialystok (1982) for L1 and L2, have argued that if learners bring about certain changes in mental representation (analysis) and control over the symbol system, then learning from positive evidence may be possible. On the basis of these arguments the data from L.W. Fillmore (1979) was re-examined to see to what extent it supported Karmiloff-Smith and Bialystok's arguments. The data provided some support for the claims but were not sufficient to demonstrate that L2 learners can derive native-like hypotheses from situationally embedded authentic data. The possibility of interaction between bottom-up hypotheses derived from initially formulaic utterances and top-down competence was proposed as a possible process in SLA which should not be ruled out but no evidence was found to positively rule it in.

Lastly, we examined the evidence relating to hypothesis revision which led to nonsystematic variability. The diffusion model was put forward as one potential explanation for the way in which nonsystematic variability would be a product of processes of hypothesis revision. It was also suggested that nonsystematic variability might be a product of two forms being learnt from two sources, one as a product of learned linguistic knowledge and one as a product of UG or a transfer of L1 competence.

12 The Development of Language Processing

In Chapter 10 we argued that there are three main causes of the variability which is characteristic of L2 learning but not of L1 learning.

In Chapter 11, we have given detailed consideration to the first of these, the multiple knowledge sources underlying hypothesis creation and revision. As a result of that consideration we have proposed two kinds of knowledge which may or may not be able to interact with each other: linguistic competence (derived from UG and L1 transfer and triggered by positive evidence) and learned linguistic knowledge (derived from explicit instruction and negative feedback). The knowledge which each generates, together or independently, must be given a form which permits language processing in real time. Schwartz (1993) has suggested that competence gives rise to performance and learned linguistic knowledge gives rise to learned linguistic behaviour. We will argue here that while these kinds of knowledge may be separate as regards the linguistic system and each may have different corresponding kinds of processing productions, it is also possible that the two will be combined in some of the productions necessary for language processing.

In Chapter 10 we also introduced an initial model for language production (Levelt, 1989) which would operate within the constraints placed on human information processing by short-term memory. That model contained knowledge stored in two different ways: declarative knowledge (encyclopedic knowledge, situational knowledge, discourse knowledge, knowledge of the lexicon) and procedural knowledge (knowledge of the processing mechanisms, especially those in the formulator). Because the model related to the production abilities of mature, monolingual, native speakers it did not contain a developmental aspect, nor did it deal directly with the different kinds of knowledge source which we now propose.

In this chapter we turn our attention to the second dimension put forward in Chapter 10: learners' need to transform knowledge of the linguistic system into productions which will allow them to process language in real-time. In order to deal with this aspect of SLA we must first present a model which enables us to conceptualise development of processing. Levelt (1989) has argued that real-time processing depends on 'automatised productions' but has not indicated how these are created or how they relate to other kinds of knowledge. First we provide a developmental framework which enables us to see how this may happen. Second we place our various kinds of knowledge within that framework and examine how each may be given the required form. This will inevitably raise questions about possible interaction once more. And finally, we examine how these processes have been and might be investigated in relation to L2 acquirers' behaviour.

There are now several theoretical frameworks which will allow consideration of these issues (for a review see R. Schmidt, 1992). The framework which we will use is based on the work of J.R. Anderson. We will set out to show how his views can be used to conceptualise the developmental mechanisms of language processing. It has to be said that Anderson's claims for his approach are much broader than the use we make of them here. The logic of his position is that learners learn the linguistic system (and not just how to process language) through the kinds of behaviour which he describes. Our view has consistently been that it is not possible to acquire native-like knowledge, i.e. competence, via these processes.

ACT*

Anderson's theory is called Adaptive Control of Thought (ACT) and the version on which this account is mainly based was put forward under the name of ACT* (Act star).

The basic framework is summed up by Figure 12.1. As can be seen there are three kinds of memory which interact with one another in specified ways. Compared with other systems, ACT* is unusual in requiring two long-term memories. Anderson believes, however, that two are necessary if important aspects of cognition are to be accounted for. In particular, Anderson believes that in this way it becomes possible to show how:

(a) over time and with practice the same knowledge can be stored in a different way so that it can be accessed more quickly. This explains the well-established effect of familiarity and practice.

(b) the process of storing different kinds of knowledge (essentially 'knowing that' — declarative knowledge — and 'knowing how' —

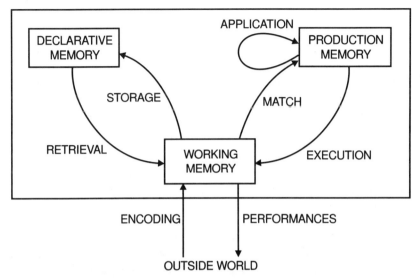

Figure 12.1 A general framework for the ACT system, identifying the major structural components and their interlinking processes

Source: J.R. Anderson (1983: 19)

procedural knowledge) is very different. A fact can be lodged in the mind in a few seconds (knowing 'that' . . .) while it can take a long time to learn how to ride a bicycle (knowing 'how' . . .).
(c) stored knowledge can be hierarchical and yet on occasions quickly accessible despite its complexity.
(d) conflict between competing possibilities can be resolved.
(e) certain kinds of information can be shown to be 'stronger' than others.

According to Anderson (1985: 232ff) all skill acquisition goes through three stages:

a cognitive stage, in which a description of the procedure is learned, an associative stage, in which a method for performing the skill is worked out and an autonomous stage, in which the skill becomes more and more rapid and automatic.

These stages will be found in the account of learning given below and will be used as a short reference system when we come to look at declarative and procedural knowledge in the context of strategies in Chapter 13.

A Production System

Anderson's is a production system in which the concept of a production has a special status. Productions are the connection between declarative knowledge and behaviour. For behaviour to happen, productions must be created. For behaviour to happen at naturalistic rates, productions must have been proceduralised (automatised). As successful proceduralised productions are created, they are stored in the production memory. As their successful use continues they will be further modified in ways described below until they become fully autonomous. The formulator in the production system of a mature native speaker will be made up of autonomous, proceduralised productions.

Production systems claim that

underlying human cognition is a set of condition–action pairs called productions. The conditions specify some data patterns and, if elements matching these patterns are in working memory, then the production can apply. The action specifies what to do in that state. The basic action is to add new data elements to working memory. (Anderson, 1983: 5–6).

Anderson's informal example of a production (Anderson, 1983: 6) is as follows:

IF   person 1 is the father of person 2
      and person 2 is the father of person 3
THEN person 1 is the grandfather of person 3.

This is to be interpreted to mean: IF, for example, you already have in store the knowledge that 'Fred is the father of Bill' and from the outside world you receive the further information that 'Bill is the father of Tom' in such a way that both these pieces of information are active in working memory at the same time, THEN you will derive the information that 'Fred is the grandfather of Tom' and deposit (action) that information in your working memory from where it can be stored in your production memory or give rise to a performance.

Thereafter a learner builds up both knowledge and skills by increasing the amount, changing the nature, and improving the accessibility of such 'condition–action' (IF . . . THEN) production pairs. However, the actual creation of productions is a long and careful process because, like Shiffrin & Schneider's (1977) automatic processes, once created they are not easily modified.

Declarative Knowledge, Working Memory and Interpretive Procedures

Productions are created, as indicated in Figure 12.1, through interaction between the memories. The working or short-term memory allows the other two memories to interact.

All knowledge, according to Anderson, is initially declarative. When information which has been stored in the declarative memory is retrieved to guide behaviour, this is done by means of general interpretive strategies. Using interpretive strategies is a very cumbersome procedure. It involves specifying all the stages of a process in great detail and in serial order. Although each of the stages is a production, the operation of productions in interpretation is very slow. They are linked to the first, 'cognitive' stage of skill acquisition and are operating on declarative knowledge. As we shall see, this is not the kind of production which might underlie fluent speech.

Anderson (1983: 218ff) posits two interpretive strategies: the use of general problem-solving and the use of analogy. To illustrate the use of analogy, Anderson uses the generation of a French sentence by means of a series of translation 'productions' which transliterate an equivalent English sentence into French. We will look in detail at his description of the workings of analogy in order to clarify the concept of production(s) and how they work in sequence.

The overall goal is to 'describe a fact' in French. The method selected involves arriving at the French sentence via translation, i.e. first produce the English sentence and then translate it. Therefore, the first subgoal is to produce the sentence in English. His example concerns the production of the French sentence: *Le banquier malin est en train de dérober la veuve pauvre,* which is offered as a translation of the English sentence: 'The smart banker is robbing the poor widow.'

The first production states the overall goal and the method to be used. (LV in productions means Local Value, i.e. a variable can be inserted at this point, in this case any particular language.)

P1 IF   the goal is to describe a fact in LV foreign-language
    THEN set as subgoals to plan a description of the fact in English
        and then to plan the translation of the English sentence into LV foreign language
        and then to generate the plan in LV foreign language

Because P1 has set as its first subgoal the production of the English sentence, the second production has to provide the basic sentence framework. It states that the appropriate syntactic shape for the sentence needed to express this type of meaning will be of the form NP Subject/Agent VP NP Object.

P2 IF   the goal is to describe (LV relation LV agent LV object) in English
    THEN set as subgoals to describe LV agent
          and then to describe LV relation
          and then to describe LV object

Within the sentence will be two sub-units, i.e. the NPs, composed of the definite article, an adjective and a noun. Production 3 sets out the framework for these:

P3 IF   the goal is to describe LV object
          and LV object is known to listener
          and LV object has a property named LV adjective
          and LV object is a member of a category named LV noun
    THEN set as subgoals to say 'the'
          and then to say LV adjective
          and then to say LV noun

The sentence also requires a VP and production 4 sets out its shape including information about number, agreement, tense and aspect:

P4 IF   the goal is to describe LV relation
          and the agent of LV relation is singular
          and LV relation is describing ongoing LV action
    THEN set as subgoals to say 'is'
          and then to say LV action
          and then to say 'ing'

The basic shape of the English sentence is now present. The second major subgoal can be attacked, i.e. the process of translation. Production 5 sets out the basic approach to translation:

P5 IF   the goal is to translate LV structure into LV language
    THEN the subgoals are to translate the elements of LV structure

The translation process begins with the translation of words which will translate directly:

P6 IF   the goal is to translate LV word into LV language
          and LV word1 is the vocabulary equivalent of LV word in LV
          language
     THEN the subgoal is to insert LV word1.

etc. etc. (Anderson, 1983: 228).

Twelve productions are cited for this sentence, some of which apply more than once. The issues become slightly more complex when genders etc. have to be decided but this example should suffice to illustrate the principle. We will not follow through the complete process in detail. The overall procedure is shown by a chart (Figure 12.2) plotting the flow of control through the operation.

The productions are thus shown to subdivide the activity into a series of serially ordered subgoals each with its specifically stated IF condition. The appropriate THEN action is taken to work through the system. They start by taking the knowledge of sentence representation in English including, for example, knowledge of how determiner reference works in English. This is knowledge held by every mature native speaker, presumably in declarative and in procedural form. Because the sentence has to be broken down into component parts for translation, it is the declarative knowledge which is accessed via interpretive mechanisms. The second stage, as shown in the flow chart in Figure 12.2, addresses the second subgoal of translation into French. Each component part (words and morphemes) of the English sentence is examined. Where it translates directly, as with adjectives, it is converted into its French equivalent. Where there is a condition, such as checking which gender the noun is or checking how to render continuous aspect, the translation process has means of elaborating more complex conditions so that the appropriate form is provided. The knowledge base will be declarative knowledge of rules of 'textbook translation' and subsequently 'rules' to generate the French sentence. The final product is, indeed, a French sentence, but one which is heavily influenced by the underlying translation.

The above description shows that producing language by means of these interpretive processes will be tedious, slow and time-consuming. Anderson explains why:

> Interpreting knowledge in declarative form . . . has serious costs in terms of time and working memory space. The process is slow because interpreting requires retrieving declarative information from long-term memory . . . The interpretive productions (i.e.

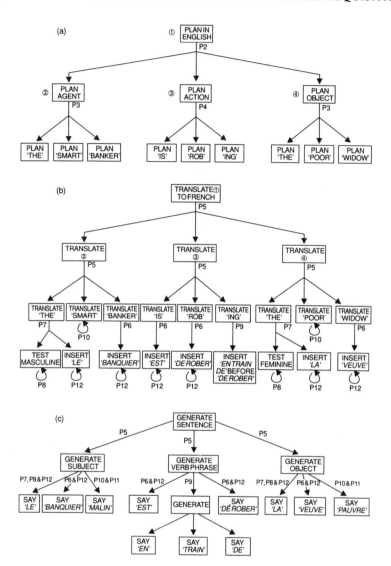

Figure 12.2 A representation of the flow of control in the sentence-generation productions for the sentence: *Le banquier malin est en train de dérober la veuve pauvre.* Part (a) illustrates the generation of the original English sentence; (b) illustrates its translation to French; and (c) illustrates the French execution plan that is the result of the translation.

Source: J.R. Anderson (1983: 227), reprinted by permission of Harvard University Press.

general problem solving and analogy) require that the declarative information be present in working memory and this can place a heavy burden on working-memory capacity. (Anderson, 1983: 231)

Given the speed required for fluent speech as described in Chapter 10, it is clear that the process by means of which the knowledge is retrieved from declarative memory into working memory and from there leads to 'performance' is far too cumbersome for the declarative memory to be the one which underlies fluent speech or comprehension. These skills, it is argued, depend critically on the proceduralisation of language productions. In the model proposed by Levelt (1989) the language processing mechanisms in all aspects of the formulator are proceduralised productions. The potentially significant information for fluent language production is in the way in which productions become proceduralised.

Production Memory and Compilation

In Anderson's theory, as we have seen, productions are constructed out of declarative knowledge which has previously been stored. They can be as laborious as the ones quoted above. However, once productions have been created, they will be examined to find ways in which they may be 'compiled', i.e. 'run together' so that larger groups of productions can be used as one unit. Compilation is made up of two subprocesses: composition and proceduralisation.

Composition 'takes a sequence of productions that follow each other in solving a particular problem and collapses them into a single production that has the effect of the sequence' (Anderson, 1983: 235) This immediately lessens the number of 'steps' referred to above and has the effect of speeding up the process.

Anderson's example for this is that of dialling a telephone number. Full interpretive procedures would require that there be a first production which has the condition:

IF   the goal is to dial LV telephone number,
        and LV digit1 is the first digit of LV telephone number
THEN dial LV digit1

a second production:

IF   the goal is to dial LV telephone number
        and LV digit1 has just been dialled
        and LV digit2 is after LV digit 1 in LV telephone number
THEN dial LV digit2

plus a third and a fourth and a fifth production, each dealing with each of the digits to be dialled in rigid sequence, providing the precise context which is necessary for the 'action' to apply, i.e. once the previous number has been dialled. A composed production would give rise to a 'macro-production' which would be able to suggest as the action part of the production that a sequence should be dialled without returning to a series of subconditions.

But note that the productions are still at this stage firmly based on the declarative knowledge and the information base from the declarative memory relative to the telephone number would still have to be called into working memory, thus taking up a lot of the limited available space. The gain represented by composition is thus limited.

The second process is proceduralisation: this 'eliminates clauses in the condition of a production that required information to be retrieved from long-term memory and held in working memory' (Anderson, 1983: 236). As a result, proceduralised knowledge is available much more quickly than non-proceduralised knowledge. In relation to telephone numbers the process of composition and proceduralisation will eventually produce:

P* IF   the goal is to dial Mary's number
     THEN dial 4-3-2-2-8-1-5

The advantages of proceduralised knowledge are clear: it makes fewer demands on working memory, it will be immediately available as a 'pattern match' (see below) and, if it has been correctly created, it will meet the needs of the situation.

It should nonetheless be noted that proceduralisation does present disadvantages as well: the procedure developed here will give rise to Mary's telephone number only. It is very specific. It will not be called forth in response to any other 'condition'. In this sense the gain in speed of production and the reduced processing load is traded off against a level of generality. However, as noted above, when this production is created the others are not 'lost', although there will be a possible subsequent conflict when 'conditions' appear in working memory to which both might apply (see below).

Anderson also suggests, as a precaution against over-hasty pro-ceduralisation, that 'It seems reasonable to propose that proceduralisation only occurs when long-term memory knowledge has achieved some threshold of strength [see below] and has been used some criterion number of times' (Anderson, 1983: 240).

This is not the end of the process by means of which information can be stored in an ever more accessible manner and through which it can be refined, but before dealing with further processes, something needs to be said about other aspects of the information in Figure 12.1, notably matching, execution, and application. These processes are all related to the production memory and application, in particular, plays a role in furthering those processes which contribute to more rapid processing.

Matching, Execution and Application

'Matching' or 'pattern match' is the mechanism through which it is decided which productions will apply. When information is active in the working memory, circumstances are present in which the production memory can be examined to see if it contains anything which matches the 'condition' side of information in the working memory. If such matching is possible, and in particular if a match is possible with a proceduralised production, then the 'action' side of the pair will deposit the production into working memory and make it immediately available for performance.

'Execution' needs little commentary as it is clearly the means by which the 'action' side of a production is delivered into working memory. The choice of term indicates, however, that the process is thought of as instantaneous and automatic.

'Application' is more significant because it relates to the process of 'strengthening' (Anderson, 1983: 249) which is thought to exist within both memories. Application is the process of using a production successfully. Each time a condition in the working memory activates a production from the production memory and causes an action to be deposited into working memory and there is no negative feedback, the production will be strengthened and will become more robust. Because it (and all other entries which are similarly strengthened) is more robust it will be able to resist occasional negative feedback and also it will be more strongly activated when it is called upon.

Tuning: Generalisation and Discrimination

These processes apply to productions which have already been compiled and assist in enabling certain productions to become more autonomous and therefore faster. The question of strength is instrumental in determining their application.

The two subprocesses of tuning are generalisation and discrimination. 'There is a generalisation process by which production rules become broader in their range of applicability, a discrimination process by which the rules become narrower' (Anderson, 1983: 241).

Generalisation is thought of as the aspect of the theory which explains what Anderson (1983: 242) calls productivity. In his presentation, this seems very close to the Chomskyan notion of creativity 'the ability to perform successfully in novel situations . . . the speaker's ability to generate and comprehend utterances never before encountered' (Anderson, 1983: 242). Where two existing productions partially overlap it may be possible to combine them to create a greater level of generality by 'deleting a condition that was different in the two original productions' (Anderson, 1983: 242). He proposes (p. 244) that whenever a production is formed 'an attempt is made to compare it to other existing productions to see if a potential generalisation exists'. The second generalising mechanism consists of replacing constants with variables.

Discrimination is intended to restrict the range of application of a production: 'The discrimination process tries to restrict the range of application of a production to just the appropriate circumstances' (Anderson, 1983: 245). Anderson argues (p. 250) that these processes account for the way in which L1 and L2 learners overgeneralise structures but then learn over time to discriminate between, for example, regular and irregular verbs.

From our point of view, the tuning processes are mechanisms which ensure that wherever possible generalisations are sought, thus creating the greatest number of 'tuned compilations' possible and that the tuned compilations are adapted with precision to the circumstances where they will be used.

All productions may on occasions give rise to internal competition. The extent to which a production has been strengthened is critical in the resolution of such conflict. Certainly in the area of language, the most obvious example being lexical meaning but also in syntax, it is quite possible that ambiguities will be present. For example, of the two meanings of 'bank', how would the system know which is the more likely? The answer has to be: the 'strongest', i.e. the one that has been accessed most frequently. A feedback process ensures that better rules are strengthened and poorer rules weakened. Strength can equally be used to differentiate between conflicting or competing possibilities: 'Newly composed productions are weak and may require multiple creations before they gain enough strength to compete successfully with the productions from which they were created' (Anderson, 1983: 239). Again the production will be applied more quickly if conflicts are immediately resolved.

All of the processes described in this section contribute to the development of the kind of automatised productions which Levelt has suggested are central to the workings of his production model and therefore essential for fluent comprehension and production. We now need to show how the various kinds of knowledge described in Chapter 11 fit into these processes.

Processing Different Kinds of Knowledge

As noted at the beginning of this chapter, Schwartz (1993) has suggested that competence gives rise to performance and learned linguistic knowledge gives rise to learned linguistic behaviour. UG and L1 transfer underlie competence, and explicit instruction with negative feedback underlies learned language behaviour.

Processing competence

We begin by examining competence. It has to be admitted that the concept of development in the context of competence is difficult to handle. In addition, in the SLA environment we have to make a distinction between competence resulting from direct access to UG and competence resulting from transfer from the L1.

Competence based on access to UG is triggered rather than developed. Triggering of innate knowledge is thought to be an automatic consequence of exposure to the appropriate positive evidence. As such, at a given time in the learner's language, triggering of a particular parameter has taken place or it has not. Normally there are no half measures.

It is assumed that, as appropriate linguistic information becomes available to the learner via perceptual processes (which are, of course, dependent to some extent on short-term memory), the innate hypotheses will be triggered by interaction between the relevant external evidence and the internal hypothesis. Relatively small amounts of data should suffice to trigger the pro-drop parameter, case theory parameters, verb movement parameters, etc.

Once triggering has taken place, if performance can, as suggested, be directly derived from competence, then there would be little delay in the consequences of that setting being converted into automatised productions for inclusion into an L2 formulator. We will assume that this is likely to be the case.

There are, however, two reservations which have to be mentioned, both of which again introduce questions about possible interaction between competence and learned linguistic knowledge.

The first deals with lexical knowledge. Grammaticality judgement tests are made up of sentences containing specific lexical items. It is not enough to have knowledge of, for example, how case theory relates to passivisation, it is also necessary to know that a particular verb has a particular pattern of case assignment. Learning the particularities of that verb is part of learned linguistic knowledge. But the application of competence knowledge may depend on it.

The second deals with the use of 'competence' in different situations. Evidence from the variability of learners' behaviour in different situations (see Chapter 10) would suggest that knowledge is not simply 'available' or 'not available'. It is available under some circumstances. Situations which require learners to pay attention to other things appear to lead them to make 'mistakes' (to call on another version of their interlanguage) which they would not make if that pressure was not there. It is an open question as to whether 'performance' derived from 'competence' knowledge is affected by this pressure or whether it affects only 'learned linguistic behaviour' derived from 'learned linguistic knowledge'. Both of these issues raise questions about interaction between the two knowledge types and this will be dealt with below.

One could argue that transfer of L1 competence, i.e. assuming that L1 parameters apply in the L2, will lead to the creation of automatised procedures in the same way. Indeed, when one listens to advanced learners who have been placed in a communicative situation which makes demands on them beyond their L2 knowledge, one frequently hears what appears to be fluent transliteration in which the settings and rules of the L1 are systematically and fluently applied to the L2.

Transfer offers obvious advantages and disadvantages. Where the parameter settings are the same, transfer may equip the learner with internally generated hypotheses which offer similar possibilities for the creation of automatised performance. The problems arise when the parameter settings are different. In these cases, as was seen with the evidence presented in Chapter 11, it is very difficult to get learners to reset the parameters on the basis of the different kinds of evidence which can be made available to them. The danger then is that learners will create productions without realising that these are not acceptable L2 utterances. And if these are allowed to continue through the procedural-isation process, they may be very difficult to modify.

Transfer probably offers one of the greatest challenges, both to learners and to researchers, because what is being transferred is deep seated, both in the sense that the parameters are part of the core of the language structure and that the settings have been transformed into well-established proceduralised productions for L1 use.

Processing learned linguistic knowledge

Learned linguistic knowledge raises two main issues of importance. The first relates to the frequent disparity between the context in which it is learnt and the use which is to be made of it and the second relates to the importance of lexical knowledge in processing.

We will first take two, perhaps extreme, forms of learned linguistic knowledge and discuss the problems which may arise from their conversion into proceduralised form in the way discussed above.

The first example is explicit information about the language provided in a classroom with or without negative feedback. We assume that this may take the form of a statement about the surface regularities of the L2. The 'rule' is presented and is 'proceduralised' by the conscientious learner in the way in which it was presented. A good learner will then be able to repeat it when asked. If the rule is proceduralised, the knowledge may be present in the same form twenty years later. The problem arises when it comes to making use of the knowledge in rapid speech. Normally this is not possible because it has been proceduralised in a way which does not allow access in those circumstances. All the learner can do is reproduce the rule in the form in which it was learnt, i.e. as a discursive statement. If use is to be made of it, the learner will have to recall the totality of the proceduralised rule and consciously extract that part of the information which is relevant.

The second example is utterances learnt in specific situations. Dialogues or exchanges based on situations may easily become pro-ceduralised. They can then be recalled when appropriate circumstances arise. When they are recalled, they are recalled in their totality but, if the learner is not able to perceive the internal relationships making up the structure of the utterance, it will not be possible for him or her to modify it. The result in extreme cases can be parrot-like answers to questions to which they do not relate.

The deceptively simple lesson to be learned is that learners will not be able to divorce the learning from the context of learning and that it is therefore essential to provide the information in the context in which it may be needed.

A second important issue relates to lexical knowledge. Lexical knowledge is to do with knowledge of the meanings of words but it is also composed of information about the syntactic values (argument structure, theta structure, agreement possibilities, i.e. all the information specified in lemmas in Chapter 10) of the lexical items. As indicated above, it is often this information which is at the root of learners' problems rather than the parameter setting. A learner might, for example, have reset the case theory parameter settings which determine passivisation in French and English, but then misclassify a particular verb because it is assumed that its case assignment properties have transferred from one language to another.

Combining different kinds of knowledge in processing

It follows from our arguments so far that learner production is the result of a complex set of interactions. In the same set of utterances produced by a learner there may be present forms which find their origin in direct UG access competence and which have been immediately proceduralised. These will probably be fluently and accurately produced in most circumstances. Other forms may be a product of transfer which have been erroneously accepted by the learner. These we would expect to be fluently produced but they could be very inaccurate. Further forms may be the result of learned linguistic knowledge. Depending on the source of the knowledge, they may be more or less fluent and/or accurate. A formula learnt in situation, for example, is likely to be fluently produced. It will, however, be totally inflexible. It can be produced only as it stands and will brook no alteration. On the other hand, a form which is an application of a learnt rule may be produced very correctly but very slowly. The learner is consulting a mental statement of the rule in order to make the utterance conform to it. It will have to be accessed through slow interpretive processes. It is not surprising if we observe a rather 'stop-go' performance in the oral language of most language learners. In addition, of course, different learning styles may lead learners towards a preference for one or other of these approaches.

The question remains of the extent to which it may be possible to propose that during the developmental processes described here performance based on competence might be modified by learned linguistic knowledge. Schwartz (1993) and others have argued for this dichotomy at the level of acquisition on principled and empirical grounds. As yet there is very little evidence to demonstrate interaction at that level between externally provided evidence and internally provided hypotheses in the acquisition process. It is, however, conceivable that during the creation of processing productions, forms derived from different sources during the mental organisation of acquisition may come together to form productions. This would lead to the gradual disappearance of surface differences while differences in the underlying knowledge (competence) remained. This would be compatible with evidence such as that cited by Coppieters (1987). This is clearly a central question for further investigation.

In the meantime, the conceptual framework provided here allows us to explain variability in more detail. Given the variety of origin and the variety in the degree of proceduralisation presented above, it is clear that items which may be present at the same time may have differential status. Depending on what source an item has come from and what its processing history may be, we should expect to find varying status for different forms. This variety is, of course, not applicable to L1 acquisition. In that case, a unique, competence-based source provides the necessary innate hypotheses which are triggered by minimal amounts of external information. Indeed, when one speaks of variety in relation to native speakers, one is largely concerned with the influence of external factors such as geographical origin, social grouping and the influence of education which relate differently to learned linguistic knowledge. L2 learners have multiple sources of knowledge and variable processing capacity: their speech is certain to display variability.

Evaluation

The presence of Anderson's theories in a book such as this may surprise some readers. It is certainly true that Anderson's work belongs to a tradition which is not easily compatible with nativist views of language acquisition. However, we are attempting to deal with approaches to language acquisition which encompass competence and performance, learned linguistic knowledge and learned linguistic behaviour, the role of internal and external sources of information for the learner.

The Levelt (1989) model of production brings together all the elements, as we argued in Chapter 10, but it does not provide a developmental aspect. Without the developmental dimension which Anderson's theories bring, it is impossible to treat the developmental aspect of three out of the four significant areas, i.e. learned linguistic knowledge, performance and learned linguistic behaviour. Once the concepts of declarative and procedural knowledge can be shown to have a contribution to make and can be shown to have their own developmental framework, then it becomes possible to construct a vision of the overall process which is necessary to cope with the multiplicity of sources available to L2 learners with mature cognitive skills.

Anderson's framework therefore provides an essential contribution to an overall theory. Hypotheses derived from explicit instruction and from formulaic language through exposure can be accommodated and placed within a developmental framework based on declarative and proceduralised knowledge. Hypotheses will be applied in more and more cases and available in more and more circumstances as more and more of the language is proceduralised. This is the most convincing account of how learners' language , especially when they are exposed to a native speaking environment, becomes more rapid, more authentic, and they become more able to produce speech at a closer approximation to native speed.

We shall now briefly examine attempts to make use of Anderson's model in L2 research.

Application

Some attempt has been made to apply these theories to SLA. This has been undertaken most by researchers in Germany, notably Dechert, Raupach and others of the Kassel school (see Möhle & Raupach, 1983; Dechert, Möhle & Raupach, 1984; Raupach, 1987). Working in different languages and working with different levels of language structure, they have attempted to build either on explicitly Andersonian distinctions (Raupach, 1987) or on similar constructs in two ways: the study of formulaic utterances in learner language and the use of temporal variables to measure learner production.

Temporal variables have been used to measure the degree to which language may have been proceduralised. There are four main temporal variables: speaking rate, articulation rate, phonation/time ratio (the amount of time actually spent speaking as a proportion of the total time), and mean length of utterance (defined as continuous speech between silent pauses of a defined duration). They are, of course, global measures and cannot indicate the degree of proceduralisation of a given structure. They were introduced by Grosjean & Deschamps (1972, 1973, 1975), who studied native speakers of English and French, individuals undertaking different tasks and compared the same speakers speaking different languages.

Raupach (1987) hoped that by using the techniques evolved by these researchers he would gain insight into the degree to which L2 learners had progressed in the ways described above, i.e. by 'proceduralising' their knowledge. Raupach (1984: 117) suggests that 'speech segments uttered between hesitation phenomena are possible candidates for processing units, if supplementary evidence can be supplied'. Thus, the study of formulaic language and the study of the significance of pausing and temporal variables are used to investigate Anderson's proposed acquisition processes. Following Fitts (1964) and J.R. Anderson (1982, 1983, 1985) the processes outlined in detail above are discussed under the three simplified stages: the cognitive stage, the associative stage and the autonomous stage.

In the cognitive stage, the learner is still dependent on declarative knowledge and is therefore using general interpretive strategies to produce the L2. The result is likely to be very slow speech involving, for example, 'verbal mediation, in which the learner rehearses the information required to execute the skill' (Raupach, 1987: 129, quoting Anderson, 1983: 217). An example would be verbal rehearsal of translation used as an interpretive strategy as outlined above.

In the associative stage, knowledge compilation, with its two subprocesses of composition and proceduralisation, comes into play.

When a task is performed repetitively, proceduralisation gradually replaces the interpretive application of declarative knowledge with productions that perform the behaviour directly. At the same time the composition process leads to a combination of a sequence of productions into a single production. (Raupach, 1987: 129)

The process of knowledge compilation through composition and proceduralisation will be taking place here.

In the autonomous stage, the proceduralised knowledge can still be refined by 'tuning':

a generalisation process by which production rules become broader in their range of applicability, a discrimination process by which the rules become narrower and a strengthening process by which better rules are strengthened and poorer rules weakened. (Raupach 1987: 130, quoting Anderson, 1983: 241)

Raupach sums up this view of language learning as follows:

Learning principally starts out with the time-consuming application of declaratively possessed language rules and data. The process of knowledge compilation and of tuning allow the learner to gradually perform parts of his language tasks automatically without activating declarative knowledge and to eventually attain a more fluent and effective performance. (Raupach, 1987: 130)

Progress is therefore seen in terms of increased fluency which is brought about by the transfer of knowledge into the procedural memory and subsequent direct access to the proceduralised productions. To assess progress of this kind the researcher needs to able to observe what knowledge compilation (composition and proceduralisation) and what tuning (generalisation and discrimination) has taken place.

Raupach (1987) cites examples of French produced by adult native speakers of German in which a not very demanding conversational task is performed at first in a way which is 'extremely hesitant and slow' (p. 137). The 'length of runs' is very small (3.25 syllables on average) and the text shows evidence of 'the learner's being inclined towards starting her utterance on the basis of German constructions' (p. 137). This manner of processing finds its expression in overt retrieval of lexical items which must sometimes be provided by the interviewer ('*fait la connaissance*', '*les habitudes*', '*oublié*'):

To speak the foreign language our learner thus constantly uses her knowledge of German plus translation rules and is, consequently, reduced to word-for-word processing. This corresponds perfectly to Anderson's examples of interpretive use of declarative knowledge in the domain of language generation. (Raupach, 1987: 137).

The actual example cited is a phrase where the learner begins: *connaissance* (euh) (.) *avec la culture* instead of *faire la connaissance de* . . . a structure which echoes the German *Bekenntschaft machen mit.* . . .

Raupach argues further that it is possible to observe learners using a 'transfer of procedural knowledge' in which they transfer stress patterns, for example, from German to French. This dependence on L1 surface structure is unlikely to 'result necessarily in idiomatic foreign language use' (Raupach, 1987: 139). As indicated by Anderson, it maintains the patterns of the procedural knowledge which underlies it.

Table 12.1 Temporal variables, related to oral interviews, showing the progression of one learner over a four year period of undergraduate study.

	Speaking rate	Articulation rate	Phonation/ time ratio	Mean length of utterance	Percentage of runs of various lengths		
					1–4 syllables	5–10 syllables	11+ syllables
Year 1	122.46	3.88	52.59	4.27	75.75	15.15	9.09
Year 2	121.50	3.75	54.69	4.69	63.63	32.95	3.40
Year 3	149.85	3.71	67.40	5.89	58.88	27.77	13.33
Year 4	177.45	3.75	78.50	6.20	50.00	38.52	11.47

Source: Towell, 1987b: 168

Comparing this kind of performance with that of learners who had been exposed to French in a native context, Raupach (1987) and Towell (1987b) are able to show by measurement of the temporal variables that the mean length of run increases and the amount of time spent pausing reduces. Towell (1987b) quotes the figures shown in Table 12.1 for the various increases associated with one learner studied over four years. He quotes the following average increases for a group of five learners, taking their highest and lowest performance on an interview tasks conducted once a year over the four years of an undergraduate course which included a year spent in France:

Speaking rate improved on average by   + 60.10%
Articulation improved on average by   + 19.70%
Phonation/time ratio improved on average by + 38.61%
Mean length of run improved on average by   +101.07%

However, he does indicate that with such a small sample and some considerable differences between individuals such averages should be treated with extreme caution. Raupach quotes the figures in Table 12.2 for increases in mean length of runs for his learners before and after a term in France.

By detailed examination of texts produced by learners before and after a period of residence in the country where the language is spoken, Raupach claims that: 'Many sequences testify that the learner's stay

Table 12.2 Increases in mean length of runs for learners before and after a term in France

L1 German	Before	After
Subject 2	5.51 syllables vs	7.54 syllables
Subject 3	6.30	10.73
Subject 4	6.00	7.87
Subject 5	4.56	7.92
Subject 6	5.55	8.70
Subject 7	7.48	7.85
L1 English		
Subject 8	4.30	8.40
Corpus d'Orléans (native speaker) 14.43		

abroad has fostered the process of knowledge compilation in many domains of her foreign language knowledge.'

He cites examples where the speaker repeats information elicited before going abroad in ways which demonstrate the increase in fluent and authentic expression. The question asked concerned the reactions of French people towards a young German:

Before going abroad:

euh (0.86) j'ai: moi j'ai déjà (1.26) euh: parlé là-dessus avec (.) quelques Français que j'ai: rencontrés (0.26) en vacances / (0.82) et: (0.40) moi je (0.56) je n'avais: jamais cru / qu'il y a (0.90) qu'il y a même / des les préjugés (0.80) euh parmi (0.32) les jeunes gens / (0.70) mais ils m'ont racon . . .(.) ils m'ont raconté / (0.68) euh que (1.90) euh: (1.60) ils ont toujours euh: (.) une opid . . . (0.32) une opinion (1.06) euh quelquefois (0.50) a . . . assez mauvais (0.32) mauvaise (0.34) des Allemands / (1.14) même des: jeunes gens / (0.62) à cause de la guerre (.)
hmm
et moi / en s . . . (0.26) en ce cas / (0.74) je leur je leur dis toujours que (0.46) ce n'ét . . . que ce n'était pas moi / s . . . ce n'était pas les jeunes gens / (0.46) qui ont fait la guerre (0.40) et pour moi c'est passé / (1.16) et: (2.04) moi je ne je n:e me sens pas (0.60) responsable pour cela (0.26)

After going abroad:

non ç:a n'avait pas d'importance (0.46) s . . . euh alors cet . . cette fois / (0.44) j'étais: euh surprise d'une manière très_agréable (.) je peux dire ça (0.84) parce que: je n'ai pas du tout remarqué: qu'i . . . qu'i . . . qu'il y a encore (0.86) des: préjugés négatifs (1.06) envers les Allemands à cause de la guerre (0.58) par exemple (1.04) j'en ai parlé à (0.68) quelques Français ils m'ont: toujours dit que (0.86) c'était pour eux que s . . . que s . . . que pour eux c'était du passé / (1.00) et: (1.50) ça ne compte plus.

While the difference can only, no doubt, be appreciated by listening to a tape recording, the second response is much more coherent, much less hesitant and there is much less searching for the way to express an idea. According to Raupach the process of procedural learning is accompanied by a reduction of hesitations in, for example, the area of gender markings. He states:

> The learner's growing ability in speeding up her foreign language processing by activating an increasing number of proceduralised productions allows her to concentrate more than before on content, not so much on form. (Raupach, 1987: 146)

Raupach also points to a number of differences in the way the learner segments the speech units and hesitates in a more 'native-like' way. Finally he argues that by comparing the language used at different points it is possible to see that:

> extensive exposure to the foreign language can have the effect of weakening or maybe even abolishing parts of the learner's knowledge that have already been encoded in procedural form. (Raupach, 1987: 147)

thus giving some backing to the notion that feedback can lead to weakening of certain forms even at the 'tuning' stage.

Raupach however is not entirely uncritical of Anderson's model.

> Foreign language learning cannot be adequately described as a uniform process of procedural learning. Rather we must acknowledge that there are different acquisition modes not only across different learners with a similar background, but also in the course of an individual's learning history . . . Anderson's stage analysis . . . is best mirrored in those learners who have acquired the foreign language in a classroom situation and who occasionally have the opportunity to practise it in a native or native-like environments before finally being exposed to it for a certain period of time as is the case with a term of residence abroad. (Raupach, 1987: 148)

He stresses, however, how frequently subjects can be observed to use a 'specific acquisition mode [which] consists in the learners developing their use of interpretive translation procedures' (p. 149) along the lines of Anderson's use of 'analogy' outlined above.

It is obviously essential to have more detailed studies of the kind which Raupach provides. It has to be admitted, however, that it is difficult to assert definitely that the procedures described by Anderson are those which underlie the observations made. At the moment, only global measures of temporal variables are available: these are no doubt of value, but they don't allow us to test in detail whether the kind of learning which is being suggested is actually taking place. It is difficult to see how one can actually measure whether or not a learner has actually 'composed', 'generalised' or 'discriminated' knowledge in the way that Anderson and Raupach claim. They suggest that in some way the knowledge of the language is being stored and accessed differently, but whether that involves the actual procedures put forward is not proven. It would be necessary to devise and carry out detailed experiments, preferably following the same learners over a considerable length of time intervening at different stages to assess the degree of language processing development to back up the temporal variables, perhaps with the aid of different kinds of tests and introspective comments from learners.

Also the observations address only the issues related to procedural-isation. In Chapter 11 we stressed the need to be able to show how mental representation of linguistic structure may also have changed if we were to show interaction between internal and external sources. We argue that the ideas presented in this chapter are most useful in showing the importance of different processing storage and access mechanisms. The changes in mental representation which allow the language system to grow are those described in Chapters 5–9 and in Chapter 11.

Summary

In this chapter we have concentrated on how learners develop the ability to process language in real-time. We have made use of Anderson's ACT* theory. This provides us with a developmental framework for processing skills which we have lacked so far. This consists of staged procedures through which knowledge is first compiled (composed and proceduralised) and then tuned (generalised and discriminated).

Although we could not accept Anderson's claims that these

processes accounted for language acquisition in the sense that they would enable learners to acquire a native-like system, we nonetheless felt that this account allowed us to integrate the multiplicity of sources previously specified as having input into SLA. The production system shows how mechanisms may be created to permit real-time language processing from competence type knowledge and from learned linguistic knowledge. The resulting mechanisms are the proceduralised productions specified in the Levelt (1989) model introduced in Chapter 10. It is argued that these are created slowly, going through stages of composition and proceduralisation. In the latter stage they become 'autonomous' and 'automatised' in the sense described by Shiffrin & Schneider (1977). However, the declarative knowledge is not lost and can be called on where necessary.

Any kind of knowledge can, in principle, be proceduralised. We examined the consequences of proceduralisation for the two main types of knowledge. Competence based on direct access to UG in a way similar to L1 acquisition should rapidly give rise to the performance of fluent and accurate speech. Competence based on L1 transfer should also prove effective in those cases where the parameter settings are identical; in cases where they are different there is a danger that productions of a fluent but inaccurate nature may result. The proceduralisation of learned linguistic knowledge was seen to give rise to different kinds of learned linguistic behaviour depending on whether the source was explicit instruction or formulaic language. The issue of whether competence-based knowledge and learned linguistic knowledge might come together during the creation of processing mechanisms was seen to be a central research question.

We then looked in some detail at an attempt to make use of the Anderson model in empirical research. The use of temporal variables did appear to give some broad support to the notions but it did not prove possible to provide explicit proof that Anderson's processes underlay the progress made. Nor was the research able to integrate changes in mental representation with the processing description. What is needed, it was felt, was research which examined both growth in linguistic knowledge and processing ability.

We will now turn to our third main explanation of variability: the question of how learners cope with the continued presence of an inadequate system and the role this has to play in relation to variability.

13 Approaches to Learner Strategies

A final aspect of learner language which bears on variability and of which L2 researchers have been aware for a number of years, is the use of strategies. Strategies have been classified under three headings (Ellis, 1985a: ch. 7): learning strategies, production strategies and communication strategies. The distinction between these three categories on a common sense basis appears evident: learning strategies are deployed by learners to ensure that they learn, production strategies to ensure that the language can be produced rapidly in a number of situations, communication strategies to compensate for the lack of knowledge of an L2 by going around the problem in some way. In fact, it has proved rather difficult to disentangle the three common sense categories. More work has been done on communication (or compensatory) strategies than on the other two, perhaps because of the relatively atheoretical nature of observation of this behaviour and the visibility of these strategies in data. Ellis, however, is rather pessimistic about the analysis of strategies: 'Peering into the "black box" to identify the different learner strategies at work in SLA is rather like stumbling blindfold around a room to find a hidden object' (Ellis, 1985a: 188).

The reason why Ellis found the activity unrewarding may have something to do with the way research into strategies had been carried out up to that point. Research into learner strategies, mainly communication strategies, began with the observation that learners could be seen to be using a number of common devices to cope with the fact that they did not have at their command sufficient language to communicate the ideas which they desired to communicate. Unlike children, most L2 learners are mature users of ideas but their L2 competence is not up to expressing those ideas, so they have to find ways around the problem. As the first step to understanding what was happening, researchers felt the need to classify the observations into a taxonomy. A fairly typical example of the results of this work can be seen in Table 13.1, taken from an article by Tarone, Cohen & Dumas, first published in *Working Papers in Bilingualism* (1976) and reprinted in Faerch & Kasper (1983).

Table 13.1 Communication strategies: a taxonomy by levels of linguistic structure and strategy type

	Phonological	Morphological	Syntactic	Lexical
Transfer from NL	/ʃip/ for /ʃɪp/	The BOOK OF JACK for *Jack's book*	Dió A ELLOS for LES *dió* A ELLOS in Spanish-L2	Je SAIS *Jean* for Je CONNAIS *Jean* in French-L2
Overgeneralization	El carro/karo/ es caro (Flap r generalized to trill contexts — Span.-L2)	He GOED Il A tombé in French-L2	I don't know WHAT IS IT	He is PRETTY (Unaware of the semantic limitations)
Prefabricated pattern	—	—	I don't know how do you do that	—
Overelaboration	/hwʌt ar ju duɪŋ/ for /wʌtʃəduɪn/	I WOULD NOT HAVE GONE	YO *quiero ir* — Span.-L2 Buddy, that's my foot WHICH you're standing on	The people next door are rather INDIGENT
Epenthesis	/sətəreɪ/ for /streɪ/	—	—	—
Avoidance (a) Topic avoidance 1. Change topic 2. No verbal response	(To avoid using certain sounds, like /l/ and /r/ in *pollution problems*.)	(Avoiding talking about what happened yesterday.)	(Avoiding talk of a hypothetical nature and *conditional* clauses.)	(Avoiding talk about one's work due to lack of *technical* vocabulary.)
(b) Semantic avoidance	It's hard to breathe for air pollution	I like to swim in response to What happened yesterday?	Q: ¿Qué quieren los pájaros que haga la mamá? R: Quieren comer. (Spanish-L2)	Il regarde et il veut boire to avoid the word for cupboard in Il ouvre l'armoire

228 APPROACHES TO SECOND LANGUAGE ACQUISITION

Table 13.1 *(continued)* Communication strategies: a taxonomy by levels of linguistic structure and strategy type

	Phonological	*Morphological*	*Syntactic*	*Lexical*
(c) Appeal to authority 1. Ask for form 2. As if correct 3. Look it up	Q: *f . . . ?* R: *fauteuil* (French-L2)	Q: *Je l'ai . . . ?* R: *prise.* (French-L2)	Q: *El quiere . . . ?* R: *que te vayas.* (Spanish-L2)	*How do you say "staple" in French?*
(d) Para-phrase	*Les garçons et les filles* for *Les enfants* (Thus avoiding liaison in French-L2)	*Il nous faut partir* for *Il faut que nous partions* (To avoid sub-junctive in French-L2)	*J'ai trois pommes* for *J'EN ai trois* (To avoid *en* in French-L2)	High cover-age word: *tool* for *wrench* Low fre-quency word: *labour* for *work* Word coin-age: *airball* Circumlo-cution: *a thing you dry your hands on*
(e) Message abandon-ment	*Les oiseaux ga . . . (gazouillent dans les arbres* was intended in French-L2)	*El queria que yo . . . (fuera a la tienda* was in-tended in Spanish-L2)	*What you . . . ?*	*If only I had a . . .*
(f) Language switch	*I want a* COUTEAU[2]	*Le livre de Paul's* (French-L2)	*Je ne pas* GO TO SCHOOL (French-L2)	*We get this* HOSTIE *from* LE PRÊTRE (English-L2)

Source: Tarone, Cohen & Dumas, 1976; reprinted in Faerch & Kasper, 1983: 6–7

This classification deals with language levels up to the lexical level (it would be perfectly possible to add a discourse and a pragmatic level to this list) and illustrates the main categories: transfer from NL, overgeneralis-ation, prefabricated patterns, epenthesis and a whole series of sub-categories under 'avoidance', including paraphrase and language switch. Useful though such taxonomies are, there are two problems which meant that research into strategies tended to stagnate.

The first problem is one of overlap between categories either within a taxonomy or between taxonomies: in this list 'transfer' is seen as a separate strategy from 'language switch' but the difference between the two may not always be obvious. Other researchers may use the term 'borrowing' to cover both. In this taxonomy, paraphrase and language switch are seen as ways of avoiding a problem, but in Faerch & Kasper (1983: 46) code switching and interlingual transfer are seen as achievement strategies.

The second problem is a lack of explanatory capacity. While it is always useful to have a classification, if the phenomenon is to be understood, it will have to be included within a theory. In the case of strategies, this will most probably have to be a theory of language use and/or production.

We shall deal here with four attempts to incorporate an account of strategies into broader theories. We will first examine the approach of Faerch & Kasper (1983); then that of Poulisse (1990), who develops and refines their approach; then that of Bialystok (1990a), who approaches the question from a different theoretical point of view; and lastly that of O'Malley & Chamot (1990), who concentrate on learning strategies from a purely cognitive perspective. Faerch & Kasper use a broad model of speech production as their basis, Poulisse uses the Levelt (1989) model presented in Chapter 10 along with elements from Grice's (1968) pragmatic principles, Bialystok (1990a) bases her views on 'analysis' and 'control' briefly presented in Chapter 11, and O'Malley & Chamot (1990) base their account on the Anderson (1983, 1985) production system outlined in Chapter 12.

Reduction and Achievement Strategies

Faerch & Kasper (1983) take as their starting point the goal of the learner. They indicate that in order to achieve that goal, the learner must first go through a planning process. At that point items appropriate to the situation will be retrieved from whatever linguistic system(s) are available to the learner, including the Interlanguage, the first language and any other languages. The learner then establishes a plan in which the linguistic items are organised and which must be executed in speech or writing. Their concept of strategies is problem-oriented and they define communication strategies as follows: 'communication strategies are potentially conscious plans for solving what to an individual presents itself as a problem in reaching a particular communicative goal' (Faerch & Kasper, 1983: 36).

The problem can be encountered by the learner at either of the two major phases of language production: the planning phase or the execution phase. The learner can react in one of two ways: either maintain the goal he or she set out to achieve and find a way of deploying the linguistic resources to meet that objective or decide that it is better to revise the goal and use whatever linguistic means are available to attain a lesser goal. The first reaction Faerch & Kasper call an achievement strategy, the second they call a reduction strategy. They also allow for the application of these strategies either to linguistic form or to functions. The most complete diagram representing these strategies is their overview of major types of communication strategies (Faerch & Kasper, 1983: 39), shown in Figure 13.1.

To place this in the context of the strategies cited above from Tarone, Cohen & Dumas, a paraphrase (e.g. 'a thing you dry your hands on' for 'towel') would be an achievement strategy based on the use of the existing interlanguage capability. An example such as 'je ne pas GO TO SCHOOL' would also be an achievement strategy based on language switch. In this approach the learner is thought to encounter a problem in achieving his or her communicative goal. The problem is situated in the (lack of an) ability to set up the right plan: the necessary forms do not exist in the L2 store. The learner chooses not to change his or her goal but to maintain it: in order to realise it, he or she must find ways of making better use of existing resources. By doing so the goal in the first example is achieved by explaining in a roundabout way what is intended in the interlanguage or, in the second example, expanding resources by using the first language. Appeals to authority ('How do you say this . . .') and retrieval strategies ('I know this word sounds like . . .') would also be forms of achievement strategies.

On the other hand the learner may decide to settle for less. Topic avoidance or message abandonment are radical versions of reduction strategies: vagueness is a less radical version (e.g. using 'tool' for 'wrench'). Again taking examples from Tarone, Cohen & Dumas: *Il nous faut partir* may be preferred by a learner to *Il faut que nous partions* ('We must go' expressed without and with the subjunctive) in order to avoid the subjunctive form. *Les garçons et les filles* may be preferred to *Les enfants* to avoid the liaison. There is, however, a sense in which formal reduction may give rise to paraphrase and it will become impossible to distinguish reduction from achievement when the one results in the other.

The Faerch & Kasper account does offer a relatively clear vision of why learners are producing these forms and what they are seeking to achieve with them. One position which, however, might be taken in

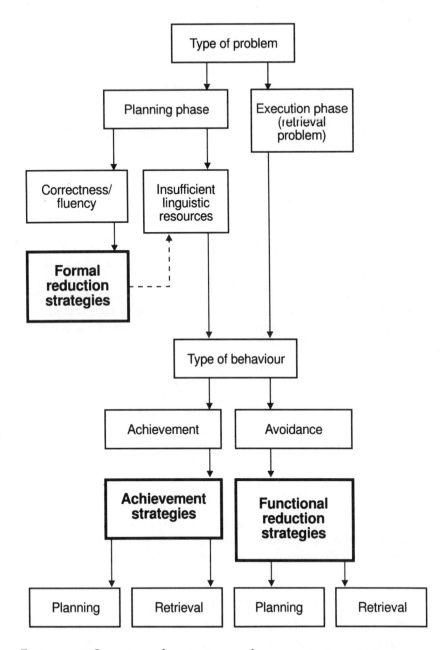

Figure 13.1 Overview of major types of communication strategies

Source: Faerch & Kasper, 1983: 39)

relation to this description is that, because they are so firmly shown to be problems in the planning and execution phases of production, the strategies have little to do with learning. Indeed, if learners became too proficient at these strategies there would be no need for them to learn the 'correct forms' of the language, given that the strategies enable them to get by quite well. And, if the learners are to have less need of these *ad hoc* solutions to immediate problems, the answer must be for them to build up their stock of linguistic knowledge: they then will not encounter these problems at the production stage.

The Nijmegen Project

A research project which refines the approach taken by Faerch & Kasper (1983) has been carried out in the last few years at the University of Nijmegen dealing with the compensatory strategies used by Dutch learners' of English. This is reported on in Poulisse (1990). As with the Faerch & Kasper approach, the report of the project takes the line that compensatory strategies are a matter of language use and not acquisition: 'the project has but few implications for second language acquisition research' (Poulisse, 1990: 196).

This is not to say, however, that the research lacks a sound theoretical base but it is rather to say that it takes its theoretical base from a view of language production (the Levelt model presented in Chapter 10) and from a pragmatic theory of language use, Gricean principles of co-operation and economy (Grice, 1968). These latter assume that in normal interaction humans obey a certain number of principles in order to provide communication which is appropriate to the situation. These include, for example, providing the amount of information which is appropriate to a situation. This depends on what knowledge is thought to be shared between the speaker and the interlocutor. To provide too much information often sounds patronising, to provide too little can be confusing. The co-operative principle assumes that in normal circumstances the speaker will attempt to get the dose right (although, of course, he or she may not succeed). The Poulisse account of compensatory strategies uses these theories to provide a more parsimonious and a more psychologically plausible taxonomy for strategies.

The argument is relatively simple. Given that strategies are used to compensate for problems encountered in language production and language use, it follows that they must be encountered at some point in the Levelt production model and that their use will be determined in large part by the rules governing normal verbal interaction. The Levelt model provides a four-step procedure.

The first step, taken within the conceptualiser is the conceptualisation of the message. This is carried out under controlled processing and gives rise to a propositionally formulated preverbal message. The second and third steps happen within the formulator. The first of these consists of the creation of a surface structure through calling lexical items from a store into the formulator where a set of mechanisms carry out the syntactic operations required to meet their specifications. The second consists of a similar set of phonological mechanisms which produce phonetic form, again accessing data from a store. The output of the formulator is finally passed to an articulator which produces the verbal output which is the fourth step (see Figure 10.1). Because all the steps beyond the conceptualiser are automatic, feedback is possible only within the conceptualiser (because the processing here is still controlled) and by monitoring the verbal output at the end. From this it follows that the only point where the process can be changed to permit reformulation to allow the intervention of strategies is at the junction between the conceptualiser and the formulator, i.e. at the stage where the preverbal message is created in propositional, largely non-linguistic form.

If there is a problem, it will occur as the formulator seeks a lexical item to fulfil the requirements of the preverbal message. If the speaker fails to find a suitable item, then the speaker must find a way round the problem. Rather than pursue the taxonomies outlined above, Poulisse proposes two archistrategies: one conceptual and one linguistic. The learner can either reconceptualise the preverbal message and put forward a new one in the hope that this time the lexical store will contain appropriate linguistic forms to enable the process to continue. Or the speaker can re-specify the linguistic means by which the preverbal message should be formulated.

If the speaker chooses a conceptual strategy, then two further possibilities open up. The first would be to look for a single means of expression which is similar to the original idea and hope that this 'approximation' will suffice for the interlocutor, with the help of the context, to grasp what is intended. The second would be to specify the component parts of the concept in as much detail as time allows and hope that the interlocutor will fill in the missing bits to make up the whole concept. These two possibilities are classified as holistic and analytical and are the substrategies on the conceptual side (Poulisse, 1990: 60).

If the speaker chooses a linguistic strategy, there are again two possibilities. The first is to switch the linguistic code radically and call on a linguistic item from another language (normally the learner's first language, but possibly any other language which is known) and trust that the interlocutor will recognise the word. The second is a less radical approach (but probably one which requires more effort) and involves constructing a new item from the knowledge of lexical items in the L2 by putting together morphemes which represent the meaning. The resulting form may or may not be an appropriate L2 form. These two linguistically based strategies are known as transfer and morphological creativity respectively (Poulisse, 1990: 62).

The long list of strategy types shown above can then be incorporated within a statement of the main categories (Poulisse, 1990: 110–13) and their use examined to see which are called upon by which learners and in which circumstances.

In her experiments, Poulisse found that the overall number of strategies reduced as learners became more proficient. In terms of the use of strategy types, however, proficiency made relatively little difference. This was not true of task types where difference in activities gave rise to quite different strategy selection. The choice depended mainly on how learners perceived the tasks, with, of course, considerable commonality in that perception. Thus, when learners were asked to carry out a picture description task in such a way that an object could be recognised by a native speaker, they recognised the need to be as explicit as possible. The fact that the task was not time limited combined with the need to be explicit led learners to use a large number of analytical conceptual strategies. In an interview, on the other hand, the topics for discussion were everyday matters, the interlocutor was present with the built-in consequence that any strategy which didn't work could be modified if necessary. Also it was not necessary for every lexical item to be totally explained. As a result, learners made use of a much greater variety of strategies including, in about 20% of the cases at all levels, the low cost, but possibly high risk, strategy of transfer. Morphological creativity was not, however, greatly in evidence at any level. Poulisse's conclusion is that learners will choose strategies which provide a balance between effort and effectiveness according to what is required by the demands of the situation in relation to the co-operative and economy principles.

The study has provided us with a more economic descriptive framework than that of Faerch & Kasper and has situated it within a recognisable theory of language production and use. It does not make claims about language acquisition *per se*, although, of course, anything which encourages language use provides input for language acquisition. The next two views of strategies which we shall examine are rather more ambitious in their claims.

Analysis and Control

Bialystok (1990a) suggests that the use of strategies depends on two dimensions: the degree of 'Analysis of linguistic knowledge' and the degree of 'control of linguistic processing'. She has worked in both L1 and L2 acquisition and argues that the these two dimensions are applicable to both. As defined by Bialystok (1990a: 118): 'Analysis of knowledge is the process of structuring mental representations of language which are organised at the level of meaning (knowledge of the world) into explicit representations of structure organised at the level of symbols (forms).' The process is gradual and continuous and certain uses of language (e.g. literate expression) depend on having the required degree of analysis. Bialystok argues that, in this sense, three-year-old children do not have a theory of grammar. What they have is an ability to use grammar. Only over time do they acquire that awareness (not necessarily conscious) which is necessary to use language in sophisticated ways. Awareness is dependent on a reorganisation of mental representations so that children become aware of the symbols they are manipulating and the relations between them: 'knowledge becomes symbolic . . . . Symbolic knowledge is independent of meanings and accessible to inspection' (Bialystok, 1990a: 121). The development of analysis requires, according to Bialystok (1990a: 125), 'self-reflection on knowledge', 'literacy instruction' and the 'presentation of rules and structure as organising principles'.

Control of linguistic processing is 'the ability to control attention to relevant and appropriate information and to integrate those forms in real-time' (Bialystok, 1990a: 125). This ability is dependent on selective attention, the ability to attend to language and to other things at the same time. Bialystok is at some pains to distinguish 'control' from other skills: 'Fluency is considered to be an emergent property of high control' (p. 125) — it is not the same as automatic or proceduralised language. It is control over high level symbols not over the means of production. 'The real consequence of high levels of control is intentional processing' (Bialystok, 1990a: 5). The demonstration of the growth of this ability in children appears to be via the ability to play language games or perform laboratory experiments where the subject has to divorce the language forms from the meanings in such a way that the form becomes available for manipulation, thus demonstrating that it is under intentional control. These skills are thought to be developed by schooling and bilingual experience.

Bialystok feels that past accounts of strategies, which have been useful in providing inventories of the kinds of surface linguistic expressions, have in essence been based on an underlying dichotomy between intention and expression. In this sense, Faerch & Kasper's division into 'reduction' and 'achievement' strategies is a particular interpretation of what is a universal dichotomy in self-expression. If the speaker encounters a problem of some kind, there are only two ways of resolving it: either settle for a lesser message (change intention), or find an alternative way of saying it (change expression). This also parallels Poulisse's (1990) 'archistrategies'. Such a dichotomy is, therefore, inherent in the process of communication, whether or not the use of specific strategies is involved. As such, communication strategies fall into the same pattern as any language use and are best described within the 'analysis' and 'control' processing account summarised above.

Once this is established, the components of analysis and control can be seen to be at the heart of the problem experienced by the learner. If the speaker cannot find the right symbols to express the concept, it may well be because the speaker has an insufficient awarensss of the relationship between the way meaning relates to language symbols, i.e. has an insufficient degree of analysis. If the speaker cannot adequately manipulate the means of expression, then this may be because the speaker has an inadequate level of control.

The learner is deemed to hold knowledge of the world as relations (presumably not dissimilar to the propositional networks of Anderson (1985)). These relations are embedded in contextualised domains of meaning. Possessing an analysed knowledge of these relations means having detached them from their meaning-based contextualised bed and having them available for different uses. 'Symbolic representation makes explicit structural relations among words, concepts and entities' (Bialystok, 1990a: 132). The awareness of these relations makes it possible to call up, for example, other forms which share certain distinctive features of an area of meaning in order to use them to compensate where such compensation is required. This is not too far from the way in which 'conceptual analytic' strategies call up component pieces of knowledge in the Poulisse model and has affinities with the 'creative morphology' strategies on the linguistic side. Both depend on an analytical awareness of internal structure. Where the degree of analysis is insufficient to enable the learner to undertake such an activity, the speaker will not be able to make use of these strategies. Making best use of them depends on a sophisticated degree of analysis. Adults learning second languages may be able to use their L1 knowledge as a guide and/or their analytic awareness of the relationship between the two symbolic systems. Bialystok would therefore include circumlocution, paraphrase, trans literation and word coinage amongst the 'analysis-based' strategies.

On the other hand, the underlying problem may be insufficient control over the means of expression. With greater control, the speaker becomes able to select the means of expression:

> In this strategy, communication is effected by holding constant the initial intention but altering the means of reference . . . the predominant means . . . [of doing this] is through switching the language. (Bialystok, 1990a: 133)

This is very much in line with Faerch & Kasper's (1983) achievement strategy and Poulisse's (1990) linguistic archistrategy, but Bialystok places it within the processing framework, thus adding a possible explanation to the account. The surface strategies which express control-based strategic decisions are language switch, gestures etc. to replace the meaning, appeal to others or consulting other sources, such as dictionaries.

The 'analysis' and 'control' account of strategies has a certain number of implications for acquisition which the previous accounts may not have. If these two factors are indeed the causes of the ability to use strategies, it follows that activities which increase analysis or control would lead to enhanced strategic use.

Instruction is often designed to make explicit structural relations and would thereby be expected to increase the degree of analysis. Instruction should then enable learners to make use of certain kinds of strategies, especially those linked to relations between two languages and to literacy skills. To discover whether this is the case might require different kinds of research strategies, most of which to date have been based on relatively simple oral data.

Evidence of increases in 'control' is difficult to obtain. In so far, however, as it may be established that certain activities increase levels of control, one would expect to see more selectivity in the use of strategies. Again, this may be the case but, as it is likely to occur at the same time as the learner is acquiring more vocabulary, and because selectivity may manifest itself through a greater ability to look ahead and avoid problems before the learner reaches them, this may be difficult to demonstrate unambiguously.

Bialystok offers an interesting possible explanation for the variability attributable to strategy use but one which is difficult to verify. We now turn finally to another account which deals specifically with learning strategies from a cognitive point of view.

Strategies Based on Declarative and Procedural Knowledge

O'Malley & Chamot (1990) embed their account of strategy use within their overall account of cognitive language learning based mainly on Anderson (1983, 1985). We will first provide a brief summary account of the Anderson framework before showing how use is made of it in relation to strategies. This account necessarily replicates some of the information provided in the more detailed analysis of Anderson's approach in Chapter 12 and the reader is referred to that section should this summary be too concise.

Anderson's system is based on three memories: one short-term memory and two long term-memories, namely a declarative memory and a production memory. All information enters via the declarative memory where it is stored in terms of meaning, as propositional representations, including propositional networks and schemata. Learning is a staged process through which information is transferred from the declarative memory to the production memory, a process which involves the creation of 'productions' which are IF . . . THEN statements. In the earliest stages of learning, only declarative knowledge can be accessed in performance and this is done by means of interpretive strategies, notably general problem solving and analogy (known as the 'cognitive' stage). As learning progresses and productions are formed through processes of composition and proceduralisation (the 'associative' stage), the information is stored in ever more economical productions which enable the learner to access the productions through matching in a much more rapid way. The creation of productions is, however, a careful one and during this associative stage it is important that any errors are weeded out because, once past this stage, declarative knowledge has little or no direct influence on the 'autonomous' productions. When the learning reaches the third 'autonomous' stage, productions no longer need to work in conjunction with declarative knowledge by calling it into working or short-term memory but are freed to be called up on their own. The gain in rapidity of production at this stage is significant: some would argue that this stage 'frees' the learner to concentrate on other aspects of learning. This is not, however, the end of the learning process because productions can be generalised and discriminated: they can be used in more than one situation if the situations overlap and they can measure their appropriateness to a situation and become more embedded within it. Key elements which cause these learning processes to happen are spreading activation, elaboration and strengthening.

Anderson (1985) also has a three-part view of production: these are construction, transformation and execution. These are not so different from the stages described in the Faerch & Kasper model (and indeed from others, such as the Clark & Clark (1977) or the Levelt model). In construction there is a selection of the knowledge which is appropriate to the goal which the learner wishes to attain with an awareness of the circumstances in which it has to be attained. In transformation this information has to be given appropriate form. Within a production system, this involves creating syntactic structures out of IF . . . THEN condition sets. (As has been repeatedly stressed in this book, this is the point at which linguists feel extreme unease at the unwillingness of writers of production systems to relate what they propose to linguistic structures and their apparent belief that semantic structures can map straight on to syntactic form.) These are then executed in ways which Anderson does not specify in any detail.

O'Malley & Chamot (1990) adapt this account to a description and classification of strategies. As did Ellis (1985a) they distinguish between learning, communication and production strategies: they then concentrate on the use of certain kinds of learning strategies especially in comprehension. They attach considerable importance to what they call elaborated 'schema-based' rules. These rules come in two categories. First, grammatical rules, discourse rules, sociocultural rules, or rules developed idiosyncratically. All of these begin as declarative knowledge but will become proceduralised as learning progresses. Second, schemata based on world knowledge, stored as meaning and originating in the ideas which a learner has assimilated working through any language he or she knows. As with other knowledge in this system, proceduralisation means that what is initially encoded in propositional networks etc. is then recoded as production systems with an IF condition and a THEN action constituent.

This is how O'Malley & Chamot characterise strategies within this system:

(a) Within a comprehension framework:

> IF   the goal is to comprehend an oral or written text, and I am unable to identify a word's meaning
>
> THEN   I will try to infer the meaning from context.
>
> IF   the goal is to comprehend a concept in a written text, and I know the concept is not at the beginning,
>
> THEN   I will scan through the text to locate the concept.

(O'Malley & Chamot, 1990: 52)

(b) Within an account of the complete process of communication including all levels of communicative competence: see Table 13.2.

Table 13.2 A production system for communicating in a second language.

P1*   IF   the goal is to engage in conversation with Sally, and Sally is monolingual in English,

      THEN the subgoal is to use my second language.

P2   IF   the goal is to use my second language,

      THEN the subgoal is to initiate a conversation.
            (sociolinguistic competence)

P3   IF   the goal is to initiate a conversation,

      THEN The subgoal is to say a memorized greeting formula.
            (discourse competence)

P4   IF   the goal is to say a memorized greeting formula, and the context is an informal one,

      THEN choose the appropriate language style.

P5   IF   the goal is to choose an appropriate language style,

      THEN The subgoal is to say, 'Hi, how's it going, Sally?'
            (sociolinguistic competence)

P6   IF   the goal is to say, 'Hi, how's it going, Sally?'

      THEN the subgoal is to pay attention to pronouncing the sentence as much like a native speaker as possible.
            (grammatical competence for pronunciation)

P7   IF   the goal is to pronounce the sentence as much like a native speaker as possible,

      THEN the subgoal is to check whether my pronunciation is accurate enough to communicate the meaning.
            (sociolinguistic competence)

Table 13.2(*continued*) A production system for communicating in a second language.

P8   IF   the goal is to check whether my pronunciation is accurate enough to communicate the meaning of my greeting,

     THEN the subgoal is to pay careful attention to Sally's response. (sociolinguistic competence)

P9   IF   the goal is to pay careful attention to Sally's response, and her response indicates that she has understood my meaning,

     THEN the subgoal is to wait for Sally to finish her conversational turn.

     (discourse competence)

P10 IF   the goal is to wait for Sally to finish her conversational turn and she completes her turn with a question,

     THEN the subgoal is to understand her question. (grammatical competence)

P11 IF   the goal is to understand Sally's question,

     THEN the subgoal is to compare what she says to what I already know in English and to my general knowledge of how conversations work.

     (grammatical competence and sociolinguistic competence)

P12 IF   the goal is to compare Sally's question to what I already know,

     and the match is good enough to understand her meaning,

     THEN the subgoal is to answer with the information requested.

P13 IF   the goal is to answer with the information requested,

     and I want to form a grammatically correct sentence,

     THEN the subgoal is to pay attention to word order and noun and verb endings as I respond.

     (grammatical competence for syntax and strategic competence)

P14 IF   the goal is to pay attention to word order and noun and verb endings,

     and I notice (or Sally's reaction suggests) that I have made a mistake that impedes comprehension,

     THEN the subgoal is to correct my mistake.

     (sociolinguistic and grammatical competence)

P15 IF   the goal is to correct my mistake,

     THEN 'pop the goal' (e.g. go back to P13).

Table 13.2(*continued*) A production system for communicating in a
second language.

P16	IF	the goal is to continue the conversation with Sally, and she responds with a question that I don't understand,
	THEN	the subgoal is to ask her to repeat or paraphrase.
P17	IF	the goal is to ask Sally to repeat or paraphrase her question, and this time I understand the question,
	THEN	'pop the goal' (e.g. go back to P12).
P18	IF	the goal is to continue the conversation with Sally, and she begins telling a long story about her activities,
	THEN	the subgoal is to pay attention to her pauses and linguistic markers and interject comments appropriately. (discourse and strategic competence)

*P1 stands for the first production system, P2 for the second, and so on.
Source: O'Malley & Chamot, 1990: 74–5

The specific strategic element intervenes towards the end of this sequence as the learner has to cope with a communication difficulty (Production 14ff).

The learning progression from cognitive, through associative to autonomous would apply to strategies as to all productions and once they had reached the autonomous stage they could generalise to similar tasks or become specialised by discrimination into quite narrow contexts. Oral comprehension strategies might therefore transfer to any comprehension tasks if similarities were discerned. As with other productions strengthening will take place and as a result conflict between productions, or between declarative and procedural forms of knowledge, will be determined by the way strengthening has related the particular production to the goal which it is able to achieve. One can imagine how, for example, reading speed could be enhanced by the creation of a series of reading strategies in which learners established productions which enabled them to pay attention to different parts of paragraphs, different parts of sentences, words which were synonyms of each other as they become more and more able to extract meaning rapidly from a text (see Anderson, 1985).

O'Malley & Chamot argue that these processes can be discerned in the development of L2 learners. As can be seen from Table 13.2, the areas dealt with by the cognitive approach of O'Malley & Chamot are quite different from the more language-based approached of most of the other researchers whose work is examined in this book. While the strategies they describe may be applicable to the process of comprehension, and indeed communication in general, it is difficult to see how they would help learners specifically to derive an awareness of how language is structured. The strategies are not so much about learning a language as about learning general communication skills. In our view, to understand language acquisition requires a more specific approach.

Discussion

Strategies are slightly different from the other areas we have dealt with. Within our treatment of variability, they cannot be neglected because it is undoubtedly true that learners make use of learning and communication strategies in normal interaction and these lead to definable patterns in language behaviour. It would seem to us, however, that, even when presented as learning strategies, these accounts bear only indirectly on the main processes of SLA. In so far as they are communication or compensatory strategies, it is questionable whether they contribute to the acquisition process at all.

It is true to say that when learners transfer certain forms from the L1 or indulge in paraphrases based on the IL, they are producing language which can only really be explained through the *ad hoc* notion of strategy. The notion is, however, in our view tangential to the acquisition process. It is difficult to see how strategies tell us how the linguistic system is built in relation to either implicit or explicit input, or how parameters might be set. We cannot however ignore the contribution of strategies to our understanding of variability as learners make use of a strategy on the occasions when they cannot find a particular form. We need to be aware of strategic use because it is an important contributor to learner language but we would not wish to claim that it is directly part of the acquisition process as we understand it.

Summary

In Chapter 13 we have examined the contribution of different theories of strategies in SLA and use. Early work on strategies limited itself to taxonomies but these suffered from overlap of categories and a lack of theoretical depth. A first attempt to provide a better framework was that of Faerch & Kasper (1983) who placed strategies within a general framework of language production and placed the multiplicity of strategies into two major categories, reduction and achievement strategies. Poulisse (1990) has refined that initial research in the sense that she has placed the concept of strategies within a more satisfactory production model, that of Levelt (1989), and related the work to more general communicative or pragmatic principles through reference to Gricean (1968) principles. She works, however, very much in the same way as Faerch & Kasper (1983) and her archistrategies can be seen to relate to defined stages in the planning process.

Bialystok (1990) has a third frame of reference, dealing with 'analysis' and 'control' of symbol systems. Her classification of strategies is not very different from that of Poulisse (1990), but she offers more in the way of an explanation of why these strategies should be as they are. Where Poulisse is happy to place them into two major categories, Bialystok is searching for the reasons why learners should be more or less successful in their use of strategies. Some, she concludes, will be improved by a greater ability to perceive relations between meaning and language symbol systems (analysis), others by a greater ability to select among potentially applicable systems (control).

O'Malley & Chamot (1990) are working in a different frame of reference and for them strategies are an exemplification of the general cognitive processes which underlie language learning. Their emphasis is on how learners can become 'fluent' in the use of strategies by allowing them to evolve along the lines set out by the Anderson theory, i.e. by compilation and tuning. They make rather different assumptions about how knowledge of the language system develops out of normal interaction.

All of these theories enrich our understanding of second language use: it is again debatable to what extent they influence acquisition.

14 Towards a Model of Second Language Acquisition

In this book we have sought to develop a consistent line of argument in response to five problem areas perceived within SLA research. These are: transfer, staged development, cross-learner systematicity, variability and incompleteness.

We have suggested that a satisfactory account of these phenomena can be obtained by examining the way the L2 learner learns the language system, learns to use the language system and, possibly, creates interaction between the two processes. We have also stressed the importance of the fact that the learner has multiple knowledge sources available to him or her. In addition, we have attached significance to the learner's need to communicate in real-time with a system which is less than perfect.

In speaking of multiple knowledge sources we are referring to the contribution made to the L2 learning process by Universal Grammar, by the L1, by explicit instruction with negative feedback and by exposure to formulaic language in context. In speaking of the need to communicate in real-time we are referring to the constraints on learning and communicative potential which are created by long-term and short-term memories and by the need for automatised production systems. In speaking of the need to communicate with a less than perfect system, we are emphasising the need to compensate for the inadequacies of the system by the use of strategies.

We have argued that all of these factors interact in the SLA process. In this final chapter we will provide an integrated, summarising, account of this interaction, followed by an examination of the research possibilities which are a consequence of viewing SLA in this way. These will be of two kinds: research designed to deepen knowledge in one area and research designed to explore interactions between different parts of the model.

An Overall Model

SLA research has to deal both with the learner's attempts to learn the system and the learner's attempts to learn to use the system. As indicated above, learners coming to SLA after the age of seven years tend to be able to call on a multiplicity of knowledge sources. These are partly internal and partly external. Internal sources are those which the learner brings to the learning process. External sources are those which provide the evidence from which knowledge has to be constructed. Research must be able to understand and investigate the potential contribution of each and the interaction of each with the others. We will first outline the nature of each contributor and attempt to situate it within a single learning model. We begin with the internal sources and our starting point is Universal Grammar:

> UNIVERSAL GRAMMAR

Given that knowledge of the underlying structure of a language cannot be derived solely from the patterns which are visible on the surface, we argue that it is not normally possible to acquire an L2 on a purely empirical basis, just as it is not possible to learn an L1 in that way. Universal Grammar is a constant background to the language learning process. It inhibits learners from entertaining 'wild' hypotheses but allows them to link together superficially disparate and idiosyncratic properties via particular parameter settings. It sets the framework within which linguistic forms in two languages can be seen to be related. It is therefore the background against which any language learning process takes place. Like any background, it conditions but does not determine what happens. The actual learning process is contingent upon the nature and abilities of the learner, the motivations of the learner, the degree of similarity between the two (or more languages in question and the kinds of exposure to the language which are available.

We have encountered evidence, however, which suggests that it is unlikely that an L2 learner after the age of seven years is going to have access to or to make use of Universal Grammar in exactly the same way as an L1 learner (see Chapters 7, 8 and 9). The learning of an L1 will have changed quite fundamentally the learner's understanding of what language is and have provided a usually satisfactory means of communication. This appears to give him or her rather fixed ideas about the nature of language. Monolingual learners typically expect other languages to conform to their own. Most frequently, therefore, in learning an L2 they will attempt to apply the parameter settings of the L1 to the L2. Where such settings come into conflict with L2 data that are encountered, learners may even construct 'rules' to mimic the surface properties of the L2, while retaining the L1 parameter setting. Such mimicking, it has been suggested (Chapter 7) is constrained by the possibilities allowed by UG. They will also make use of the L1 as a starting point for transliterations or translations which enable them to derive L2 forms: a long and complicated process, but better than nothing when no alternative is available.

Our second source, to be combined with the first, is, then:

THE FIRST LANGUAGE

Learners may transfer (t) a parameter setting, or UG may make possible a kind of mimicking (m). These two then combine to produce internally derived hypotheses by two possible routes. This process can be presented in a diagram combining the elements.

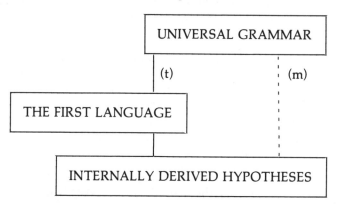

The straight line from UG through L1 to internally derived hypotheses suggests direct transfer (t) and the dashed line the potential mimicking (m) of L2 rules. The lines from UG are continuous where we can be certain of the input of UG into L1 learning but dashed where we cannot be certain that there is a direct input into L2 learning. These sources combine to produce a rich harvest of linguistically based, internally produced, direct and indirect hypotheses about how the L2 might work.

Initial hypotheses will, of course, be inadequate and they have to be confirmed or denied, strengthened or modified and transformed into productions usable in real time. However, the way in which internally derived hypotheses are reinforced and turned into usable mechanisms depends critically on two more essential elements: data and information processing mechanisms.

Relevant data for the acquisition process come in a variety of forms. We have examined the importance of explicit instruction with negative feedback and exposure to formulaic language in context (Chapter 11). We will examine the potential influence of each of these in turn in more detail below. Both of these kinds of data, however, are made available to learners in a manner different from the internally derived hypotheses. They are a result of information processing mechanisms which condition the way in which input provides data for hypotheses, the way in which hypotheses must be turned into productions for fluent use and the final output of productions. The main factors in information processing are the way memory works and the way knowledge is stored differently for different purposes. Post-seven-year-old learners have developed sophisticated memory capacity and information processing systems. These are employed in both understanding and producing language. Acquisition depends to some extent on the kinds of interaction with the internally developed hypotheses which the information processing framework permits.

In order to illustrate this clearly within the overall model, we now need to combine the mechanisms by means of which the internal hypotheses are developed with an additional set of information processing components which allow us to indicate the role of external input and output. These components are based on what has been said about declarative and procedural knowledge, controlled and automatic processing and short-term and long-term memories.

Although the shape of this model (see Figure 14.1) is quite different, we believe that it incorporates the insights derived from that of Levelt (1989) as presented in Chapter 10. It is also intended that it should be able to deal with the concept of the re-organisation of mental knowledge as presented in the discussion of the work of Karmiloff-Smith (1986a) in Chapter 11, with the creation of productions as outlined in relation to the work of Anderson (1983) in Chapter 12, and with the development in the ability to use strategies as described in Chapter 13.

In this model input and output always have to pass through short-term memory, as indicated by the arrows at the bottom of the diagram.

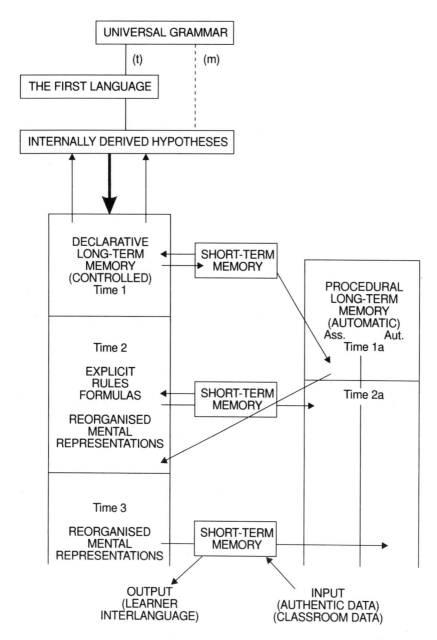

Figure 14.1 A model of second language acquisition

This is the mechanism which determines the information which is available to long-term memories and which is used in passing information between the two kinds of long-term memory proposed: the declarative memory and the procedural memory.

Interaction between short-term memory and declarative knowledge is controlled and functions via interpretive mechanisms. As a result it is slow but flexible because the user is paying attention to the forms. Interaction between short-term memory and procedural memory will be very fast but inflexible because the productions in procedural memory are compiled wholes which may not be modified easily.

All knowledge (internally and externally derived) initially goes into declarative memory. It is there that the internally derived hypotheses 'deposit' the information they can provide. Equally, externally derived information, i.e. explicit instruction and form-function pairs (formulas) passes through the STM into the declarative memory. It has been argued (Chapter 11) that declarative memory may operate at several levels of implicitness and explicitness and, if this can happen at all, it is there that information from multiple sources may over time be integrated, revised and moved from one level to another as suggested by Karmiloff-Smith (1986a).

The internally derived hypotheses derived from UG and L1 will, by definition, offer substantive suggestions for the 'core' of linguistic knowledge and those parameters which are applicable to the two languages. The working of other areas of the language will have to be understood from data in interaction with the internally derived hypotheses, notably by revising the inapplicable settings, lemmas and forms proposed by the first language. The model suggests four possible learning routes. We will briefly list them here and three of them will be explored below through a more detailed examination of the interaction with authentic data and explicit instruction.

Route one would be confirmation by external data of an internal hypothesis leading to the creation of a production to be stored in procedural memory first in associative form and then in autonomous form for rapid use via the short-term memory.

Route two would be initial storage of a form-function pair in declarative memory as an unanalysed whole. If it cannot be analysed by the learner's grammar but it can be remembered for use in a given context, it may be shifted to procedural memory at the associative level. It then can be used in situations and it may be re-called at a later date into declarative memory where, under controlled processing, it may be re-examined to see if it can be reorganised to take into account what the learner now knows about the L2. If it is now analysable, it may be converted to another level of mental organisation before being passed back to the procedural memory. If it is not, it can be returned to the procedural grammar for continued availability as an unanalysed whole.

Route three concerns explicit rules. Explicit rules are taken to be conceptual knowledge (like knowledge of scientific laws or historical events) and may be proceduralised as such. Verb paradigms, vocabulary lists, rules for the agreement of the past participle or lists of prepositions which take particular cases may be learnt by heart in this way. They may be recalled very rapidly but only in the form in which they were learnt. The whole sequence of knowledge has to be reproduced and out of that sequence the learner can extract the relevant information, rather like repeating a mnemonic rhyme to remember how many days a given month has. It is a useful way of remembering knowledge but only usable when time is available. In terms of language use, it requires time and can be used for purposes of revision or correction. In the proceduralised form this knowledge is unlikely to interact with other kinds of knowledge. In the declarative form, however, interaction with internally derived hypotheses may be possible and may contribute to mental reorganisation, although this has yet to be demonstrated.

Route four concerns strategies. Strategies in the O'Malley & Chamot (1990) sense are largely a matter of proceduralising mechanisms for faster processing of comprehension. This happens almost entirely within the information processing part of our diagram. As learners repeatedly carry out the same kind of operations to extract meaning from texts, these will go through the stages of proceduralisation towards autonomous knowledge. It would not seem that these mechanisms are dependent on or need to interact with internal hypotheses. In the Poulisse (1990) theory, those 'conceptual' aspects of strategy use which depend on the conceptualiser would be outside this model, while the linguistic aspects would depend on what language was stored in the declarative and procedural memories. In the Bialystok (1990a) framework, 'analysis' would be akin to mental reorganisation. It is not entirely clear where 'control' would fit. It appears to be close to what we have indicated when suggesting that learners will be able to make more use of controlled processing as a result of possessing greater proceduralised knowledge. Control is not the same as proceduralisation. As, in our view, strategies do not interact directly with internal hypotheses, we will now examine the first three of these routes by looking at the role of the two main kinds of data, authentic data and classroom data.

The role of exposure to authentic data

Authentic data are the essential means by which learners confirm or deny hypotheses. Authentic data are essential in the progression described above as route one and route two.

We argue that hypotheses derived from UG either directly or via L1 will be available initially as declarative knowledge, that is, as hypotheses to be tentatively tried out via controlled processing where learners pay attention to what they are receiving and what they are producing. If the hypotheses are confirmed, they can quickly be launched on the staged progression described by Anderson (1983, 1985). They would then progress through stages of associative and autonomous knowledge until they are realised as autonomous productions, available for real-time use to meet all of the language learner's requirements. However, as indicated in Chapter 12, this process must have a number of checks and balances included to stop wrong forms being given autonomy. Nonetheless, the conceptual framework is relatively clear and in the model it is represented by arrows crossing and re-crossing from one memory to the other. We will try to describe this process in more detail.

Internal hypotheses which have their roots in UG and the L1 come into declarative knowledge (which, of course, should not in any way be confused with conscious knowledge). This is thought of as the major input of hypotheses to the L2 learning process and is represented in the model in Figure 14.1 by a large descending arrow. These hypotheses are then matched against observations of the regularities of the authentic data and other declarative information sources. Smaller upwards pointing arrows show how these are interfaced with the internal hypothesis generating process. This interaction may permit triggering of internally derived UG hypotheses on the basis of appropriate positive evidence. Internally derived L1 hypotheses may also be transferred where the parameter settings are the same. Where the setting is different, a process of revision leading to resetting could, in principle, begin: the extent to which this process can be demonstrated is the focus of much current research. Hypotheses which are confirmed would quickly move through short-term memory into the associative and over time, by strengthening, into the autonomous parts of the proceduralised long-term memory. Hypotheses which are not confirmed may remain as declarative hypotheses. These may be used to modify awareness of the system at some future date. As for all declarative knowledge they may be used to give rise to output of a controlled kind when all else fails. It would also seem, however, that some of these 'incorrect' hypotheses may nonetheless become proceduralised, at least at the associative stage, and give rise to fluent learner output which is directly influenced by L1 parameter settings.

Not all authentic data will serve to confirm or deny existing hypotheses. Because the learner's existing knowledge may be insufficient to provide an awareness of the internal structure of an utterance and because short-term memory is limited in capacity, learners are often unable to decipher the internal structure of utterances when these are first heard in context. However, learners post age seven years may well have sufficient memory capacity to enable them to store utterances as undifferentiated wholes. These would normally be stored initially as declarative knowledge. If, however, they are repeatedly found to be useful and usable in situations, they would quickly become proceduralised knowledge. This process, which is the beginning of route two, is also shown as an arrow from declarative knowledge crossing from left to right through short-term memory into the associative part of the procedural memory. Learners can be expected to proceduralise such formulaic utterances before they can divide them into component parts. The proceduralised formulaic language will remain as such unless or until it is re-examined in some way. As indicated above, following Karmiloff-Smith (1986a), we argue that this re-examination can take place. It is shown in Figure 14.1 as an arrow returning from the associative part of the automatised long-term memory, going through short-term memory and back into declarative memory. There, under controlled processing, the learner may reorganise the knowledge before returning it to the procedural long-term memory with its relation to the rest of the language system more securely established at a higher level of explicitness.

Knowledge taken in, stored and then reorganised in this way would give rise to staged development of knowledge as described by Karmiloff-Smith (1986a). The initial storage would provide the learner with a necessary ability to produce language in situations with the degree of fluency which is required, without having internalised very much of the linguistic system. But for the knowledge which is available from such examples to become part of the linguistic system, it would need to be given a different mental representation through which it could be related to the rest of that system. At some subsequent time, preferably when information relevant to it is present in declarative knowledge, it would need to be taken out of its associatively proceduralised form and passed back into declarative knowledge. Recognising the time at which this is possible may depend on the kind of analytical awareness described by Bialystok (1990a). Once in the declarative knowledge framework, while the learner is paying attention to that part of the system under controlled processing, if the processes described by Karmiloff-Smith (1986a) are applicable in SLA, it may be possible for that knowledge to be reorganised into more explicit levels and integrated into the linguistic system. We would wish to argue that this reorganisation of mental representation, while being a declarative cognitive process which takes place under 'control' is dependent on an interaction between internally derived hypotheses (from UG (±L1)) and the externally provided evidence, hence the potentially additional significance of the arrows above declarative long-term memory pointing upwards towards internally derived hypotheses. The revised hypothesis with a more explicit level of mental organisation would then be available for conversion into automatised productions to be contained in a proceduralised long-term memory or Levelt-type formulator for L2.

We argue, then, that interaction with external data provides two main contributions to the L2 learning process. First, it provides a mechanism whereby the internally derived hypotheses may be tested against 'reality': if they are found acceptable they will be turned into productions suitable for fluent language use. If they are found unacceptable they may remain in declarative knowledge until such time as they are either modified or rejected, or, less happily, they may be turned into production rules for fluent but inaccurate use. Second, it provides a mechanism whereby formulaic language can be retained so as to allow the learners to achieve an immediate interactive capability on the basis of an implicit knowledge of utterances. That knowledge is then available as a basis for subsequent mental reorganisation. As the learner develops greater awareness of the linguistic system, it may be possible to re-examine the formulaic utterance and reinterpret its internal structure as part of the learning of the language system. The whole process is guided by the background knowledge coming from UG (± L1) which prevents learners from making up 'wild' grammars which would contravene the rules of natural language.

To illustrate: in the case of L2 learners learning languages with similar structures to their L1, such as speakers of Romance languages learning other Romance languages, it will be possible for hypotheses which are derived from L1 transfer to be rapidly confirmed as successful parts of the L2 system. In such cases, we would expect that for a short time the learner would use the hypotheses (formulated as declarative knowledge) to derive the specific forms of the language by interpretive methods in a rather slow, controlled manner. This would, however, very quickly be superseded by more fluent productions as the forms were shifted through the associative into the autonomous stages of pro-ceduralisation. Where the transfer process turns out not to work so smoothly, or where certain forms transfer some but not all of their characteristics, we would expect those forms not to be fully automatised. They may be passed to the procedural memory and therefore be available for rapid use but for successful development they should not become autonomous. If they did, they would fossilise in the learner's grammar. As long as they remain associative, they can be passed back into the declarative grammar for reorganisation in the developing system.

In the cases where the L1 has no relevant parameter, the learner may or may not have direct access to a UG parameter which can be triggered by authentic data. If triggering is possible the learner will have the hypothesis confirmed and it may immediately begin the process towards becoming readily available, secure, proceduralised knowledge in the automatised memory/formulator.

In the cases where neither UG nor the L1 provides an hypothesis, i.e. for those parts of the language system which are 'peripheral' in UG terms, the learner has to construct hypothesis on the basis of the information available. This can be found only in the authentic utterances which the learner has encountered in situations. These must be 'unpackaged'. We have argued that this may be possible by changes in mental representation.

The role of explicit instruction

We have seen in Chapter 11 that the classroom is a very powerful instrument of instruction and that it can control language learning in a very direct way. There is relatively little evidence, however, to show that most classroom learners become good language users, rather the opposite.

We would wish to follow Doughty (1991) in arguing that classroom instruction can be successful. Learners can use information about language provided in a classroom to construct hypotheses which eventually may guide their language use. There is good evidence to show that instruction has an immediate effect as conscientious learners apply what is taught. Evidence indicates, however that what is taught does not enable them to build up knowledge of the language system. Also, current evidence suggests that whatever effect classroom learning produces may wear off after a certain time.

There seem to be two main ways in which data is provided for learners learning in classrooms. In many cases, learners are exposed to carefully crafted examples of the language system and are asked to undertake structured activities with the examples. The basis on which the examples have been selected may vary, as may the techniques of presentation. They may have been selected because they illustrate points defined in a pedagogic grammar. They are then designed to bring such information to a level of consciousness and thereafter to practise it with further examples until the rules are known. They may or may not be accompanied by explicit information about the surface structure of the language. In other cases, the examples may have been selected because of their use to achieve certain functions in defined contexts and not because they illustrate a grammatical point. In these classrooms the emphasis is likely to be more on using the examples in situation and less on explicit instruction. Over a period of learning more than one emphasis may be employed.

We will discuss here the influence of the two kinds of input normally provided by classrooms in order to place this teaching and learning in the context of our model.

As input classroom data play the same role as authentic data although they are differently selected. They are external in the same way as authentic data are external. They differ in their dense concentration on certain forms in a structured manner. Most often negative feedback is provided. Frequently the data are accompanied by explanations.

In terms of Figure 14.1, the classroom input data feed into declarative controlled knowledge via the short-term memory exactly like authentic data. They may then be turned into productions along the lines described briefly above and in detail in Chapter 12.

We perhaps need to be reminded that productions can be created out of all kinds of knowledge. As O'Malley & Chamot have pointed out (see Chapter 13), strategic competence can be taught and turned into a set of productions. So can explicit rules. Most teachers have a set of mnemonic devices which are used to enable learners to retain knowledge of rules. Because the cognitive mechanisms we are dealing with here are general, knowledge of all kinds can be put into the declarative memory and then converted into productions. The open question is whether or not, and how, learners equipped with, for example, mnemonic devices to remind them of the position and order of French personal pronouns, word order in German or which German prepositions take the dative, can convert that knowledge into the same kind of knowledge that enables native speakers to perform so fluently and accurately.

We would argue, as indicated in route three above, that such learning does not usually convert itself into the same kind of knowledge that native speakers of the language have. It is our belief that for that to happen the external evidence, be it rules, explanations of the grammar or examples in situation, would have to interact productively with the internally derived hypotheses from UG (± L1) in the declarative memory. Such an interaction would enable the learner to revise the L2 system in the light of knowledge provided by UG. Most frequently this appears not to happen.

This can be briefly illustrated with an example. Viewed from the perspective of UG the position of the French negator *pas* following both main verb and auxiliary verb in tensed clauses, but occurring before main verbs and either before or after auxiliary verb in infinitive clauses, depends on the setting of a parameter determining verb movement (see Chapter 6). All a pedagogic grammar can offer is a statement of when *pas* occurs with the auxiliary and with the main verb. The learner may learn the rule from the pedagogic grammar and turn it into a production. It can then be recalled in the form in which it was learnt. The learner could, for example, repeat the rule verbatim. The information within it can then be extracted and applied in context as long as time allows. This does not, however, constitute native-like knowledge. The learner may proceduralise the knowledge provided by the pedagogic grammar and even make reasonably rapid use of it in producing language. But without having interfaced that knowledge with internal hypotheses and thus permitting the kind of reorganisation we have been considering, this piece of knowledge cannot fit into the knowledge of the language in the same way that the native speaker 'knows' that the position of the clitic pronoun is a by-product of the general verb movement parameter. This is not to say that the language could not be produced on the basis of this learned linguistic knowledge. But it will be slower and subject to inaccuracies where this 'surface' rule does not suffice.

Effective teaching often ensures that learners learn precisely what is taught. It is, however, unfortunately in the nature of SLA that they will be unable to relate explicit instruction about the language to the creation of linguistic competence. Classroom reliance on explicit instruction and illustrative examples will produce learners who have turned the grammatical rules and examples they have been given into productions.

They will be able to apply the rules to the kinds of exercises they have been taught, such as translating or completing sentences which illustrate the forms taught. Similarly, classroom reliance on phrases in situations will give rise to learners who, given the appropriate situation, will produce, with considerable and commendable fluency, the exact phrases dealt with in the classrooms. In both cases, however, as Felix & Weigl (1991) have demonstrated, whenever learners are asked to deal with language which is outside what they have experienced in the classroom there will be an inability to generalise the learning and a consequential resorting to transliteration of L1 forms.

Expressed in the terminology of our model, if learners follow route three they will create productions from the two kinds of declarative knowledge provided by the classroom, i.e. explicit rules and formulas. They will do so in such a way that the result is Karmiloff-Smith's (1986a) 'implicit' knowledge, i.e. knowledge which, like all productions, is context-dependent and whose internal structure is opaque. They can repeat the rules and/or they know the forms but they cannot relate these to the rest of the language system.

Karmiloff-Smith's evidence opens up the possibility that, when learners are exposed to conditions which promote interaction between the external evidence of whatever kind and the internal hypotheses where UG constraints can come into play, effective acquisition could take place. If that interaction is not possible, the results would be the creation of productions from inadequate evidence, i.e. one set of productions derived from internal hypotheses (competence based on UG and L1 transfer) and a second set of productions derived from external evidence (learned linguistic knowledge based on instruction and negative feedback). It may be that the inadequacies generally observed demonstrate that totally effective acquisition is not possible. It is not our task here to suggest in detail how such obstacles might be overcome in classrooms, but it seems likely that the barriers might be breached if the learner were encouraged to try out a maximum of language production and were not constrained to use only the 'correct' forms taught in the class.

Lest this should seem too pessimistic we should add that it is our belief that a large number of quite effective L2 users are in essence gifted users of productions created from learned linguistic knowledge based on L1 surface transfers (transliterations or translations), ultra-rapid application of rules and compensatory strategies. It is quite possible to communicate up to a certain level in this way, especially if the use of the L2 is in a limited set of contexts. It is not, however, possible to attain native-like competence. We have also suggested, that, over time, interaction between declarative and procedural memories may enable learners to produce surface utterances based on composite productions which hide remaining differences in underlying competence.

Research Methods and Directions for Further Research

The views outlined in the previous section have been distilled from the detailed examination of different kinds of research in SLA carried out in the rest of this book. It is now time to examine how research could be carried forward on the basis of the model presented, taking first its constituent elements and second their interaction.

Investigating the role of Universal Grammar

In our view UG is a fundamental contributor to the analysis of SLA and therefore to research into SLA. Only through UG is it possible to obtain a view of the nature of the subject of investigation, i.e. language. Any attempt to investigate surface forms of language, as in the case of the morpheme studies (see Chapter 2), for example, without an understanding of the interrelated nature of the underlying hypotheses which learners may have been provided with in advance, is always going to be open to a possible alternative explanation from UG.

From the learner's point of view, UG is simply always present (without, of course, any degree of consciousness). The learner cannot entertain certain 'wild' hypotheses about the L2 because UG will not 'allow' him or her to do so. The learner may perceive easily certain relationships between structures in the language, structures perhaps which pedagogic grammars would never relate to one another, because they are part of a single parameter. By virtue of setting or resetting a parameter in one part of the grammar a learner may automatically 'know' how another part of the grammar must work. By perceiving that a particular relationship which obtains between a pair of languages, and which depends, for example, on 'movement' a learner may suddenly 'learn' a series of structures which were previously unknown. All of these developments may be attributable to UG.

In relation to our problem areas, UG is especially influential when considering transfer, staged development and cross-learner systematicity, all of which could be seen in Chapters 5–9 to be accounted for when one understood the relationship between languages as defined by UG.

There is clearly, however, an immense amount of groundwork which has to be carried out to improve research based on UG. Our linguistic analyses are still too limited in the amount of the grammar they cover and the boundaries of the influence of UG are still too ill-defined. Books talk of 'core' and 'periphery' in grammars, but it is virtually impossible to discover where one ends and the other begins. Quite frequently parts of a language system which might be thought to be 'odd', turn out to be significant in understanding how the system works. On the other hand, some of the most frequently used parts of a language system defy description. The analyses change too frequently and too fundamentally for secure applications to be developed before the latest theoretical insight has uprooted the system.

These criticisms of UG-based research are no doubt well-founded in many cases, but they do not remove the necessity to base SLA research on sound linguistic premises.

The great advantage of UG-based research is that it is 'experimental' and hypothesis-driven in a more precise way than most other kinds of SLA research. The UG scholar can use UG to make a prediction as to what should be happening. Most frequently this will take one of three forms. The first is a prediction that one form should be learnt before another form because UG shows that the learning of the second form depends on knowledge of the first. The second is that the learning of the forms which make up a parameter should be linked in some way. If the values of a parameter are organised hierarchically, for example via the 'subset' principle (see Chapter 6), then learning an item higher up on the hierarchy should provoke learning of items further down. The third is a cross-linguistic prediction based on the previous two kinds of insights: if L1 has set a parameter in one way and L2 in another, then UG may be used to predict the task of the learner in resetting the parameter. The task of the UG researcher is to devise intelligent methods of finding out whether the prediction is correct. The further advantage of UG-based work is that, if the hypothesis is shown to be proven or not proven, it will inform both about the value of the linguistic theory and about the process of SLA.

In terms of methodology, UG based studies of SLA most frequently make use of written grammaticality judgement tests. UG-based researchers find this inevitable, mainly because the structures they wish to investigate would never occur with sufficient frequency if they had to be found in spontaneous speech. In early research, these were of a 'grammatical/ungrammatical' variety and interpretations were offered on the simple basis of how many sentences were accepted as grammatical. More recently, use has been made of scaled judgements (e.g. 1–5 on a scale of grammaticality) where learners are asked to indicate which part of the sentence they find ungrammatical and to correct it and of grammaticality preference tests where learners are asked to judge which of two or more sentences they 'prefer'. Also, alongside grammaticality judgements, other tests have been used to confirm or deny hypotheses which might arise from them. These include gap-filling, sentence manipulation and sentence combining, depending on the kind of structure being investigated. The interpretations are also becoming more sophisticated as researchers look not only at the sentences which are accepted but also at those which are rejected and look for revealing patterns in the decisions which are being made.

The number of studies of this kind being carried out is increasing. Most serious studies are to be found in the journals *Second Language Research* and *Studies in Second Language Acquisition* and references can be taken up from published collections such as Flynn & O'Neil (1988) and Gass & Schachter (1989). White's (1989a) account of research in this area provides evidence of the methodologies used.

Investigating the role of the first language

We have argued at various points in the book that the first language is the cause of many of the major differences between L1 and L2 acquisition. In conjunction with UG, the role of which we have just considered, the L1 provides the learner with settings for all the parameters which are shared by the two languages in question. In Chapter 6 it was argued that the learner's first inclination will always be to assume that the L2 settings are going to be the same as the L1 settings. Only where there is no setting to guide him or her is the learner likely to be 'open-minded'. The process of language learning is then one of resetting parameters, or making the L1 parameter setting do the job of a different L2 parameter setting (mimicking) or learning anew in those areas where there is no L1 setting.

These tasks are going to be more or less difficult depending on the relationship between the two languages and the ease with which differences may be perceived. Some differences will be so easily perceived that resetting will be very fast indeed. Other differences will be invisible if the learner has only the surface language to go on and may take a long time to reset. They may never do so. If the learner can mimic the L2 by applying a device made available by UG to a different range of forms, the learner may well be satisfied with the results for a long time.

Research into this area is dependent on cross-linguistic comparisons based on UG theories. Investigations based on verb movement and the pro-drop parameter, for example, have proved particularly fruitful. Depending on the languages which are chosen, various areas can be investigated. If the L1 and the L2 are very different in the parameters which they make use of, then it is possible to investigate what happens when the L1 provides very little 'guidance' to the L2 learner. Is it possible, for example, for the learner to access UG principles in the same way as a child in these circumstances? Languages which have different settings of the same parameters present a different kind of research question: is it possible, or under what conditions, will a learner reset a parameter which is different from the L1 settings in precise ways? Is it possible to establish, for example, whether explicit instruction in the forms in the parameter will cause it to reset? And what does 'reset' mean in such a context?

The methods used in such investigations tend to be similar to those used in other UG-based investigations, i.e. grammaticality judgement tests etc. The reasons for this choice are the same. It is essential to gather information about learners' 'knowledge' (or competence) in relation to a defined set of structures, many of which are frequently quite unusual, especially in oral language. They can not be elicited in natural oral exchanges.

The UG based investigations do not exhaust the possible investigations into the role of the L1. As we have seen in Chapters 12 and 13, the L1 may give rise to surface transliterations and may be part of strategy use.

The hypothesis in relation to transliteration is that learners will generate a sentence in the L1 and then rapidly transliterate it into the L2 (see Chapter 12). Learners who adopt this tactic would develop a set of procedures to govern the process. They would have a set of lexical equivalents and a series of devices of the IF . . . THEN kind which would enable them to convert certain kinds of L1 structures into L2 structures. In theory, if they were extremely good translators, they might evolve the kind of systematic relationships which are described in Vinay & Darbelnet's (1958) book *La stylistique comparée du français et de l'anglais*. It is conceivable that some learners, especially those brought up on a diet of translation, might evolve successful techniques of this kind. We think, however, that these would be rare and that it is much more likely that learners will keep a great deal of the L1 structures in the L2 forms they produce, thus revealing the mechanism at work.

To our knowledge, there has been relatively little recent work in this area. In the days when error analysis was popular, considerable collections were made of 'transfer errors' which researchers thought must be transliterations of this kind. Most, however, tended to be single words rather than utterances. These collections were subject to the kind of reinterpretation offered by Richards (1974), because they had no more than surface plausibility to back up the assertion that these were indeed transliterations. The problem still exists, of course. It is very difficult to claim for certain that a production from a learner must be a transliteration. Even when the L1 is 'transparently visible', an alternative explanation is very frequently possible. It would, however, be interesting to establish the extent to which this process is used. In the strategy research by Poulisse (1990), methods were used in which raters were given training in recognition of certain kinds of strategies, including L1-based strategies and it is conceivable that a method could be found to investigate the prevalence of transliteration.

It will, of course, never have the potential theoretical significance of UG-based transfer research, but it could be an area of significance. Of interest, for example, is the observation that learners appear to be able to call on the L1 forms with no hesitation. It would seem that the L1 is never very far below the surface of language production and that there is a switching mechanism which allows access to it. Investigations into areas such as bilingual aphasia have developed very sophisticated testing techniques, notably the Bilingual Aphasic Test, developed by Paradis (1987). Rather than pursue further investigations into the use of strategies, which, in our view, does not lead to a much greater understanding of acquisition processes, it might be of interest to set up projects which would investigate whether or not the L1 was present in the way suggested by writers such as Paradis.

The research techniques would be very different from those explored up to now. They would probably be borrowed much more from psychology and would rely on detailed measurement of the time taken to respond to certain forms etc. They would, however, provide original insights into an area which has not been much investigated.

Investigating the role of information processing

The importance of this area has been somewhat neglected, perhaps because of the difficulty of carrying out investigations. As was indicated in Chapter 11 and in Chapter 13, Bialystok has been interested for at least twenty years in the way in which analysis and control of L2s determine what can be learnt. The difficulty she encountered from her 1982 experiments onwards seems to have been that of specifying the nature of the information processing skills required by a given task. The arguments are reasonably clear but the experimental evidence is difficult to interpret. When the predicted results do not appear, it is difficult to know whether this is because the tasks did not in fact require the kind of analysis and control predicted or because the methods of measurement did not measure what they were thought to measure. Tarone (1988) has argued that the enterprise is inherently impossible. McLaughlin (1987, 1990) has argued for an information processing approach but has generally stopped short of explaining how it could be carried out. Hulstijn & Hulstijn (1984) have made use of an experimental method involving imitation by means of which they were able seriously to undermine some of the more ambitious claims of Krashen's (1981) monitor model.

As we have outlined it here, the objectives of research into this area would be to establish one main point: the nature of the storage of all kinds of information in declarative and procedural forms. We need more evidence and different ways of investigating the different kinds of productions learners create and how they create them.

The methods associated with this investigation must rely on finding ways on discovering how learners have processed and stored knowledge. Investigations using temporal variables (Chapter 11) are quite helpful in establishing global measurements of learners processing capabilities. Four kinds of comparisons would be especially useful. Comparisons between different learners would help us establish an awareness of the degrees of difference in individual processing characteristics. Comparison between the same learners carrying out the same kind of processing in native and second languages would enable us to find out whether our predicted differences actually exist. Comparison of the same learners at different points in the learning cycle would enable us to judge progression. Comparison of the same learners undertaking a variety of tasks would enable us to become aware of the impact of the task, even if we are unable to specify exactly what characteristics of the task produce observed effects.

The temporal variables, however, only inform about global processing. They do not isolate the processing of particular forms or the processing of particular 'rules'. They give us a global assessment of the learner's processing ability but not of the learner's ability to process those parts of the language in which we might be especially interested. Nor do they separate out aspects of processing ability. A subject who is a fast producer of language can legitimately be presumed to have proceduralised a large amount of the language. But how does that relate to the use of short-term and long term memory? What is it that the learner recalls into short-term memory? Is it productions of set phrases, linked to contexts? Is it a set of rules in compiled form? In order to answer questions such as these we would need to concentrate on methods which test the content of short-term memory. Methods such as imitation, shadowing, placing bleeps on tape recordings have been used by psycholinguists in relation to the use of the L1. Such techniques may well have a role in the investigation of L2 processing, especially if they can be made to relate to the model of production provided by Levelt (1989).

Investigating interaction between the parts of the model

This area is to do with the very important questions surrounding interaction between the externally provided data (of both our major kinds) and the internally derived hypotheses. We need more evidence and different ways of investigating what hypotheses learners generate internally and what is the impact of various kinds of evidence on those hypotheses. UG-type investigations described above using grammaticality judgement tests can give us information about some of the hypotheses learners hold. We then need to know what external evidence will lead to changes in those hypotheses.

The external evidence is related to explicit instruction and authentic data. The first tends to come either by explicit rules or by formulas embedded in a classroom situation, the second by formulas embedded in situations. It is therefore essential that we should know whether learners can unpackage formulas and if so, how. It is equally essential that we should know at what level, if at all, explicit explanation can modify hypotheses.

Our model suggests that both may be possible under certain conditions. How can we know whether this is so? Karmiloff-Smith's (1986a, b) studies of L1 learners suggest that it should be so. In looking closely at the evidence from L.W. Fillmore's (1979) studies, however, we did not feel that this could be affirmed for L2 learners without doubt. The studies of classroom learners by White (1991a, b) followed up by Trahey & White (1993) show that learners do proceduralise the information they are given. However, they forget it over time when it is not used and it is suggested that this is because it is not integrated with knowledge of the linguistic system. Doughty's (1991) study, however, suggests that classroom explanations can help to modify hypotheses if learners are ready for this to be done. But Felix & Weigl's (1991) study demonstrates that it frequently does not happen. The research question becomes: what kinds of presentation and the use of what kinds of information would give the best chance of interaction between the internal and external sources in order to provoke hypothesis creation and revision? Some current interest is being shown in techniques of input processing (Sharwood Smith, 1993; Van Patten & Cadierno, 1993).

Summary

We have attempted in this final chapter to bring together in a single model the strands of evidence presented in the preceding chapters. We have interpreted the model in relation to the ways in which it may be used by learners to approach SLA along various routes: the development of competence on the basis of internally derived hypotheses from UG and L1, the development of learned linguistic knowledge on the basis of external evidence, the development of information processing skills on the basis of both sources of knowledge, the development of interaction between the multiple sources. We have shown how following some possible routes leads to acquisition which remains distant from native-like knowledge. As with all research, the final statement reveals those areas where there are more questions than answers. We have outlined some of the main questions: there is still much more to be done in investigating the role of UG, the role of the L1 at various stages in the process, the contribution of the information processing dimension and the need to understand interaction between the parts of the whole. We have finally set out some of the ways in which these questions may be answered through renewed research efforts.

Bibliography

Adiv, E. (1984) Language learning strategies: the relationship between L1 operating principles and language transfer in L2 development. In R. Andersen (ed.) *Second Languages: A Cross-Linguistic Perspective*. Rowley, MA: Newbury House.

Anderson, J. (1978) Order of difficulty in adult second language acquisition. In W. Ritchie (ed.) *Second Language Acquisition Research: Issues and Implications*. London: Academic Press.

Anderson, J.R. (1982) Acquisition of cognitive skill. *Psychological Review* 89, 4, 369–406.

— (1983) *The Architecture of Cognition*. Cambridge, MA: Harvard University Press.

— (1985) *Cognitive Psychology and its Implications*. New York: Freeman.

Appel, R. and Muysken, P. (1987) *Language Contact and Bilingualism*. London: Edward Arnold.

Atkinson, M. (1992) *Children's Syntax*. Oxford: Blackwell.

Authier, J-M. (1991) V-governed expletives, case theory, and the projection principle. *Linguistic Inquiry* 22, 721–40.

Bailey, N., Madden, C. and Krashen, S. (1974) Is there a 'natural sequence' in adult second language learning? *Language Learning* 21, 235–43.

Bardovi-Hartig, K. (1987) Markedness and salience in second language acquisition. *Language Learning* 37, 385–407.

Berwick, R. (1985) *The Acquisition of Syntactic Knowledge*. Cambridge, MA: MIT Press.

Bialystok, E. (1978) A theoretical model of second language learning. *Language Learning* 28, 69–83.

— (1982) On the relationship between knowing and using forms. *Applied Linguistics* 3, 181–206.

— (1986) Factors in the growth of linguistic awareness. *Child Development*. 57, 498–510.

— (1988) Levels of bilingualism and levels of linguistic awareness. *Developmental Psychology* 24, 560–7.

— (1990a) *Communication Strategies*. Oxford: Blackwell.

— (1990b) The dangers of dichotomy: A reply to Hulstijn. *Applied Linguistics* 11, 1, 46–51.

— (1991) Metalinguistic dimensions of bilingual language proficiency. In E. Bialystok (ed.) *Language Processing in Bilingual Children*. Cambridge: Cambridge University Press.

Bialystok, E. and Sharwood Smith, M. (1985) Interlanguage is not a state of mind. *Applied Linguistics* 6, 2, 101–17.

Bickerton, D. and Givón, T. (1976) Pidginisation and syntactic change: from SVX and VSX to SVX. In S. Stever, C. Walker and S. Mufwene (eds.) *Papers from the Parasession on Diachronic Syntax*. Chicago Linguistic Society.

Bley-Vroman, R. (1983) The comparative fallacy in interlanguage studies: The case of systematicity *Language Learning* 33, 1–17.

— (1989) What is the logical problem of foreign language learning? In S. Gass and J. Schachter (eds.) *Linguistic Perspectives on Second Language Acquisition*. Cambridge: Cambridge University Press.

Bloom, L. (1970) *Language Development: Form and Function in Emerging Grammars.* Cambridge, MA: MIT Press.

Bot, K. de (1992) A bilingual production model: Levelt's 'Speaking' model adapted. *Applied Linguisitics* 13, 1, 1–24.

Brown, R. (1973) *A First Language.* Cambridge MA: Harvard University Press.

Brown, R. and Hanlon, C. (1970) Derivational complexity and order of acquisition in child speech. In J. Hayes (ed.) *Cognition and the Development of Language.* New York: Wiley.

Burt, M., Dulay, H. and Hernandez-Chavez, E. (1975) *Bilingual Syntax Measure 1.* New York: Harcourt Brace Jovanovich.

Cazden, C., Cancino, H., Rosansky, E. and Schumann, J. (1975) Second language acquisition sequences in children, adolescents and adults. Final Report, US Department of Health, Education and Welfare, NIE; Office of Research Grants, Project #730 744, Grant #NE-6-00-3-0014.

Chomsky, N. (1957) *Syntactic Structures.* The Hague: Mouton.

— (1981) *Lectures on Government and Binding.* Dordrecht: Foris.

— (1982) *Some Concepts and Consequences of the Theory of Government and Binding.* Cambridge, MA: MIT Press.

— (1986a) *Knowledge of Language: Its Nature, Origin and Use.* New York: Praeger.

— (1986b) *Barriers.* Cambridge, MA: MIT Press.

— (1989) Some notes on economy of derivation and representation. *MIT Working Papers in Linguistics* 10, 43–74.

Clahsen, H. (1984) The acquisition of German word order: A test case for cognitive approaches to L2 development. In R. Andersen (ed.) *Second Languages: A Cross-linguistic Perspective.* Rowley, MA: Newbury House.

— (1988) Parametrized grammatical theory and language acquisition: A study of verb placement and inflection by children and adults. In S. Flynn and W. O'Neil (eds.) *Linguistic Theory in Second Language Acquisition.* Dordrecht: Kluwer.

Clahsen, H. and Muysken, P. (1986) The availability of universal grammar to adult and child learners: A study of the acquisition of German word order. *Second Language Research* 2, 93–119.

Clahsen, H., Meisel, J. and Pienemann, M. (1983) *Deutsch als Zweitsprache: der Spracherwerb auslandischer Arbeiter.* Tübingen: Gunter Narr.

Clark, E. (1985) The acquisition of Romance, with special reference to French. In D. Slobin (ed.) *The Crosslinguistic Study of Language Acquisition, Vol. 2: Theoretical Issues.* Hillsdale, NJ: Lawrence Erlbaum Associates.

Clark, H. and Clark, E. (1977) *Psychology and Language.* New York: Harcourt Brace Jovanovich.

Clark, R. (1974) Performing without competence. *Journal of Child Language* 1, 1–10.

Cook, V. (1985) Universal Grammar and second language learning. *Applied Linguistics* 6, 1, 2–18.

Coppieters, R. (1987) Competence differences between native and fluent non-native speakers. *Language* 63, 544–73.

Corder, S. (1967) The significance of learners' errors. *International Review of Applied Linguistics* 5, 161–70.

Crookes, G. (1991) Second language speech production research: A methodically oriented review. *Studies in Second Language Acquisition* 13, 2, 113–33.

Dechert, H., Möhle, D. and Raupach, M. (eds.) (1984) *Second Language Productions.* Tübingen: Gunter Narr Verlag.

de Villiers, J. and de Villiers, P. (1973) A cross-sectional study of the acquisition of grammatical morphemes in child speech. *Journal of Psycholinguistic Research* 2, 267–78.

Dickerson, L. (1975) The learner's interlanguage as a system of variable rules. *TESOL Quarterly* 9, 410–07.

Dickerson, L. and Dickerson, W. (1977) Interlanguage phonology: Current research and future directions. In S. Corder and E. Roulet (eds) *Interlanguages and Pidgins and Their relation to Second Language Pedagogy*. Neuchatel: Librairie Droz.

Doughty, C. (1991) Second language instruction does make a difference: Evidence from an empirical study of SL relativization. *Studies in Second Language Acquisition* 13, 4, 431–71.

Dulay, H. and Burt, M. (1972) Goofing: An indicator of children's second language strategies. *Language Learning* 22, 234–52. Reprinted in S. Gass and L. Selinker (eds.) (1983) *Language Transfer in Language Learning*. Rowley, MA: Newbury House.

— (1973) Should we teach children syntax? *Language Learning* 23, 245–58.

— (1974) Natural sequences in child second language acquisition. *Language Learning* 23, 245–58.

Dulay, H., Burt, M. and Krashen, S. (1982) *Language Two*. Oxford: Oxford University Press.

duPlessis, J. (1986) Universal grammar and L2 acquisition of Afrikaans word order. Paper presented at LARS, Utrecht, September 1986.

duPlessis, J., Solin, D., Travis, L and White, L. (1987) UG or not UG, that is the question: a reply to Clahsen and Muysken. *Second Language Research* 3, 56–75.

Eckman, F. (1977) Markedness and the contrastive analysis hypothesis. *Language Learning* 27, 315–30.

Ellis, R. (1984a) *Classroom Second Language Development*. Hemel Hempstead: Prentice Hall.

— (1984b) Can syntax be taught? A study of the effects of formal instruction on the acquisition of WH questions by children. *Applied Linguisitics* 5, 138–55.

— (1985a) *Understanding Second Language Acquisition*. Oxford: Oxford University Press.

— (1985b) Sources of variability in interlanguage. *Applied Linguistics* 6, 118–31.

— (ed.) (1987a) *Second Language Acquisition in Context*. London: Prentice Hall.

— (1987b) Interlanguage variability in narrative discourse: Style shifting in the use of the past tense. *Studies in Second Language Acquisition* 9, 12–20.

— (1988) The effects of linguistic environment on the second language acquisition of grammatical rules. *Applied Linguistics* 9, 257–74.

— (1989) Sources of intra-language variability in language use and their relationship to second language acquisition. In S. Gass, C. Madden, D. Preston and L. Selinker (eds) *Variation in Second Language Acquisition Vol.II*. Clevedon: Multilingual Matters. Reprinted in R. Ellis (1992) *Second Language Acquisition and Language Pedagogy*. Clevedon: Multilingual Matters.

— (1990) *Instructed Second Language Acquisition*. Oxford: Blackwell.

— (1992) *Second Language Acquisition and Language Pedagogy*. Clevedon: Multilingual Matters.

Eubank, L. (ed.) (1991) *Point Counterpoint: Universal Grammar in the Second Language*. Amsterdam: John Benjamins.

Faerch, C. and Kasper, G. (1983) Plans and strategies in foreign language communication. In C. Faerch and G. Kasper (eds.) *Strategies in Interlanguage Communication*. London: Longman.

Farwell, B. (1963) *Burton*. New York: Holt, Rinehart and Winston.

Felix, S. (1987) *Cognition and Language Growth*. Dordrecht: Foris.

Felix, S. and Weigl, W. (1991) Universal Grammar in the classroom: The effects of formal instruction on second language acquisition. *Second Language Research* 7, 2, 162–81.
Fillmore, L.W. (1976) The second time around: cognitive and social strategies in second language acquisition. Unpublished Doctoral Dissertation. Stanford University.
— (1979) Individual differences in second language acquisition. In C. Fillmore, D. Kempler and W. Y-S Wang (eds) *Individual Differences in Language Ability and Language Behavior.* New York: Academic Press.
Fitts, P. (1964) Perceptual-motor skill learning. In A. Melton (ed.) *Categories of Human Learning.* New York: Academic Press.
Flynn, S. and O'Neil, W. (1988) *Linguistic Theory in Second Language Acquisition.* Dordrecht: Kluwer.
Fodor, J. (1983) *Modularity of Mind.* Cambridge, MA: MIT Press.
French, M. (1985) Markedness and the acquisition of pied-piping and preposition stranding. *McGill Working Papers in Linguistics* 2, 131–44.
Gass, J. and Schachter, J. (eds) (1989) *Linguistic Perspectives on Second Language Acquisition.* Cambridge: Cambridge University Press.
Gatbonton, E. (1978) Patterned phonetic variability in second language speech: A gradual diffusion model. *Canadian Modern Language Review* 34, 3, 335–47.
Green, D. (1986) Control, activation and resource: A framework and a model for the control of speech in bilinguals. *Brain and Language* 27, 210–23.
Greenberg, J. (ed.) (1966) *Universals of Language.* Cambridge, MA: MIT Press.
Gregg, K. (1984) Krashen's monitor theory and Occam's razor. *Applied Linguistics* 5, 75–100.
— (1990) The variable competence model of second language acquisition and why it isn't. *Applied Linguistics* 11, 364–83.
Grice, H.P. (1968) Utterer's meaning, sentence meaning and word meaning. *Foundations of Language* 4, 225–42.
Grosjean, F. and Deschamps, A. (1972) Analyse des variables temporelles du français spontané. *Phonetica* 26, 129–56.
— (1973) Analyse des variables temporelles du française spontané II. Comparaison du français oral dans la description avec l'anglais (description) et avec le français (interview radiophonique). *Phonetica* 28, 191–226.
— (1975) Analyse contrastive des variables temporelles de l'anglais et du français: vitesse de parole et variables composantes, phénomènes d'hésitation. *Phonetica* 31, 144–84.
Haegeman, L. (1991) *Introduction to Government and Binding Theory.* Oxford: Blackwell.
Hakuta, K. (1976) A case study of a Japanese child learning English as a second language. *Lanaguage Learning* 26, 321–51.
Hanania, E. and Gradman, H. (1977) Acquisition of English structures: a case study of an adult native speaker in an English-speaking environment. *Language Learning* 27, 75–92.
Harrington, M. and Sawyer, M. (1992) L2 working memory capacity and L2 reading skill. *Studies in Second Language Acquisition.* 14, 1, 25–39.
Hawkins, J.A. (1980) On implicational and distributional universals of word order. *Journal of Linguistics* 16, 193–235.
Hawkins, R. (1990) Variability in second language learning: The interaction of linguistic knowledge with language processing capacity. Unpublished. Ms., University of Essex.

Hawkins, R., Towell, R. and Bazergui, N. (1993) Universal grammar and the acquisition of French verb movement. *Second Language Research*. 9, 189–233.

Hornstein, N. and Weinberg, A. (1981) Case theory and preposition stranding. *Linguistic Inquiry* 12, 55–92.

Huang, J. and Hatch, E. (1978) A Chinese child's acquisition of English. In E. Hatch (ed.) *Second Language Acquisition*. Rowley, MA: Newbury House.

Huebner, T. (1980) Creative construction and the case of the misguided pattern. In J. Fisher, M. Clark and J. Schachter (eds.) *On TESOL '80*. Washington DC: TESOL.

— (1983a) *A Longitudinal Analysis of the Acquisition of English*. Ann Arbor: Karoma Publishers.

— (1983b) Linguistic systems and linguistic change in an interlanguage. *Studies in Second Language Acquisition* 6, 1, 33–53.

— (1985) System and variability in interlanguage syntax. *Language Learning* 35, 2, 141–63.

Hulk, A. (1991) Parameter setting and the acquisition of word order in L2 French. *Second Language Research* 7, 1–34.

Hulstijn, J. and Hulstijn, W. (1984) Grammatical errors as a function of processing constraints and explicit knowledge. *Language Learning* 34, 23–43.

Hyams, N. (1986) *Language Acquisition and the Theory of Parameters*. Dordrecht: Reidel.

— (1991) Seven not-so-trivial trivia of language acquisition: Comments on Wolfgang Klein. In L. Eubank (ed.) *Point Counterpoint: Universal Grammar in the Second Language*. Amsterdam: John Benjamins.

Hyltenstam, K. (1983) Data types and second language variabilty. In H. Ringbom (ed.) *Psycholinguistics and Foreign Language Learning*. Abo Akademi.

Iatridou, S. (1990) About Agr(P). *Linguistic Inquiry* 21, 551–7.

Ingram, D. (1989) *First Language Acquisition: Method Description and Explanation*. Cambridge: Cambridge University Press.

Jackson, H. (1981) Contrastive analysis as a predictor of errors, with reference to Punjabi learners of English. In J. Fisiak (ed.) *Contrastive Linguistics and the Language Teacher*. Oxford: Pergamon.

Johnson, J. and Newport, E. (1989) Critical period effects in second language learning: The influence of maturational state on the acquisition of English as a second language. *Cognitive Psychology* 21, 60–90.

Kadia, K. (1988) The effect of formal instruction on monitored and spontaneous naturalistic interlanguage performance. *TESOL Quarterly* 22, 509–15.

Karmiloff-Smith, A. (1979) *A Functional Approach to Child Language*. Cambridge: Cambridge University Press.

— (1985) Language and cognitive processes from a development perspective. *Language and Cognitive Processes* 1, 1, 60–85.

—(1986a) Stage/structure versus phase/process in modelling linguistic and cognitive development. In I. Levin (ed.) *Stage and Structure: Re-opening the Debate*. Norwood, NJ: Ablex Press.

— (1986b) From meta-process to conscious access: Evidence from children's metalinguistic and repair data. *Cognition* 23, 95–147.

Kayne, R. (1975) *French Syntax*. Cambridge, MA: MIT Press.

— (1989) Null subjects and clitic climbing. In O. Jaeggli and K. Safir (eds.) *The Null Subject Parameter*. Dordrecht: Kluwer.

Keenan, E. and Comrie, B. (1977) Noun phrase accessibility and universal grammar. *Linguistic Inquiry* 8, 63–99.

Krashen, S. (1976) Formal and informal linguistic environments in language learning and language acquisition. *TESOL Quarterly* 10, 157–68.
— (1977a) Some issues relating to the Monitor Model. In H. Brown, C. Yorio and R. Crymes (eds) *On TESOL 77: Teaching and Learning English as a Second Language: Trends in Research and Practice.* Washington, TESOL.
— (1977b) The Monitor Model for adult second language performance. In M. Burt, H. Dulay and M. Finocchario (eds.) *Viewpoints on English as a Second Language.* New York: Regents.
— (1982) *Principles and Practice in Second Language Acquisition.* Oxford: Pergamon.
— (1985) *The Input Hypothesis: Issues and Implications.* London: Longman.
— (1988) *Second Language Acquisition and Second Language Learning.* Oxford: Pergamon Press.
Krashen, S. and Scarcella, R. (1978) On routines and patterns in language acquisition and performance. *Language Learning* 28, 283–300.
Labov, W. (1970) The study of language in its social context. *Studium Generale* 23, 30–87.
Larsen-Freeman, D. (1975) The acquisition of grammatical morphemes by adult ESL students. *TESOL Quarterly* 9, 409–19.
Larsen-Freeman, D. and Long, M. (1991) *An Introduction to Second Language Acquisition Research.* London: Longman.
Levelt, W. (1989) *Speaking: From Intention to Articulation.* Cambridge, MA: MIT Press.
Liceras, J. (1988) On some properties of the 'pro-drop' parameter: Looking for missing subjects in non-native Spanish. In S. Gass and J. Schachter (eds) *Linguistic Perspectives on Second Language Acquisition.* Cambridge: Cambridge University Press.
Lightbown, P., Spada, N. and Wallace, R. (1980) Some effects of instruction on child and adolescent ESL learners. In R. Scarcella and S. Krashen (eds) *Research in Second Language Acquisition.* Rowley, MA: Newbury House.
Lococo, V. (1975) Analysis of Spanish and German learners' errors. *Working Papers in Bilingualism* 7, 96–124.
— (1976) A Comparison of three methods for the collection of second language data: Free composition, translation and picture description. *Working Papers in Bilingualism* 8, 59–86.
Long, M. (1983) Does second language instruction make a difference? A review of the research. *TESOL Quarterly* 17, 359–82.
— (1988) Instructed interlanguage development. In L. Beebe (ed.) *Issues in Second Language Acquisition: Multiple Perspectives.* Rowley, MA: Newbury House.
Luján, M., Minaya, L. and Sankoff, D. (1984) The universal consistency hypothesis and the prediction of word order acquisition stages in the speech of bilingual children. *Language* 60, 343–71.
McLaughlin, B. (1987) *Theories of Second Language Learning.* London: Edward Arnold.
— (1990) Restructuring. *Applied Linguistics* 11, 2, 113–28.
McNeill, D. (1966) Developmental psycholinguistics. In F. Smith and G. Miller (eds) *The Genesis of Language: A Psycholinguistic Approach.* Cambridge, MA: MIT Press.
Makino, T. (1980) Acquisition order of English morphemes by Japanese secondary school students. *Journal of Hokkaido University of Education* 30, 101–48.
Mazurkewich, I. (1984a) The acquisition of the dative alternation by second language learners and linguistic theory. *Language Learning* 34, 91–109.

— (1984b) Dative questions and markedness. In F. Eckman, L. Bell and D. Nelson (eds) *Universals of Second Language Acquisition*. Rowley, MA: Newbury House.

— (1985) Syntactic markedness and language acquisition. *Studies in Second Language Acquisition* 7, 15–36.

Meisel, J. (1991) Principles of universal grammar and strategies of language learning: some similarities and differences between first and second language acquisition. In L. Eubank (ed.) *Point Counterpoint: Universal Grammar in the Second Language*. Amsterdam: John Benjamins.

Meisel, J., Clahsen, H. and Pienemann, M. (1981) On determining developmental stages in natural second language acquisition. *Studies in Second Language Acquisition* 3, 109–35.

Miller, G.A. and McKean, K.O. (1964) A chronometric study of some relations between sentences. *Quarterly Journal of Experimental Psychology* 16, 297–308.

Möhle, D. and Raupach, M. (1983) *Planen in der Fremdsprache*. Frankfurt am Main: Verlag Peter Lang.

Nagara, S. (1972) *Japanese Pidgin English in Hawaii: A Bilingual Description*. Honolulu: University Press of Hawaii.

Obler, L. (1989) Exceptional second language learners. In S. Gass, C. Madden, D. Preston and L. Selinker (eds) *Variation in Second Language Acquisition, Vol. II*. Cambridge: Cambridge University Press.

Odlin, T. (1989) *Language Transfer: Cross-linguistic Influence in Language Learning*. Cambridge: Cambridge University Press.

O'Malley, J. and Chamot, A. (1990) *Learning Strategies in Second Language Acquisition*. Cambridge: Cambridge University Press.

Paradis, M. (1987) *The Assessment of Bilingual Aphasia*. Hillsdale, NJ: Erlbaum.

Parker, K. (1989) Learnability theory and the acquisition of syntax. *University of Hawaii Working Papers in ESL* 8, 49–78.

Phinney, M. (1987) The pro-drop parameter in second language acquisition. In T. Roeper and E. Williams (eds) *Parameter Setting*. Dordrecht: Reidel.

Piaget, J. (1923) *Le langage et la pensée chez l'enfant*. Neuchâtel: Delachaux and Niestle.

Pienemann, M. (1985) Learnability and syllabus construction. *Modelling and Assessing Second Language Acquisition*. In K. Hyltenstam, and M. Pienemann (eds) Clevedon: Multilingual Matters.

— (1987) Determining the influence of instruction on L2 speech processing. *Australian Review of Applied Linguistics* 10, 83–113.

— (1989) Is language teachable? *Applied Linguistics* 10, 52–79.

Pierce, A. (1989) *On the Emergence of Syntax: A Cross-linguistic Study*. Unpublished doctoral dissertation, MIT.

Pollock, J-Y. (1989) Verb movement, universal grammar, and the structure of IP. *Linguistic Inquiry* 20, 365–424.

Poulisse, N. (1990) *The Use of Compensatory Strategies by Dutch Learners of English*. Dordrecht: Foris.

Pye, C. (1983) Mayan motherese: an ethnography of Quiché Mayan speech to young children. Unpublished ms.

Radford, A. (1990) *Syntactic Theory and the Acquisition of English Syntax*. Oxford: Blackwell.

Raupach, M. (1984) Formulae in second language speech production. In H. Dechert, D. Möhle, M. Raupach (eds.) *Second Language Productions*. Tübingen: Gunter Narr Verlag.

— (1987) Procedural learning in advanced learners of a foreign language. In J. Coleman and R. Towell (eds) *The Advanced Language Learner*. London: AFLS/SUFLRA/CILT.

Ravem, R. (1974) The development of wh- questions in first and second language learners. In J. Richards (ed.) *Error Analysis*. London: Longman.

Richards, J. (1974) *Error Analysis*. London: Longman.

Riemsdijk, H. van (1978) *A Case Study in Syntactic Markedness*. Dordrecht: Foris.

Riley, P. (1981) Towards a contrastive pragma-linguistics. In J. Fisiak (ed.) *Contrastive Linguistics and the Language Teacher*. Oxford: Pergamon.

Rizzi, L. (1982) *Issues in Italian Syntax*. Dordrecht: Foris.

— (1986) Null objects in Italian and the theory of *pro*. *Linguistic Inquiry* 17, 501–57.

— (1990) *Relativized Minimality*. Cambridge, MA: MIT Press.

Rosansky, E. (1976) Methods and morphemes in second language acquisition research. *Language Learning* 26, 409–25.

Ross, J. (1967) *Constraints on Variables in Syntax*. Unpublished doctoral dissertation, MIT.

— (1970) On declarative sentences. In R. Jacobs and P. Rosenbaum (eds) *Readings in English Transformational Grammar*. Waltham, MA: Ginn.

Schachter, J. (1986) In search of systematicity in interlanguage production. *Studies in Second Language Acquisition* 8, 119–34.

— (1990) On the issue of completeness in second language acquisition. *Second Language Research* 6, 93–124.

Schiff, N. (1979) The influence of deviant maternal input on the development of language during the preschool years. *Journal of Speech and Hearing Research* 22, 572–80.

Schlyter, S. (1986) Surextension et sous-extension dans l'acquisition des verbes de mouvement/déplacement. In A. Giacomi and D. Véronique (eds) *Acquisition d'une langue étrangère*. Aix-en-Provence: Université de Provence.

Schmidt, M. (1980) Coordinate structures and language universals in interlanguage. *Language Learning* 30, 2, 397–416.

Schmidt, R. (1992) Psychological mechanisms underlying second language fluency. *Studies in Second Language Acquisition* 14, 4, 357–87.

Schmidt, R.W. (1977) Sociolinguistic variation and language transfer in phonology. *Working Papers in Bilingualism* 12 (pp. 79–95). Toronto: OISE. Also in Ioup and Weinberger (eds) (1977) *Interlanguage Phonology: The Acquisition of a Second Language Sound System* (pp. 365–77). Cambridge, MA: Newbury House.

Schumann, J. (1978) *The Pidginization Process: A Model for Second Language Acquisition*. Rowley, MA: Newbury House.

Schwartz, B. (1993) On explicit and negative data effecting and affecting competence and linguistic behaviour. *Studies in Second Language Acquisition* 15, 2, 147–65.

Schwartz, B. and Tomaselli, (1988) Some implications from an analysis of German word order. In W. Abraham and E. Reuland (eds.) *Proceedings of the Fifth Workshop on Comparative Germanic Syntax*. Gronigen.

Selinker, L. (1972) Interlanguage. *IRAL* 10, 3, 209–31.

— (1983) Language transfer. In S. Gass and L. Selinker (eds) *Language Transfer in Language Learning*. Rowley, MA: Newbury House.

Selinker, L., Swain, M. and Dumas, G. (1975) The interlanguage hypothesis extended to children. *Language Learning* 25, 139–52.

Sharwood-Smith, M. (1993) Input enhancement in instructional SLA. *Studies in Second Language Acquisition* 15 (2), 165–79.

Shiffrin, R. and Schneider, W. (1977) Controlled and automatic human information processing: II Perceptual learning, automatic attending and a general theory. *Psychological Review* 84, 2, 127–90.

Slobin, D. (1979) *Psycholinguistics.* Glenview, IL: Scott, Forseman and Co.

— (1985) Crosslinguistic evidence for the language-making capacity. In D. Slobin (ed.) *The Crosslinguistic Study of Language Acquisition, Vol. 2: Theoretical Issues.* Hillsdale, NJ: Lawrence Erlbaum Associates.

Sorace, A. (1993) Unaccusativity and auxiliary choice in nonnative grammars of Italian and French: asymmetries and predictable indeterminacy. *Journal of French Language Studies* 3, 71–93.

Sorenson, A. (1967) Multilingualism in the northwest Amazon. *American Anthropologist.*

Stowell, T. (1981) *Origins of Phrase Structure.* Unpublished doctoral dissertation, MIT.

Tarone, E. (1982) Systematicity and attention in interlanguage. *Language Learning* 29, 1, 181–91.

— (1983) On the variability of interlanguge systems. *Applied Linguistics* 4, 143–63.

— (1985) Variability in interlanguage use: a study of style-shifting in morphology and syntax. *Language Learning* 35, 3, 373–404.

— (1988) *Variation in Interlanguage.* London: Edward Arnold.

Tarone, E., Cohen, A. and Dumas, G. (1976) A closer look at some interlanguage terminology: a framework for communication strategies. *Working Papers on Bilingualism* 9, 76–90. Also in C. Faerch and G. Kasper (eds) (1983) *Strategies in Interlanguage Communication.* London: Longman.

Taylor, I. (1976) *Introduction to Psycholinguistics.* New York: Holt, Rinehart and Winston.

Towell, R. (1987a) Approaches to the analysis of the oral language development of the advanced learner. In J. Coleman and R. Towell (eds) *The Advanced Language Learner.* London: AFLS/SUFLRA/CILT.

— (1987b) Variability and progress in the language development of advanced learners of a foreign language. In R. Ellis (ed.) *Second Language Acquisition in Context.* London: Prentice—Hall.

— (1987c) A discussion of the psycholinguistic bases for communicative language teaching in a foreign language situation. *British Journal of Language Teaching* 25, 2, 91–9.

Towell, R., Bazergui, N. and Hawkins, R. (1992) Systematic and non-systematic variability in non-instructed learning. *Working Papers in Language and Learning* 3. 55pp. University of Salford.

Towell, R., Hawkins, R. and Bazergui, N. (1993) Systematic and non-systematic variability in advanced language learning. *Studies in Second Language Acquisition* 15, 439–60.

Trahey, M. and White, L. (1993) Positive eveidence and preemption in the second language classroom. *Studies in Second Language Acquisition* 15, 2, 181–205.

Tsimpli, I-M. (1991) Functional categories and maturation: The prefunctional stage of language acquisition. *UCL Working Papers in Linguistics* 3, 123–48.

Tsimpli, I-M. and Roussou, A. (1991) Parameter resetting in L2? *UCL Working Papers in Linguistics* 3, 149–69.

Tsimpli, I-M. and Smith, N. (1991) Second language learning: evidence from a polyglot savant. *UCL Working Papers in Linguistics* 3, 171–83.

VanPatten, B. and Cadierno, T. (1993) Explicit instruction and input processing. *Studies in Second Language Acquisition* 15, 2, 225–61.

Véronique, D. (1986) L'apprentissage du français par des travailleurs marocains et les processus de pidginisation et de créolisation. In A. Giacomi and D. Véronique (eds) *Acquisition d'une langue étrangère*. Aix-en-Provence: Université de Provence.

Vinay, J. and Darbelnet, J. (1958) *La stylistique comparée du français et de l'anglais*. Paris: Didier.

Wexler, K. and Manzini, R. (1987) Parameters and learnability in binding theory. In T. Roeper and E. Williams (eds) *Parameter Setting*. Dordrecht: Reidel.

White, L. (1986a) Implications of parametric variation for adult second language acquisition: An investigation of the 'pro-drop' parameter. In V. Cook (ed.) *Experimental Approaches to Second Language Acquisition*. Oxford: Pergamon.

— (1986b) Markedness and parameter setting: Some implications for a theory of adult second language acquisition. In F. Eckman, E. Moravscik and J. Wirth (eds) *Markedness*. New York: Plenum Press.

— (1989a) The principle of adjacency in second language acquisition: Do L2 learners observe the subset principle? In S. Gass and J. Schachter (eds) *Linguistic Perspectives on Second Language Acquisition*. Cambridge: Cambridge University Press.

— (1989b) *Universal Grammar and Second Language Acquisition*. Amsterdam: John Benjamins.

— (1991a) Adverb placement in second language acquisition: some effects of positive and negative evidence in the classroom. *Second Language Research* 7, 133–61.

— (1991b) Second language competence versus second language performance: UG or processing strategies? In L. Eubank (ed.) *Point Counterpoint: Universal Grammar in the Second Language*. Amsterdam: John Benjamins.

— (1991c) Argument structure in second language acquisition. *Journal of French Language Studies* 1, 189–207.

— (1991d) The verb movement parameter in second language acquisition. *Language Acquisition* 1, 337–60.

— (1992) Long and short verb movement in second language acquisition. *Canadian Journal of Linguistics* 37, 273–86.

Wode, H. (1976) Developmental sequences in naturalistic L2 acquisition. *Working Papers on Bilingualism* 11, 1–31.

Wolfe Quintero, K. (1992) Learnability and the acquisition of extraction in relative clauses and wh- questions. *Studies in Second Language Acquisition* 14, 1, 39–71.

Zobl, H. (1980) The formal and developmental selectivity of L1 influence on L2 acquisition. *Language Learning* 30, 43–57.

— (1984) Cross-language generalisations and the contrastive dimension of the interlanguage hypothesis. In A. Davies, C. Criper and A. Howatt (eds) *Interlanguage*. Edinburgh: Edinburgh University Press.

— (1990) Evidence for parameter-sensitive acquisition: a contribution to the domain-specific versus central processes debate. *Second Language Research* 6, 39–59.

— (1992) Sources of linguistic knowledge and uniformity of nonnative performance. *Studies in Second Language Acquisition* 14, 2, 387–402.

Index

Acculturation/Pidginisation Hypothesis, 37, 42
accuracy order, 24, 25
achievement strategies, 230, 236, 244
Acquisition-Learning Hypothesis, 6, 26, 27
Adaptive Control of Thought (ACT), 202
adverb placement, 104
Affective Filter Hypothesis, 27, 30, 31
age of initial exposure, 15, 112
analysis and control, 156, 191, 200, 229, 233, 235-237, 244, 251, 254, 264
application, 211
archistrategies, 233, 236, 237, 244
articulator, 169, 233
associative memory and knowledge, 242, 250, 252, 253, 255
associative stage, 203, 219, 238, 255
automatised long-term memory, 253
automatised memory/formulator, 255
automatic processing, 162-165, 167, 170-173, 175, 188, 197, 202, 204, 213, 214, 220, 235, 245, 248, 254, 255
autonomous knowledge, 250, 252
autonomous learning, 242
autonomous procedures, 225
autonomous stage, 203, 219, 238, 255

behaviourist psychology, 17
Bilingual Syntax Measure, 24
Burton, Sir Richard, 1

C^0, 79, 82-84, 86, 93-95, 139, 140
Canonical Order Strategy, 47, 52
capability continuum, 34, 35, 41, 153
careful style, 34, 35
clauses, 75-77
co-operative principles, 234

code-switching, 171
cognition, 202
cognitive abilities, 155, 175
cognitive approaches, 4, 45, 46, 54, 101
cognitive bias, 153
cognitive capacities, 155
cognitive language learning, 238, 242
cognitive mechanisms, 256
cognitive processes, 244
cognitive skills, 180, 218
cognitive stage, 203, 205, 219, 238
cognitive strategies, 192, 193, 196, 238
communication strategies, 159, 226, 229, 239, 243
compensatory strategies, 159, 162, 226, 232, 243, 258
competence, 33, 36, 174, 175, 182, 185, 186, 191, 199-202, 213, 214, 217, 225, 257, 259, 266
compilation, 209, 219, 220, 222, 224, 265
complementiser or C^0, 77
composition, 209, 210, 219, 224, 225, 238
conceptual analytic strategies, 236
conceptual strategy, 233
conceptualiser, 168, 169, 233, 251
conscious knowledge, 29
conservatism, 46, 49, 53
continuity, 46, 48, 49, 52, 53
Contrastive Analysis Hypothesis, 17-19, 31, 153
control, 191, 200, 229, 235-237, 244, 251, 254, 264
controlled knowledge, 156, 167, 253
controlled processing, 162, 163, 165, 172, 233, 248, 250, 252, 254
creation of productions, 248
creative morphology, 236
cross-category harmony, 67

cross-learner systematicity, 52, 153, 245, 259
cumulative development, 49

declarative knowledge, 165, 167, 168, 171, 172, 175, 201, 202, 205, 207, 209, 210, 218-220, 225, 238, 239, 242, 248, 252-255, 258, 264
declarative memory, 238, 250, 251, 259
determiners, 9
development of knowledge, 253
development of processing, 202
developmental aspect, 218
developmental framework, 224
developmental problem, 130-132
different knowledge sources, 174
diffusion model, 198, 200
discriminated knowledge, 224
discriminated productions, 239
discrimination, 211, 212, 220
Dutch, 29, 80-84

economy principle, 234
Empty Category Principle, 97, 117, 135
encapsulated module, 174, 191
exclusive parameter values, 103, 124
execution, 211
explicit knowledge, 186
explicit rules, 251, 258, 265

first language acquisition, 58, 65, 97, 98
focus of attention, 157
formulaic language, 151, 158, 174, 176, 183-186, 192-194, 200, 216, 218, 225, 245, 248, 250, 253, 254, 258, 265
formulator, 168-170, 173, 201, 204, 209, 214, 233
fossilisation, 2, 110, 255
fossilised grammar, 38
free variation, 37, 40, 198
French, 3, 7-9, 13, 18, 19, 34, 40, 41, 51, 66-69, 80-86, 89, 90, 96-98, 104, 105, 120-126, 136-138, 143

generalisation, 49, 211, 212, 220
generalised knowledge, 224, 239
German, 10, 11, 46, 66, 70, 71, 80-84, 86, 88, 90, 126, 132, 138, 139, 145, 147-150
grammatical morphology, 12, 23, 24

head position parameter, 138, 149
holistic strategy, 233
hypothesis construction, 174, 180, 182, 199, 200, 201

I^0, 76, 82, 84, 94
implicit knowledge, 186-188
inclusive parameter values, 103, 124
incompleteness, 2, 5, 30, 37-39, 42, 54, 110, 119, 153, 245
Indians, Vaupes River, 1
Infl or I^0, 75
information processing, 162
Initialisation-Finalisation Strategy, 47, 52
input frequency, 134, 140
instruction, 174-178, 180-183, 189, 201, 213, 215, 218, 225, 245, 248, 250, 255, 262, 265
interlanguage grammar, 23
interpretive method, 255
interpretive processes, 216
interpretive strategies, 205, 207, 219, 238, 250
interpretive translation procedures, 224
interpretive use of declarative knowledge, 220

Krashen's five hypotheses, 25

language faculty, 33, 54, 60, 130, 131
language production, 165, 167, 172, 173, 230, 232, 234, 243
learnability, 120, 124
learned L2 knowledge, 26
learned linguistic behaviour, 174, 176, 183, 201, 213, 214, 218, 225
learned linguistic knowledge, 174-177, 182, 199-201, 213-218, 2225, 258, 266
learner production, 216
learning environment, 155
learning principles, 49
learning strategies, 226, 239, 243
lemmas, 167-169, 250
lexical knowledge, 214, 216
lexicon, 169, 170, 175
linguistic approaches, 4, 17, 54
linguistic competence, 177, 201
linguistic strategy, 233

logical and developmental problems, 129
long-term memory, 202, 245, 248, 250, 162, 163, 172, 238, 265

macroplanning, 168
markedness, 98
matching, 211, 238
Mauritius, 2
mental representation, 185, 186, 188, 190, 191, 200, 224, 225, 253-255
mental restructuring, 176, 251, 254
metaprocess, 189, 190
microplanning, 168, 169
mimicking, 247, 261
modularity, 175
Monitor Hypothesis, 27, 30
morpheme studies, 23, 154, 259
morphological creativity, 234
multi-L2 situation, 2
multiple sources of knowledge, 160, 201, 217, 218, 225, 245, 246, 250, 266

Natural Order Hypothesis, 23, 25-28
negation, 13
negative evidence, 182
negative feedback, 174-177, 181, 183, 199, 201, 213, 215, 245, 248, 256, 258
no negative evidence condition, 59
nonsystematic variability, 144, 182, 197-200
Norwegian children, 59
null subjects, 91, 92

operating principles, 131

parameter, 149, 174, 255, 259, 260, 262
parameter activation, 106
parameter resetting, 116, 129, 259, 262
parameter setting, 153, 246, 247, 252, 259
parameters with exclusive values, 93, 97
parameters with inclusive values, 93, 97, 98
perceptual saliency, 46, 47
performance, 33, 174, 175, 201, 213, 214, 217, 225
phrase structure, 61, 65, 68, 69, 71
positive evidence, 110, 112, 113, 120, 174, 175, 181, 182, 186, 191, 200, 201, 252

positive feedback, 189
pre-emption, 49
principles and parameters, 61, 71
principles of co-operation and economy, 232
pro-drop parameter, 113, 115, 117, 262
procedural knowledge, 165, 166, 168, 171, 172, 201, 203, 207, 218, 242, 248, 264
proceduralisation, 204, 209, 210, 219, 223-225, 235, 238, 239, 250, 251, 253-255, 257, 259, 265
procedure, 161, 210
procedures, 160, 167, 167, 169, 170, 187, 224
processing units, 219
processing, 168
production memory, 211, 238
production strategies, 226, 239
production system, 204
productions, 161, 170, 201, 207, 209, 210, 217, 232, 238, 239, 256-259, 263-265
projection, 66
proper government, 96

Quiché people of Guatemala, 59

rate of speech, 161
reduction strategies, 230, 236, 244
reorganisation of mental knowledge, 248, 257
resetting parameters, 252, 261
restructuring, 185, 186, 191, 198, 199

short-term memory, 162, 163, 165, 167, 168, 172, 201, 205, 213, 238, 245, 248, 250, 252, 253, 256, 265
social distance, 38, 39, 42
sociolinguistic approaches, 4, 33, 54
sources of knowledge, 266
Spanish, 115
staged development, 5, 10, 28, 36, 41, 45, 52, 129, 133, 153, 245, 259
strategies, 162, 232, 234, 237-239, 242, 243, 248, 251, 263
strength, 171, 210, 211
strengthening, 211, 212, 220, 239, 242, 252
subject pronouns, 9, 10
Subordinate Clause Strategy, 48, 52

subset principle, 101, 102, 104, 119, 120
subset, 113, 260
superset, 113
switching, 263
systematic variability, 37, 40, 144
systematicity, 5, 11, 28, 45, 129

talented L2 learners, 2
task-based variability, 156
temporal variables, 218, 219, 221, 224, 225, 264
transfer, 5, 7-9, 18, 28, 31, 39, 74, 84, 87, 117, 153, 174, 214-216, 220, 229, 243, 245, 255, 258, 259, 263
transliteration, 214, 247, 258, 262, 263
triggering, 174, 176, 185, 191, 197, 199, 213, 214, 217, 252, 255
tuning, 211, 212, 219, 220, 223, 224

unanalysed wholes, 176, 183, 186, 251
uniqueness, 49

Universal Grammar, 57, 58, 153, 174, 246, 254, 258-260, 262, 266
unpackaging, 176, 183, 185, 192, 255, 265

variability, 5, 13, 26, 29, 33, 35, 40, 41, 54, 142, 143, 145, 150, 154, 160, 171, 172, 198, 214, 217, 225, 238, 243, 245
variable competence model, 36, 41, 153
variable rules, 36
verb movement, 120, 125, 262
verb-final, 10, 11, 80, 83-85, 87-89
verb-second (V2), 10, 11, 80, 83-89
verb-separation, 10, 11, 80, 84, 86, 88, 89
vernacular style, 34, 35

word order, 10
working memory, 164, 165, 204, 205, 209, 210

X-bar theory, 61, 63, 69, 116